EUROPE AND WORLD TRADE

EUROPE AND WORLD TRADE

KLAUS HEIDENSOHN

Pinter
London and New York

PINTER
A Cassell imprint
Wellington House, 125 Strand, London WC2R 0BB, England
215 Park Avenue South, New York, NY 10003, USA

First published 1995

British Library Cataloguing in Publication Data

A catalogue record for this book is available from The British Library

ISBN 1 85567 121 2 (hardback)
1 85567 122 0 (paperback)

Library of Congress Cataloging-in-Publication Data

Heidensohn, Klaus.
Europe and world trade / Klaus Heidensohn.
p. cm.
Includes bibliographical references and index.
ISBN 1-85567-121-2 (hb). – ISBN 1-85567-122-0 (pb)
1. European Union countries – Commerce. 2. European Union countries – Commercial policy. 3. International trade. I. Title.
HF3496.5.H44 1995
382′.3′0941–dc20 95-14314
CIP

Typeset by Mayhew Typesetting, Rhayader, Powys
Printed and bound in Great Britain by
Biddles Ltd, Guildford and King's Lynn

To FRANCES,
our daughter Christina
and our son Martin

CONTENTS

ABBREVIATIONS

ACP	African, Caribbean and Pacific Ocean countries
APEC	Asia-Pacific Cooperation
ASEAN	Association of South-East Asian Nations
ASIAN NICs(4)	Hong Kong, Singapore, South Korea, Taiwan
BENELUX	Belgium, Netherlands and Luxemburg
BEUC	Bureau Européen des Unions des Consommateurs
bn	billion
CAP	common agricultural policy
CCP	common commercial policy
CCT	common customs tariff
CEA	Chinese Economic Area
CEC	Commission of the European Communities
CEECs	Central and East European countries
CEECs(4)	Czech Republic, Hungary, Poland, Slovakia
CEFTA	Central European Free Trade Area
CEPR	Centre for Economic Policy Research
CET	common external tariff
CITES	Convention on International Trade in Endangered Species
CMEA	Council for Mutual Economic Assistance
COMECOM	Council for Mutual Economic Assistance (alternative nomenclature)
DIW	Deutsches Institut für Wirtschaftsforschung
DTI	Department of Trade and Industry (UK)
EBRD	European Bank for Reconstruction and Development
EC	European Community
ECE	Economic Commission for Europe
ECSC	European Coal and Steel Community
ECU	European Currency Unit
EEA	European Economic Area
EEC	European Economic Community
EFTA	European Free Trade Area
EU	European Union
EUR 6	European Union, six original member states

EUR 9	European Union, excluding Greece, Portugal and Spain
EUR 10	European Union, excluding Portugal and Spain
EUR 12	European Union, twelve member states
EUROSTAT	Statistical Office of the European Communities
GATS	General Agreement on Trade in Services
GATT	General Agreement on Tariffs and Trade
GDP	gross domestic product
GNP	gross national product
GSP	General System of Preferences
G–7	Group of seven western industrial countries (USA, UK, Japan, Italy, Germany, France, Canada)
IBRD	International Bank for Reconstruction and Development
IFS	Institute for Fiscal Studies
IMF	International Monetary Fund
ITC	International Trade Commission
ITO	International Trade Organisation
MFA	Multi-Fibre Arrangement
MFN	most favoured nation
mio	million
MMC	Monopolies and Mergers Commission
MNE	multinational enterprise
NAFTA	North American Free Trade Agreement
NCC	National Consumer Council
NCPI	New Commercial Policy Instrument
NICs	newly industrialised countries
NTB	non-tariff barrier
OECD	Organisation for Economic Co-operation and Development
OOPEC	Office for Official Publications of the European Communities
OPEC	Organisation of Petroleum Exporting Countries
p.a.	per annum
p.c.	per cent
R&D	Research and Development
SITC	Standard International Trade Classification
STABEX	Stabilisation of Export Earnings Scheme
SYSMIN	Stabilisation Scheme for Mineral Products
TREMs	Trade-Related Environmental Measures
TRIMs	Trade-Related Investment Measures
TRIPs	Trade-Related Aspects of Intellectual Property Rights
UK	United Kingdom
UN	United Nations

UNCTAD	United Nations Conference on Trade and Development
US	United States (of America)
USA	United States of America
USITC	United States International Trade Commission
USSR	Union of Soviet Socialist Republics
VAT	value added tax
VER	voluntary export restraint
VIE	voluntary import expansion
VISEGRAD Group	Czech Republic, Hungary, Poland and Slovakia
VRA	voluntary restraint agreement
WB	World Bank
WTO	World Trade Organisation

LIST OF FIGURES

LIST OF TABLES

PREFACE

Europe has emerged as the most powerful world trader. Yet there is no book that deals with the position and role of Europe in world trade. This book aims to fill the gap by offering a comprehensive and up-to-date treatment of *Europe and World Trade*. The idea of writing a book on this topic stems from the latent demand I identified for such a text while teaching economics to students on degree courses with a distinct European dimension.

I was encouraged to write this book by Michael Driscoll. But I am also indebted to a number of colleagues and friends who spent time commenting on draft versions of parts of this book. I am particularly grateful to Jiten Borkakoti, Len Gomes, Alan Gully, Lionel Fontagné, Nigel Grimwade, Valerio Lintner and Alan Winters for their valuable suggestions and positive comments.

Sylvanus Madujibeya made it possible for me to shift the balance of my job more towards research and writing by giving me reasonable teaching duties and a sabbatical. The task of carrying out the research for this book was facilitated by the help I received from staff at the GATT Secretariat, the Commission of the European Communities, Eurostat, the EFTA Secretariat and the Economic Commission for Europe. The librarians at Middlesex University gave me generous support in my search for material, and I would particularly like to thank Laurie Greenfield, Bettina Langlois and Joan Woollatt for their help.

My students at Middlesex provided me with valuable feedback on my international trade course, convinced me of the need for this book and contributed towards improving the finished product.

Marcos Baer, Mike Chapman, Jesus Encinar Rodriguez, Alberto Garcia Elias and Alistair Hall provided much appreciated technical assistance in preparing figures and tables for this book.

Edmund and Lucy Pereira coped admirably with a difficult manuscript and I gratefully acknowledge their characteristic skill and efficiency in producing the final text.

GATT kindly gave permission to reproduce texts from the General Agreement and Uruguay Round Agreement (appendices A–C).

Last but not least I am extremely grateful to my family without whose support it would have been impossible for me to complete this book. Their much appreciated help consisted of encouragement and genuine interest in my work (including a free newspaper cutting service). They also wisely reminded me of the need not to let the book project get out of proportion. Frances Heidensohn gave me unstinting love and support, and showed exemplary patience and understanding.

While I am grateful to everyone mentioned, I alone am, needless to say, responsible for the content of the book.

Klaus Heidensohn
November 1994

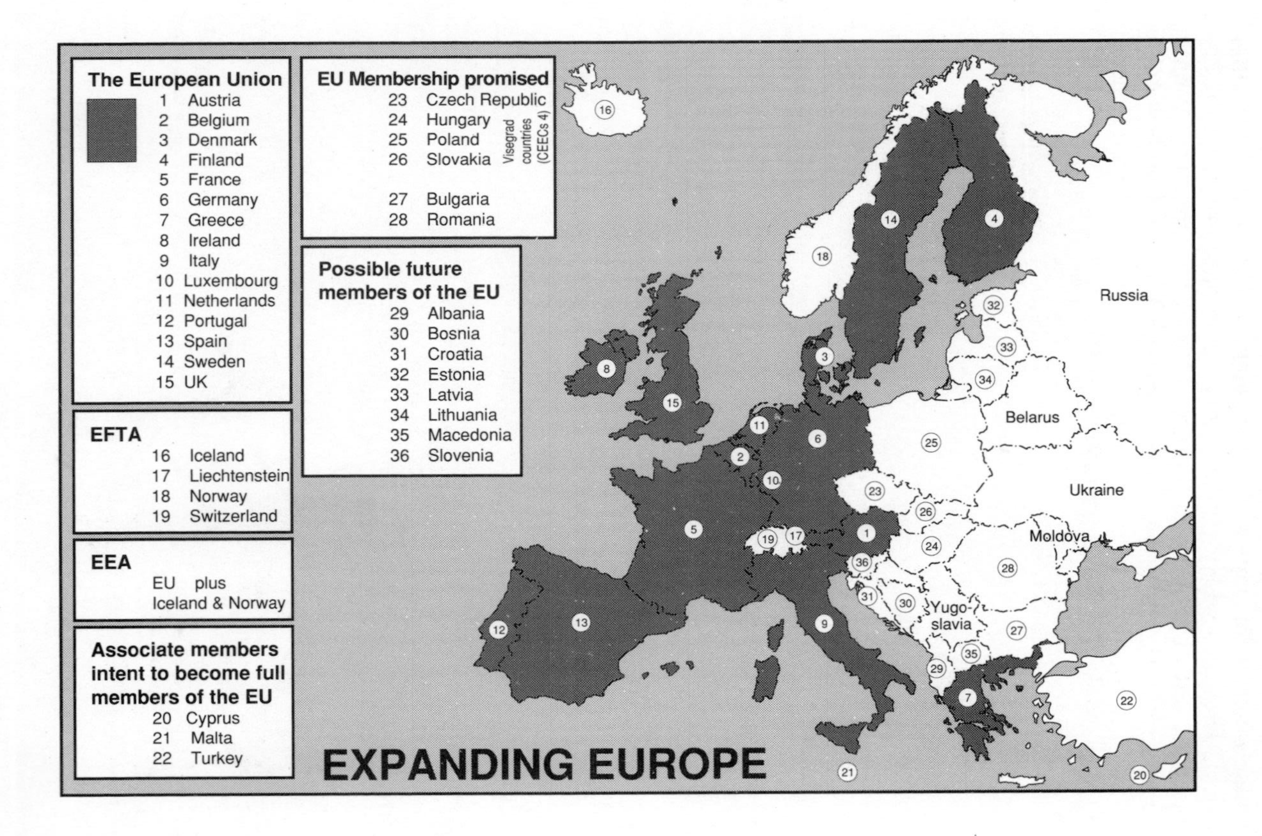

The European Union
1 Austria
2 Belgium
3 Denmark
4 Finland
5 France
6 Germany
7 Greece
8 Ireland
9 Italy
10 Luxembourg
11 Netherlands
12 Portugal
13 Spain
14 Sweden
15 UK
EFTA
16 Iceland
17 Liechtenstein
18 Norway
19 Switzerland
EEA
EU plus
Iceland & Norway
Associate members intent to become full members of the EU
20 Cyprus
21 Malta
22 Turkey
EU Membership promised
23 Czech Republic
24 Hungary
25 Poland
26 Slovakia
Visegrad countries (CEECs 4)
27 Bulgaria
28 Romania
Possible future members of the EU
29 Albania
30 Bosnia
31 Croatia
32 Estonia
33 Latvia
34 Lithuania
35 Macedonia
36 Slovenia
Russia
Belarus
Ukraine
Moldova
Yugo-slavia
EXPANDING EUROPE

1
INTRODUCTION

While what is meant by *world trade* hardly requires any explanation, defining *Europe* is somewhat problematic. For more than forty years (from the end of the Second World War until the late 1980s) the Iron Curtain divided the continent of Europe into two hostile blocs – capitalist Western Europe and communist Eastern Europe. Since then the political and economic map of Europe has been reshaped – in Eastern Europe communism ended; Germany was reunited; two independent states – the Czech Republic and Slovakia – replaced Czechoslovakia; Yugoslavia has been split up into several independent countries; the Soviet Union broke up and there are a number of successor states to the USSR which want to be part of Europe; the European Economic Area (EEA) – comprising the European Communities and the EFTA (European Free Trade Area) countries – came into being; since 1 January 1995 the *European Union* (EU) have been enlarged to include most of the EFTA group; more European states can be expected to become members of the EU before the end of the millenium.

At present there is in our view not enough cohesiveness between the various economic groupings in Europe – the EU, EFTA and the Central and East European transition economies – to talk about *a Europe*. Europe is still divided; the concept of Europe as an entity (embracing both the old Western and Eastern Europe) exists only on maps or as a vision of the future. Western Europe (the EU plus EFTA) does not as yet form a whole. In dealing with the theme of this book – Europe and world trade – we shall, therefore, focus on the *European Union*. The EU is the most powerful economic grouping within the new Europe; it is, despite differences in culture, language and emphasis on nationalism, both socially and economically more integrated than the rest of Europe; and it has been in a position to negotiate and operate as a whole in its external economic relations. Although the European Union did not start to exist until January 1994 when it replaced the European Community, we shall use the 'Union' or the 'European Union' consistently in referring to both the pre and post 1994 situation; the term 'European Community' will only be used in quotations and in the bibliography. To avoid excessive repetition, however, we shall also use the 'European Communities' and 'Europe' to describe the EU. The key issues surrounding Europe and world trade will be explored in seven chapters.

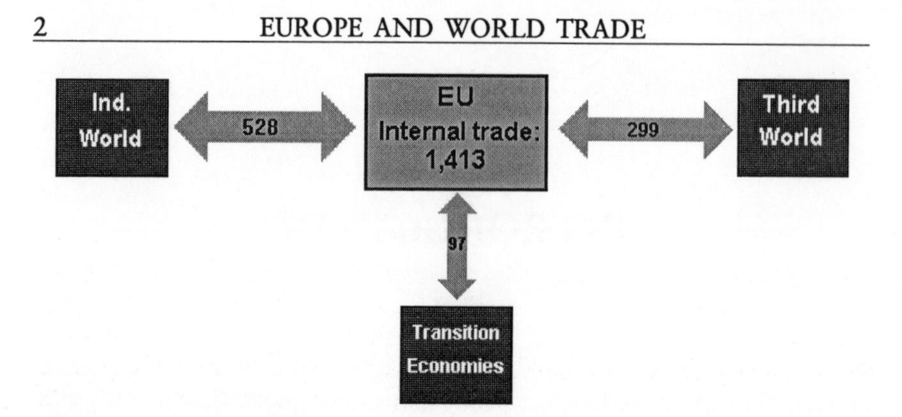

Figure 1 EU trade flows of merchandise (exports plus imports), 1992, in bn ECU (figures have been rounded up to the nearest billion)

Source: Eurostat (1993)

Chapter 2 will deal with Europe's patterns of trade. *Figure 1* serves to illustrate both the importance of trade within the EU (internal trade) and the magnitude of the trade flows (exports plus imports) between Europe and the rest of the world (external trade). In 1992, intra-EU trade accounted for as much as 1,413 billion ECU. But while internal trade is clearly more significant for the EU than its external trade, the trade flows between the EU and its principal trading partners – the developed countries (528 billion ECU), the Third World (299 billion ECU) and the transition economies of the former Eastern Bloc (97 billion ECU) – are also very large. Chapter 2 will, by way of providing an overall perspective to the theme of the book, discuss the EU's position in world trade, its export markets and import sources, and its principal trade partners. It will also consider the Union's merchandise trade by product, and its terms of trade and competitiveness.

In Chapter 3 we shall consider '1992': the Single European Act; non-tariff barriers to Europe's internal trade; the single market programme; '1992' and internal trade; obstacles to success; and the single market's external trade implications.

The trade policies of the EU will be the subject of Chapter 4. The discussion in this chapter will involve us in a consideration of Europe's trade policy objectives, the policy framework, trade policy measures and special agreements and preference schemes. This will be followed by a discussion of the impact of the EU's trade policy including its welfare implications.

Chapters 5 to 7 will cover Europe's external economic relations. In Chapter 5 we shall be concerned with the EU's trade with the rest of Europe. Treatment of this aspect of Europe's trade will involve us in discussions of EFTA and the EEA, of Central and Eastern Europe, and the question of EU enlargement. The trade links between Europe and two other giants in world trade – Japan and the United States – are the object of enquiry in Chapter 6. Here we shall discuss the EU–Japan patterns of trade, Japan's trade policy and surplus, EU–US structure of trade, US trade policies, and market access conflicts in EU–US relations. The trade links between Europe and the Third World will be considered in Chapter 7 which will cover the following specific aspects of trade between the EU and the developing countries: the ACP (African, Caribbean and Pacific Ocean Countries) group, the Mediterranean basin, UNCTAD (United Nations Conference on Trade and Development) and Europe's generalised system of preferences (GSP), and the newly industrialised countries (NICs).

In the concluding Chapter 8 we shall discuss Europe within the world trading system. Four important issues will be considered in this chapter: GATT (General Agreement on Tariffs and Trade); the Uruguay round and its outcome; future agendas of multilateral trade negotiations; and 'protectionism versus liberalisation'.

2
PATTERNS OF EU TRADE

Introduction
•
Europe's position in world trade
•
The Union's export markets and import sources
•
The EU's principal trade partners
•
Merchandise trade by products
•
Internal trade
•
Intra-industry trade
•
Terms of trade and competitiveness
•
Guide to further reading

INTRODUCTION

How significant is the EU's involvement in world trade? Who are the Union's principal trade partners, export markets and import sources? What is the EU's pattern of trade by product? What is the Union's balance between internal and external trade? How significant is intra-industry trade for the Communities? How have the EU's terms of trade and international competitiveness changed over time? These are the issues we shall consider in this chapter on Europe's patterns of trade.

EUROPE'S POSITION IN WORLD TRADE

In Chapter 1 we learnt about the magnitude of the EU's external and internal trade flows (*Figure 1*). In order to obtain a global view of the Union's trading position in the world economy it is useful to look at its shares in world merchandise (*Table 2.1* and *Figure 2.1*). In 1992, the

Table 2.1 Shares of world merchandise exports including EU-internal trade, 1992

Western industrialised countries	72.8
Europe (EC + EFTA)	45.7
European Union[1]	38.9
Germany	11.5
France	6.3
Italy	4.8
UK	5.1
EFTA[2]	6.8
USA	12.0
Japan	9.1
Canada	3.6
Others[3]	2.4
Developing market economies	19.2
Asia	12.9
Asian NICs (4)[4]	9.2*
Latin America	4.1
Africa	2.2
Rest of the world	8.0
China	2.3
Russian Federation	1.0
CEECs (4)[5]	0.9
Europe (EC/EFTA/CEECs)	46.6

Notes:
* Including re-exports.
1 Belgium, Denmark, France, Germany, Greece, Ireland, Italy, Luxembourg, Netherlands, Portugal, Spain, UK.
2 Austria, Finland, Iceland, Norway, Sweden, Switzerland, Liechtenstein.
3 Australia, South Africa, New Zealand, Turkey.
4 Hong Kong, Singapore, South Korea, Taiwan.
5 Czech Republic, Slovakia, Hungary, Poland.

Source: GATT (1993a)

Union's share in total world merchandise exports amounted to 39 per cent including internal trade. The EU and EFTA combined contributed as much as 46 per cent to world exports. Even after ignoring intra-EU trade, exports from the EU accounted for 20 per cent of world merchandise exports (*Table* 2.2 and *Figure* 2.2). The Union and EFTA between them had a share of world exports amounting to 28 per cent and, if we also include the Central and East European Countries (CEECs), an enlarged Europe generated nearly three tenths of world merchandise exports in that year. The Communities are also the main exporters of commercial services in the world. In 1992, their share of world exports in services amounted to 43 per cent; they played a significantly larger role in exporting services than the USA which

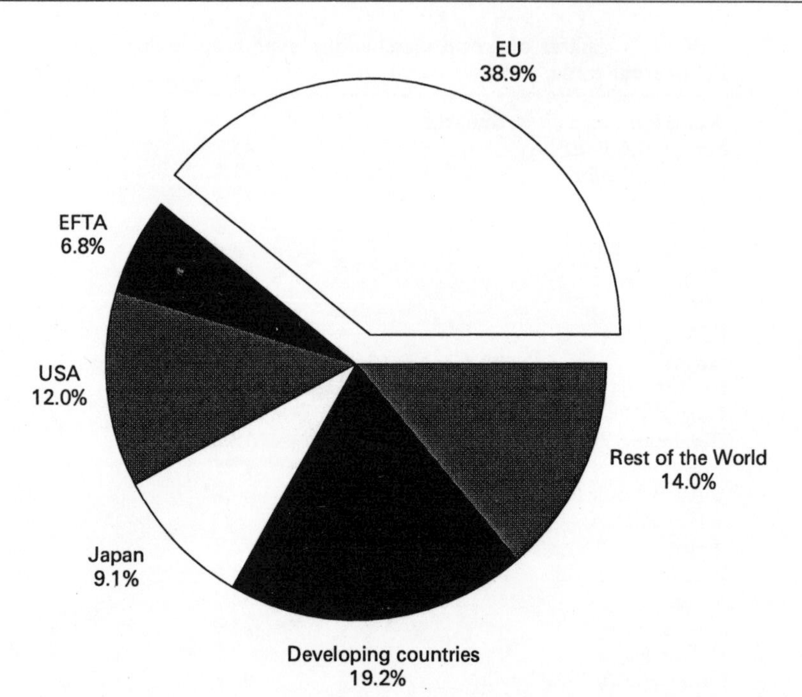

Figure 2.1 Shares of world merchandise exports including EU-internal trade, 1992

Source: GATT (1993a)

contributed 16 per cent to world exports in commercial services (*Table 2.3*). EFTA and the EU combined accounted for more than half of world exports (51 per cent) in commercial services.

THE UNION'S EXPORT MARKETS AND IMPORT SOURCES

Tables 2.4 and *2.5* provide information about the Union's main trade partners and the relative significance of Europe's internal and external trade.

The Communities' shares of major export markets have changed considerably since 1958 (*Table 2.4* and *Figure 2.3*). The importance of the Western industrialised countries increased. In 1958, 45 per cent of the Union's exports went to Western industrialised countries; by 1992 the share had increased to 55 per cent. Exports to the Third World, on the other hand, grew much less rapidly. In 1958, 44 per cent of all the Union's exports were destined for developing market economies; by 1992 the 'South' imported only 35 per cent of the Union's

Table 2.2 Shares of world merchandise exports excluding EU-internal trade: leading exporters, 1992

European Union	20.0
USA	15.8
Asian NICs (4)	12.1
Japan	12.0
EFTA	7.9
Canada	4.7
China	3.0
CEECs (4)	1.3
Russian Federation	1.0
Rest of the world	22.2

Source: GATT (1993a)

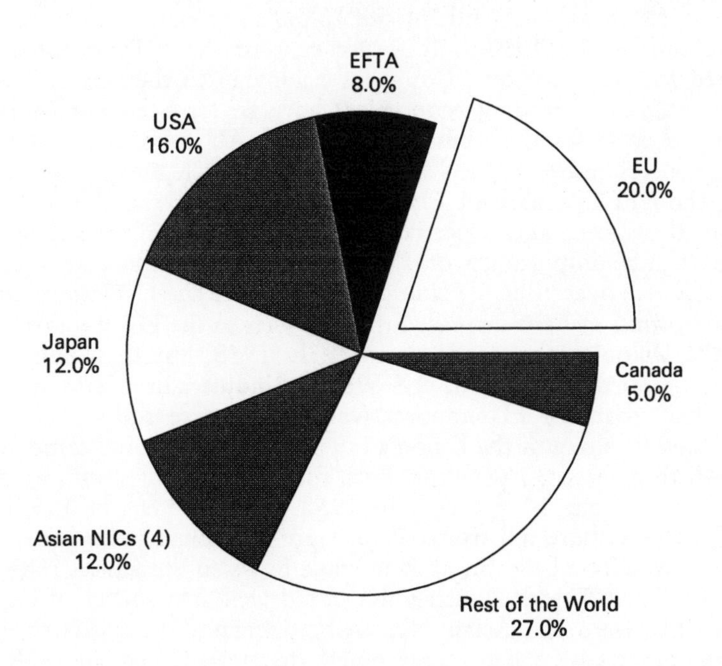

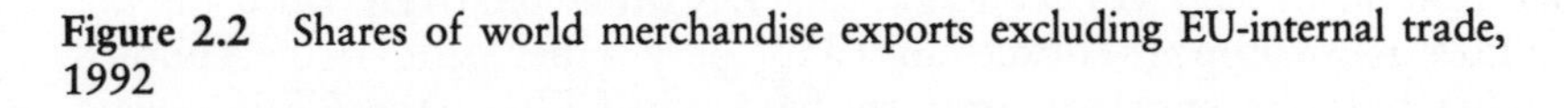
Figure 2.2 Shares of world merchandise exports excluding EU-internal trade, 1992

Source: GATT (1993a)

Table 2.3 Shares of world exports of commercial services: leading exporters, 1992

European Union	42.6
USA	16.2
EFTA	8.3
Asian NICs (4)	5.9
Japan	5.0
Canada	1.6
CEECs (4)	1.1
China	0.9
Rest of the world	18.4

Source: GATT (1993a)

exports. The ACP group of developing countries, in particular, appear to have been increasingly less involved in trading with the Union. In 1958, as much as one tenth of the Union's external exports went to ACP countries; by 1992 only 4 per cent of the EU's exports were destined for ACP markets. Countries belonging to the former Eastern bloc (or the state trading economies) have so far been but negligible trading partners for the members of the EU. About 10 per cent of the Union's merchandise exports have tended to reach these countries. In 1958, the CEECs' share of EU exports was as little as 2 per cent; it reached 6 per cent and 5 per cent in 1975 and 1992 respectively.

The relative importance of Europe's principal import sources has also changed over time. (*Table 2.5* and *Figure 2.4*). Western industrialised countries have increased their exports to the EU at a faster rate than the Union's other trade partners. In 1958, less than half of the Union's imports came from the Western industrialised countries; by 1992 their share of EU imports was nearly three fifths. The Third World saw its share of the Union's imports shrink over the same period from 46 to a mere 30 per cent. Both the ACP countries (whose share was reduced from 10 per cent in 1958 to 4 per cent in 1992) and OPEC (whose share fell from 17 to 9 per cent during this time) were particularly affected by this shift in trade flows to the Union. The only group of Third World countries that fared well as a source of imports for the EU were the Asian NICs who increased their share of the Union's imports by 5 percentage points (from 1 per cent in 1958 to 6 per cent in 1992). Up to 1992, the EU drew relatively little on the CEECs as an import source. In 1992, only 4 per cent of the Union's import bill was spent on imports from the CEECs; the CEECs were even less significant for the EU in 1958 and 1975. The state – trading Republic of China, on the other hand, trebled its share of the EU import bill between 1975 and 1992.

Table 2.4 EU exports of merchandise, % of EU trade

		1958	1975	1992
Internal		37	52	61
Shares of	Germany	26	26	26
	France	12	17	17
	UK	–	10	12
	Italy	7	11	11
External		63	48	39
Shares of	Germany	25	33	35
	France	16	17	16
	UK	–	19	15
	Italy	8	12	13
Destination of exports				
Western industrialised countries		45	48	55
	EFTA	20	22	25
	USA	13	12	17
	Japan	1	2	5
Developing market economies		44	39	35
	OPEC (13)[1]*	12	16	10
	Mediterranean Basin (12)[2]*	12	14	10
	ACP (69)[3]	10	7	4
	Asian NICs (4)	2	2	6
	Latin America	9	7	5
Rest of the world		11	13	10
	CEECs (4)	2	6	5
	USSR\Successor States of USSR	2	4	3
	China	2	1	2

Notes:

* Algeria is a member of both OPEC and the Mediterranean Basin.

1 Algeria, Libya, Nigeria, Gabon, Venezuela, Ecuador, Iraq, Iran Saudi Arabia, Kuwait, Qatar, United Arab Emirates, Indonesia.

2 Algeria, Morocco, Tunisia, Egypt, Jordan, Lebanon, Syria, Turkey, Israel, Cyprus, Malta, Yugoslavia.

3 Angola, Antigua & Barbuda, Bahamas, Barbados, Belize, Benin, Botswana, Burkina Faso, Burundi, Cameroon, Cape Verde, Central African Republic, Chad, Comoros, Congo, Côte d'Ivoire, Djibouti, Dominica, Dominican Republic, Equatorial Guinea, Ethiopia, Fiji, Gabon, Gambia, Ghana, Grenada, Guinea, Guinea Bissau, Guyana, Haiti, Jamaica, Kenya, Kiribati, Lesotho, Liberia, Madagascar, Malawi, Mali, Mauritiana, Mauritius, Mozambique, Namibia, Niger, Nigeria, Papua New Guinea, Rwanda, St Christopher & Nevis, St Lucia, St Vincent & the Grenadines, São Tomé & Principe, Senegal, Seychelles, Sierra Leone, Solomon Islands, Somalia, Sudan, Suriname, Swaziland, Tanzania, Togo, Tonga, Trinidad & Tobago, Tuvalu, Uganda, Western Samoa, Vanuatu, Zaïre, Zambia, Zimbabwe.

Source: Eurostat (1993)

Table 2.5 EU imports of merchandise, % of EU trade

		1958	1975	1992
Internal		35	49	59
Shares of	Germany	20	24	24
	France	12	17	18
	UK	–	11	12
	Italy	7	11	12
External		65	51	41
Shares of	Germany	19	22	29
	France	17	16	14
	UK	–	21	17
	Italy	9	13	12
Sources of Imports				
Western industrialised countries		48	47	59
	EFTA	14	16	23
	USA	18	18	18
	Japan	1	4	11
Developing market economies		46	46	30
	ACP (69)	10	7	4
	Mediterranean Basin	7	8	8
	Asian NICs (4)	1	2	6
	OPEC	17	28	9
Rest of the world		6	7	11
	CEECs (4)	2	3	4
	USSR\Successor States of USSR	2	3	3
	China	1	1	3

Source: Eurostat (1993)

Another feature emerging from *Tables 2.4* and *2.5* is that trade among member states of the EU has gained at the expense of external trade flows, and this applies to both exports and imports. In 1958, the ratio between internal and external exports (*Table 2.4* and *Figure 2.5*) was approximately three fifths (internal and external exports accounted for 37 and 63 per cent respectively). By 1992, the ratio had been reversed in favour of internal exports with internal exports contributing three fifths of total EU exports. The balance between internal and external imports (*Table 2.5* and *Figure 2.6*) changed in the same direction and by about the same magnitude. In 1958, imports from third countries were nearly twice as large as imports from within the Union (65 and 35 per cent respectively); by 1992 internal imports were 50 per cent larger than external imports (59 and 41 per cent respectively). While there is no doubt that the formation of a customs union lead to the Communities' internal trade growing at a faster rate than their external trade, the data are somewhat misleading in that they

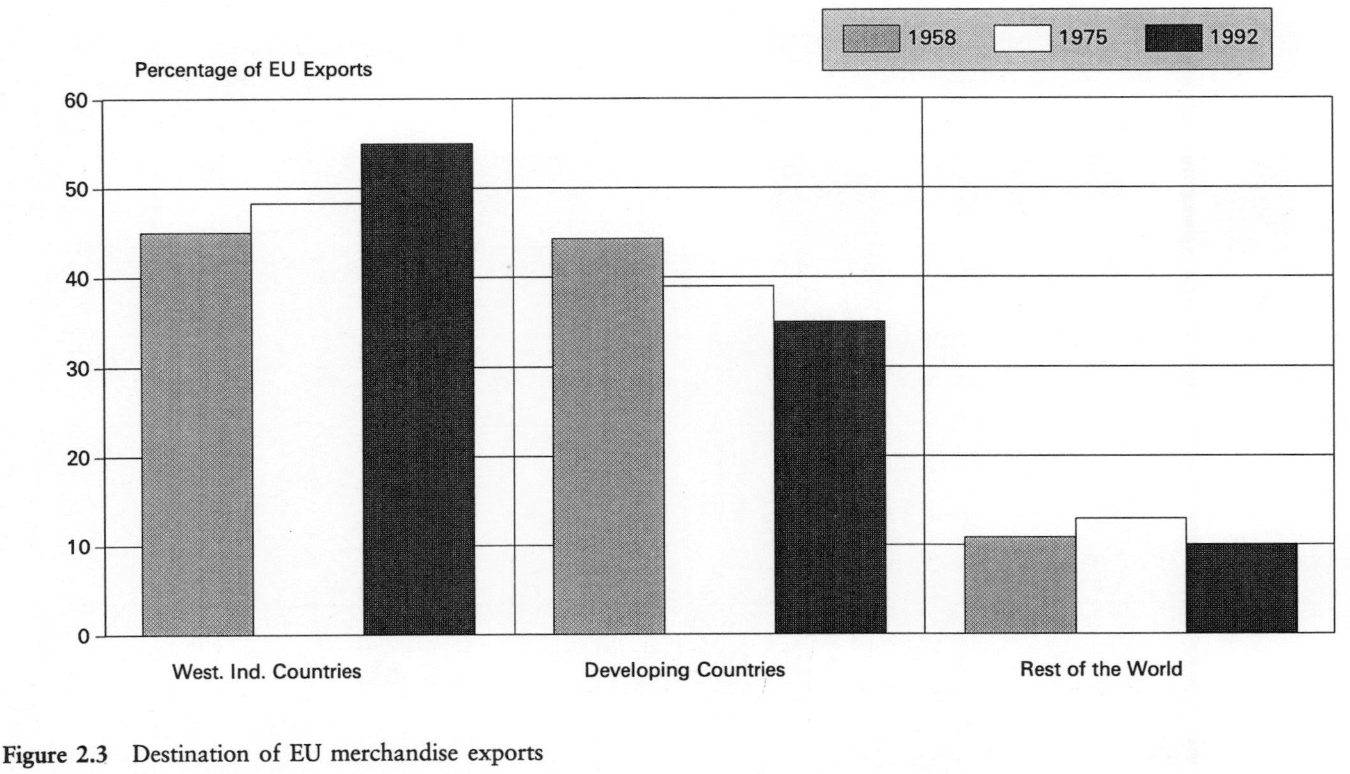

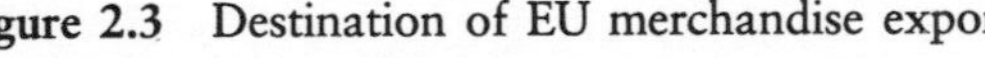

Figure 2.3 Destination of EU merchandise exports

Source: Eurostat (1993)

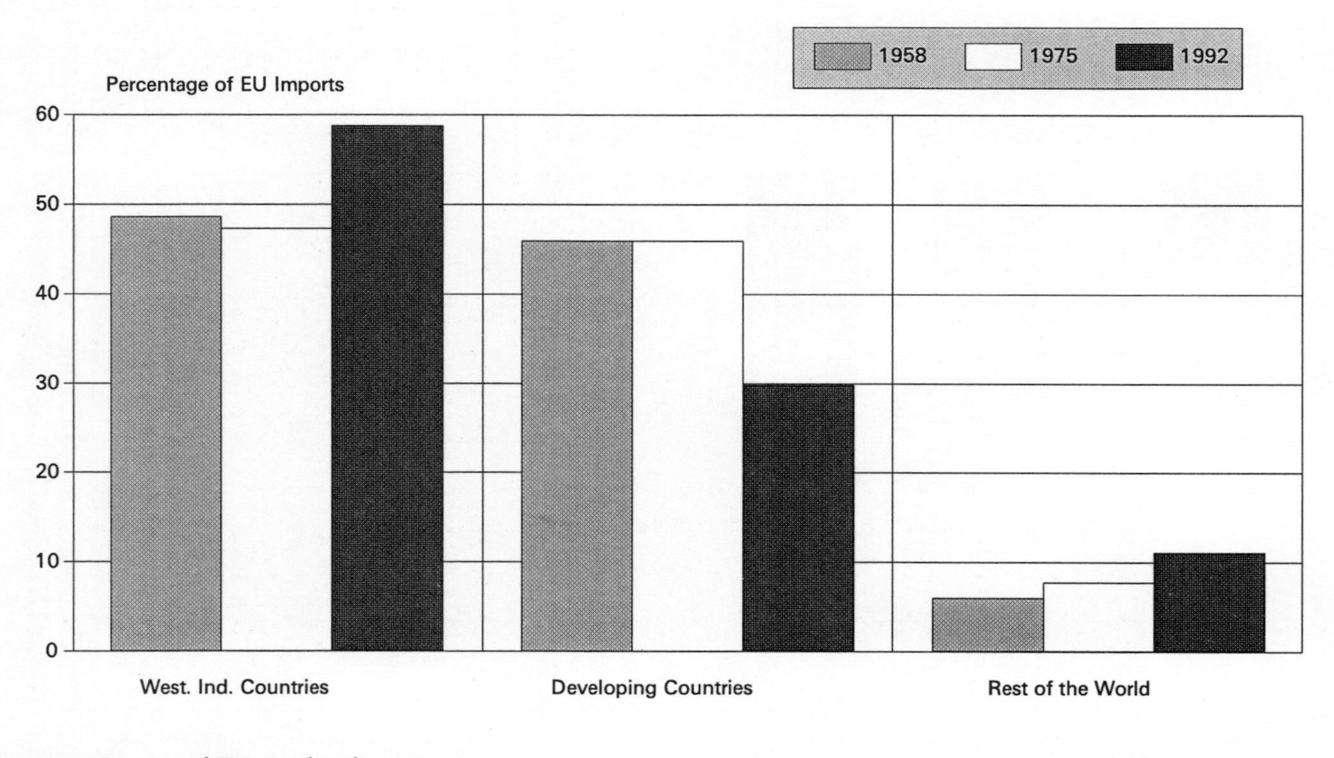

Figure 2.4 Sources of EU merchandise imports

Source: Eurostat (1993)

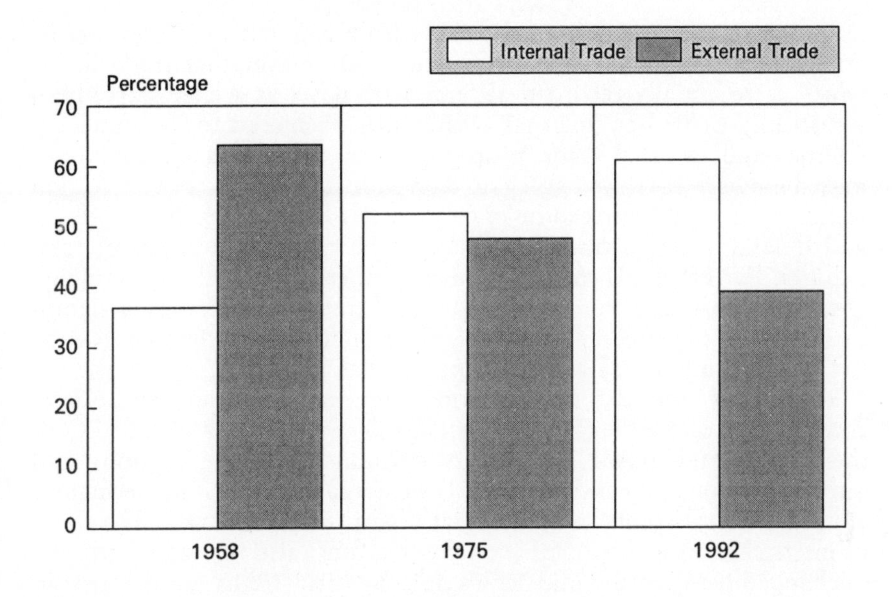

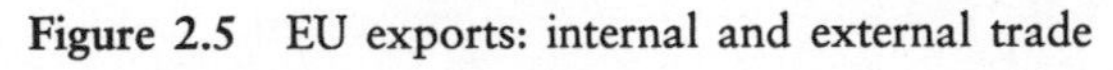

Figure 2.5 EU exports: internal and external trade

Source: Eurostat (1993)

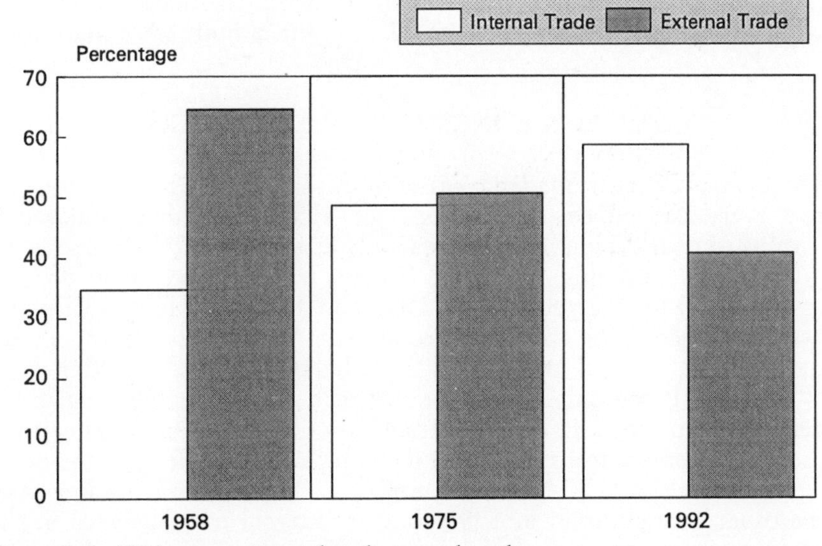

Figure 2.6 EU imports: internal and external trade

Source: Eurostat (1993)

exaggerate the magnitude of the shifts from external to internal trade. For the enlargement of the Union inevitably meant that trade flows, which were initially recorded as 'external', have, at a later stage, been statistically treated as 'internal'. While it is of interest to look into the internal and external trade proportions for the EU as an entity, we must be aware that the aggregate data hide differences between Union members. In 1992, for example, in countries like the Benelux, Portugal and Ireland, internal trade amounted to nearly three quarters of total exports. For other EU members, on the other hand, such as Germany, Denmark, Italy and the UK, the share of internal exports was significantly below the Union's average. Similar inter-country differences exist for internal imports as a percentage of total imports.

Tables 2.4 and *2.5* also provide information about the relative contribution of the 'big four' (Germany, France, Italy and the UK) to the Union's trade flows. In the years 1975 and 1992, the 'big four' had a share of about four fifths of the EU's external exports with Germany's exports to third countries growing at a particularly fast rate. The share of internal exports attributable to the 'big four' also remained virtually unchanged between the mid 1970s and the early 1990s (64 per cent in 1975 and 66 per cent in 1992). A very similar picture presents itself if we consider the contributions of the 'big four' to the Union's import flows. The combined shares of German, French, Italian and UK internal imports remained virtually unchanged between 1975 and 1992 (it increased by 3 percentage points from 63 to 66 per cent). The share of the Union's imports from the rest of the world destined for markets within the 'big four' amounted to 72 per cent in both 1975 and 1992.

THE EU'S PRINCIPAL TRADE PARTNERS

The Communities' trade balances with third countries have been negative every year since 1958 except for 1986 when they achieved a surplus of over 7 billion ECUs (generally attributed to the decline in oil prices). *Table 2.6* summarises the Union's trade balances with the rest of the world for the years 1960, 1980 and 1990 (in million ECUs and as percentages of the countries' gross domestic products). It also shows the external, internal and overall trade balances of the 'big four'.

Germany is the only Union country that, except for the small trade deficit it incurred in its external trade flows in 1980, has been earning foreign currencies from trading with both third countries and the other Union states. The UK had a favourable trade position in trading with the other Communities in 1980. But its external trade balance in the same year was negative and its overall trading position resulted in a trade balance deficit. In 1990, the UK incurred trade deficits in trading with both its Union partners and the rest of the world.

Table 2.6 EU trade balances of visible goods, in mio ECU/as % of gross domestic product

	1960	1980	1990
External balances			
European Union	−3,445/−1.24	−65,862/−2.93	−42,906/−0.90
Germany	+719/+1.05	−1,111/−0.18	+23,003/+1.95
France	+139/+0.24	−10,811/−2.26	+1,960/+0.21
UK	–	−5,553/−1.44	−17,978/−0.58
Italy	−803/−2.28	−12,269/−3.78	−5,001/−2.29
Internal balances			
Germany	+593/+0.87	+4,163/+0.71	+24,003/+2.04
France	+445/+0.78	−6,077/−1.27	−14,887/−1.59
UK	–	+1,891/+0.49	−14,002/−1.64
Italy	−274/−0.78	−4,196/−1.28	−4,261/−0.54
Total trade balances			
Germany	+1,312/+1.92	+3,052/+0.53	+47,006/+3.99
France	+584/+1.02	−16,888/−3.53	−16,847/−0.99
UK	−2,365/−3.47	−3,662/−0.95	−31,980/−1.97
Italy	−1,077/−3.06	−16,465/−5.06	−9,262/−4.08

Sources: Eurostat (1993); CEC (1994: 113)

Table 2.7 Main EU trade partners: shares of EU trade (exports plus imports)

Trading partner	1958	1975	1992
EFTA	17	19	24
USA	15	15	17
Mediterranean Basin	10	11	9
OPEC	15	22	9
Japan	1	3	8
CEECs (4)	2	4	4
USSR\Successor States of USSR	2	4	3
China	1	1	3

Source: Eurostat (1993)

At the risk of oversimplifying the complex and widespread trade links of the EU, it can be argued that there are eight major EU trade partners (*Table* 2.7 and *Figure* 2.7). If we consider trade flows as a whole (i.e. the value of all merchandise exports plus imports), we see that trade with EFTA, the USA, the Mediterranean basin, OPEC, Japan, the CEECs, China and the successor states of the USSR accounted for approximately four fifths of the value of the Union's total trade both in 1975 and 1992.

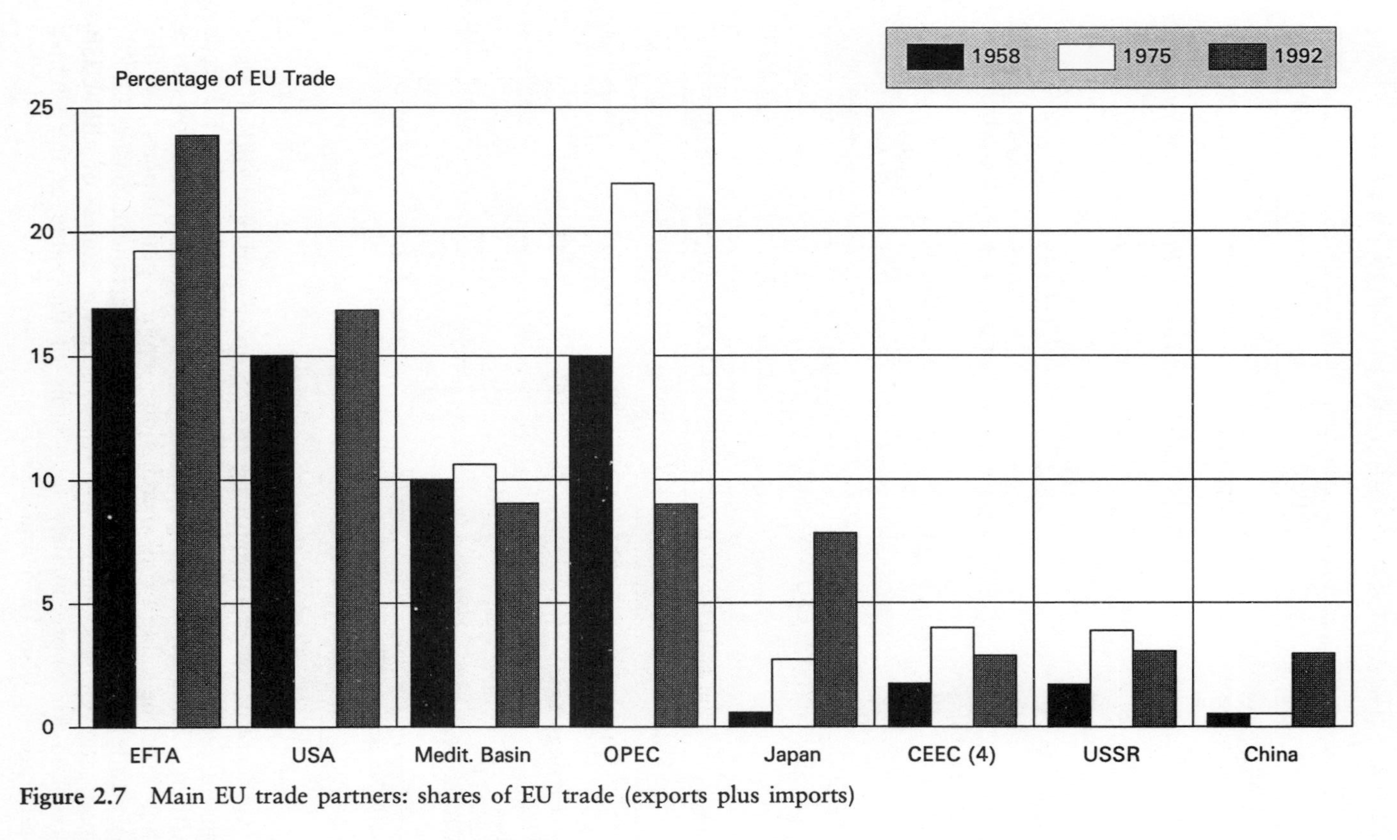

Figure 2.7 Main EU trade partners: shares of EU trade (exports plus imports)

Source: Eurostat (1993)

Table 2.8 EU trade balances of visible goods, in mio ECU

Trading partner	1958	1975	1983–1992 Average
Mediterranean Basin	+1,002	+6,710	+3,929
EFTA	+777	+5,864	+2,853
USA	−1,526	−9,333	+651
CEECs (4)	−37	+1,474	+27
China	+220	+477	−2,215
Asian NICs (4)	+171	−806	−3,439
ACP (69)	−255	−994	−4,309
USSR\Successor States of USSR	−91	+1,000	−4,922
OPEC	−1,372	−17,678	−9,033
Japan	−47	−3,253	−22,558

Source: Eurostat (1993)

It is also interesting to look at the trade balances between the EU and its main trade partners. *Table 2.8* and *Figure 2.8* summarise the EU's trade balances with ten main trade partners: the eight included in *Table 2.7* plus ACP and the group of 'miracle economies' of south-east Asia – the four Asian NICs. If, instead of singling out a particular year, we take the averages of the Union's trade balances with these ten principal trading partners, we find that the EU was, between 1983 and 1992, on average in a deficit situation with six countries/trade groups: Japan, OPEC, USSR (or its successor states), ACP, the Asian NICs and China with the average trade deficits with Japan (22,558 million ECU) and OPEC (9,033 million ECU) being particularly large. In trading with the group of countries belonging to the Mediterranean Basin, EFTA, the USA and the CEECs, the EU was, on the other hand, on average a net exporter, between 1983 and 1992. The average figures do, however, disguise the fact that the EU, in trading with EFTA, became a net importer in 1991 and 1992 (Eurostat 1993: 6).

MERCHANDISE TRADE BY PRODUCTS

Manufacturing (machinery, transport equipment and other manufactured goods) accounts for about three quarters of all EU exports to third countries (*Table 2.9* and *Figure 2.9*) and the structure of the Union's exports has not changed very much despite the fact that the period between 1958 and 1992 witnessed considerable changes in technology. The composition of imports into EU countries by products, on the other hand, has undergone major changes (*Table 2.10* and *Figure 2.10*). Imports of primary goods have become relatively less

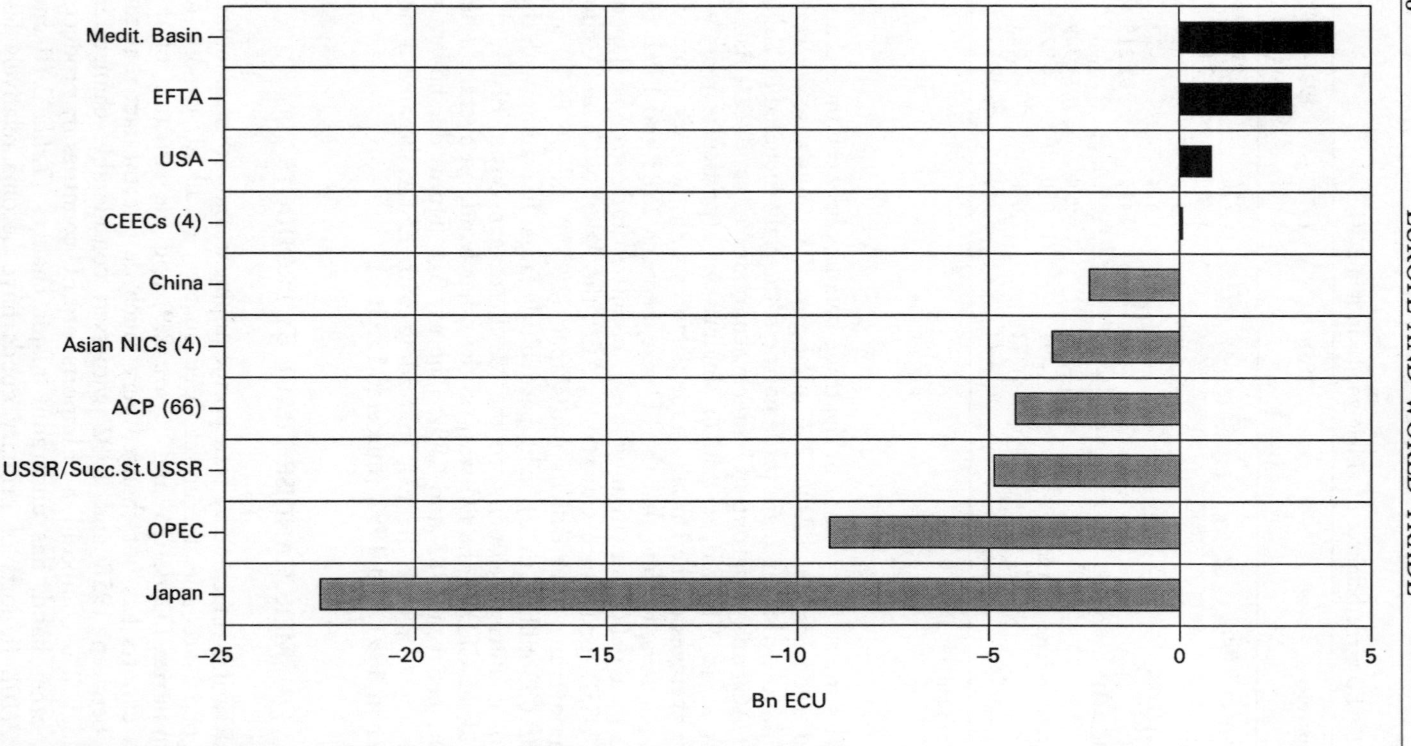

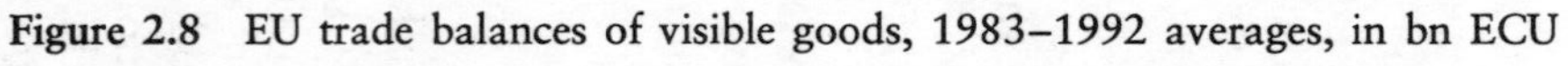

Figure 2.8 EU trade balances of visible goods, 1983–1992 averages, in bn ECU

Source: Eurostat (1993)

Table 2.9 EU external trade: exports by products, in %

	1958	1975	1992
Machinery, transport equipment	37	43	41
Other manufactured goods	37	30	30
Chemicals	9	11	12
Food, beverages, tobacco	9	7	8
Fuel, other raw materials	8	6	5
Miscellaneous	–	3	4

Source: Eurostat (1993)

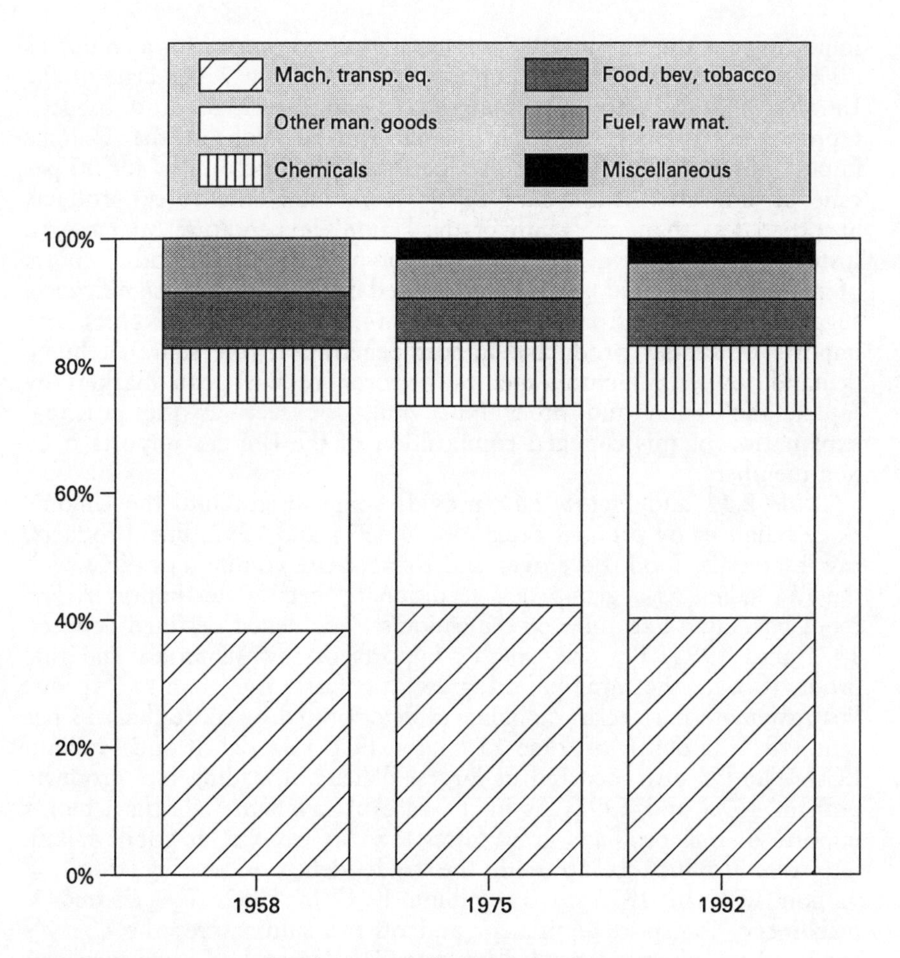

Figure 2.9 EU external trade: exports by products, in %

Source: Eurostat (1993)

Table 2.10 EU external trade: imports by product groups, in %

	1958	1975	1992
Chemicals, other manufactures	17	24	37
Machinery, transport equipment	6	13	30
Fuel	16	32	13
Food, beverages, tobacco	30	13	8
Other raw materials	30	14	7
Miscellaneous	1	4	5

Source: Eurostat (1993)

important for the EU. In 1958, raw materials accounted for as much as 30 per cent of the Union's imports; by 1992 only 7 per cent of the Union's imports were raw materials. Food, beverages and tobacco represented product categories which ranked high in the Union's import bill in 1958; the three products combined accounted for 30 per cent of imports. More than thirty years later, the three products absorbed less than one tenth of the Union's expenditure on imports. Instead of exchanging raw materials for manufactured goods imports of manufactured and semi-manufactured have gained in significance, suggesting a shift from inter- to intra-industry trade (exports and imports of similar products). Import penetration (the share of home demand for manufactures met by imports) of European markets by Japan, the Asian and other NICs must be seen as the principal explanation of this changed composition of the Union's imports from non-members.

Table 2.11 and *Figure 2.11* provide some insight into the Union's trade balances by product categories in 1975 and 1992. Fuel products, raw materials, food, beverages and tobacco are commodities in which the EU, taken as a group, has traditionally been a net importer. For food, beverages and tobacco the Union's trade deficit declined between 1975 and 1992. But the Union's imports of raw materials and fuel products, over the same period, grew at a faster rate than its exports. For raw materials the trade balances deteriorated by more than 50 per cent – from a deficit of some 15 million ECU to a deficit of 24 million ECU. The EU also incurred its largest deficits in trading fuel products both in 1975 and 1992. As in the case of raw materials the Union's imports of fuel products grew faster than its exports of goods falling into this product group with the trade deficit increasing from 38 million ECU in 1975 to 54 million ECU in 1992. For chemicals, machinery, transport equipment and other manufactures the Union's exports have always exceeded imports. The Union had large surpluses of over 30 million ECU in trading machinery and transport equipment both in 1975 and 1992. For chemicals and manufactures the Union's

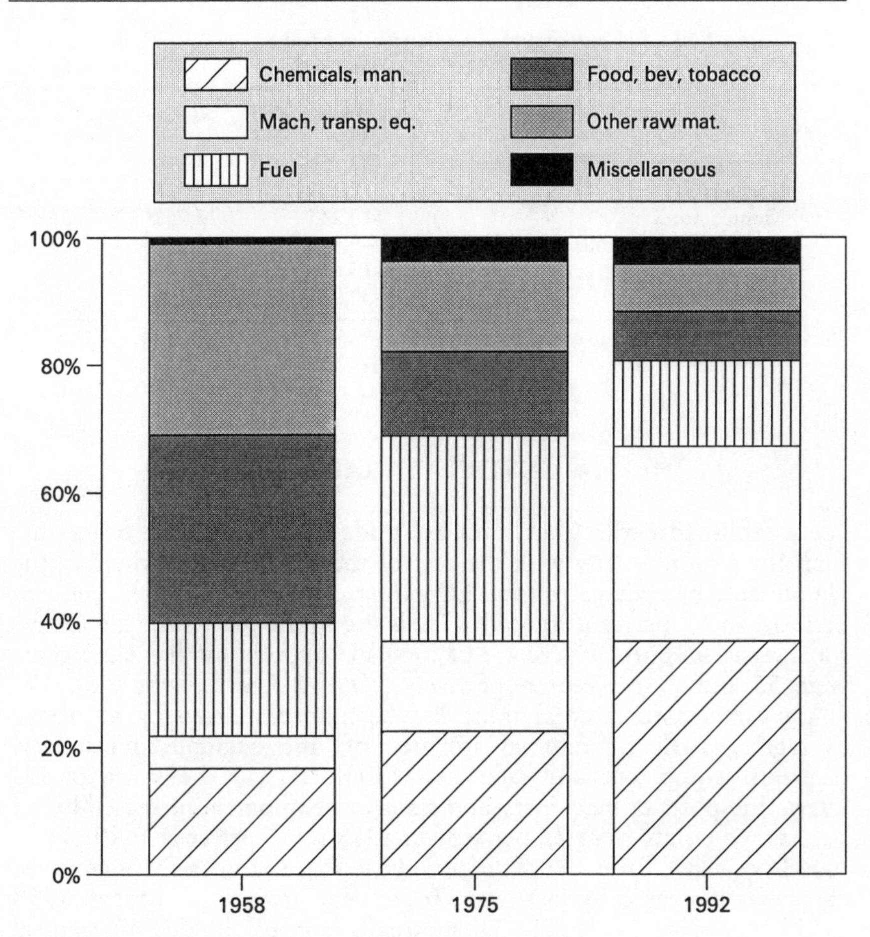

Figure 2.10 External trade: imports by products, in %

Source: Eurostat (1993)

trade surplus increased between 1975 and 1992. The Union's surplus resulting from trading in chemicals nearly trebled between the mid-1970s and the early 1990s (from 7 million ECU in 1975 to 20 million ECU in 1992). Manufactures yielded a larger trade surplus (10 million ECU) than chemicals (7 million ECU) in 1975. But the Union's trade position in manufactures improved less dramatically than its trade performance for chemicals (in trading chemicals the EU increased its surplus between 1975 and 1992 by 13 million ECU; for manufactures the Union's increase in net exports amounted to 5 million ECU over the same period).

Table 2.11 EU external trade balances by product group, in mio ECU

	1975	1992
Machinery, transport equipment	+33,301	+34,370
Chemicals	+7,209	+20,315
Manufactures	+10,245	+15,782
Food, beverages, tobacco	−9,424	−4,848
Raw materials	−15,611	−24,120
Fuel products	−38,321	−54,306

Source: Eurostat (1993)

INTERNAL TRADE

We established earlier that intra-EU trade has grown at a faster rate than the Union's trade with the rest of the world. Exports within the Union, as a percentage of total EU exports, increased from 37 per cent in 1958 to 61 per cent in 1992 (*Table 2.4* and *Figure 2.5*); the figures for internal imports as a share of total EU imports for the same years were 35 and 59 per cent respectively (*Table 2.5* and *Figure 2.6*). The Union's increased internal trade has been accompanied by an above average growth of internal imports of, for example, machinery, transport equipment and chemicals (*Table 2.12*). The share of EU internal imports of machinery and transport equipment increased by 15 percentage points from 22 per cent in 1958 to 37 per cent in 1992 (i.e. by 68 per cent). Over the same period the share of intra-EU imports of chemicals increased by just over 70 per cent (from 7 per cent in 1958 to 12 per cent in 1992). These trends are partly due to natural economic phenomena such as factor endowments and technological progress which, according to Winters (1987), are the most important explanatory variables for the broad pattern of world trade in manufacturing goods. The trend would also seem to reflect the increasing economic integration that has resulted from the gradual removal of tariffs and quantitative trading restrictions within the EU. While tariffs and quantitative limits on trade within the EU are by now virtually non-existent, trade between EU states continued to be subject to other internal barriers up to the end of 1992. The Council of Ministers' single European act (1985) – establishment of an integrated European domestic market by the end 1992 – aimed at dismantling the remaining barriers in order to allow for a genuinely uninhibited flow of goods and services to take place between the twelve member states. We shall discuss in Chapter 3 how the remaining barriers to trade between member states curtailed trade up to 1992 (by increasing the supply

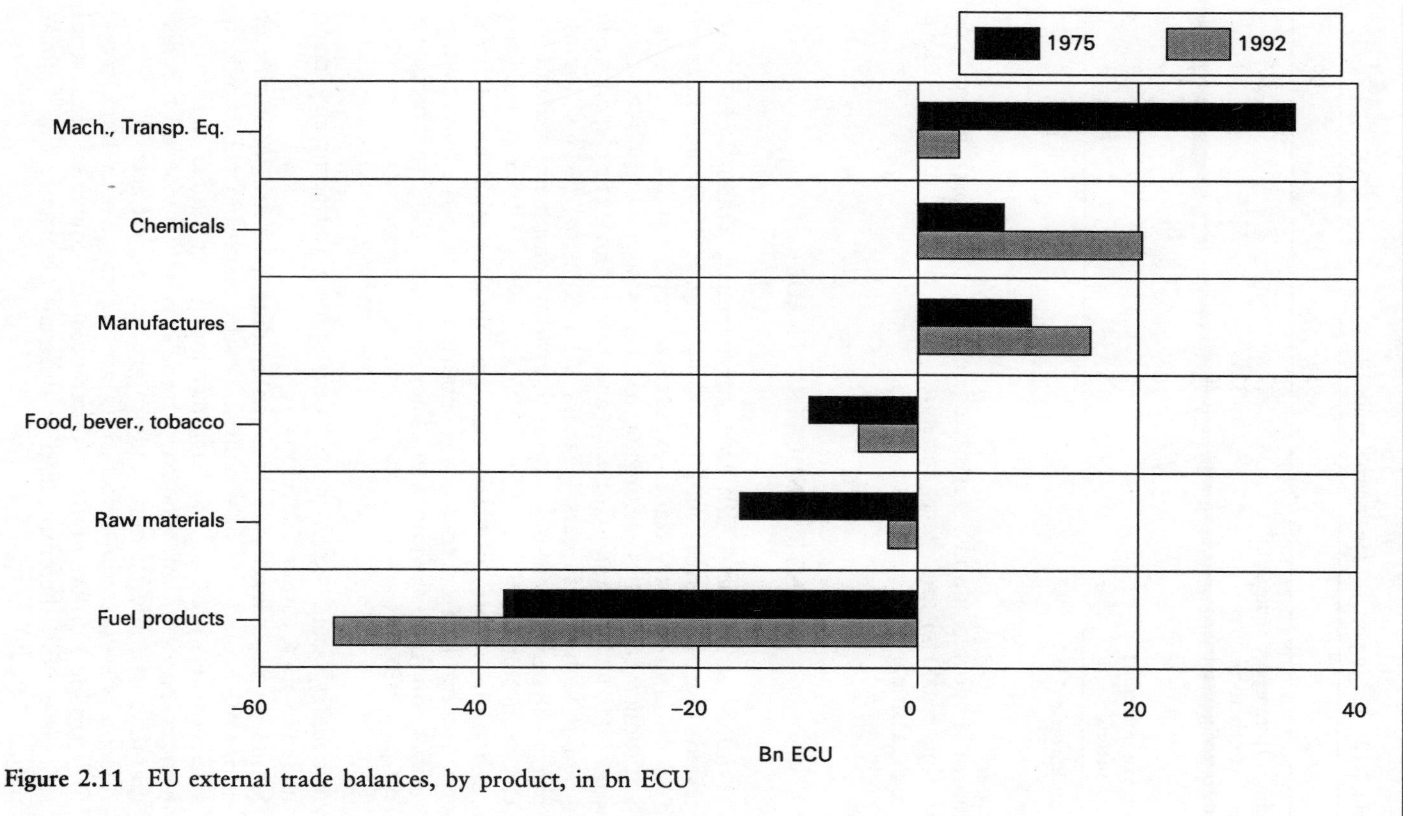

Figure 2.11 EU external trade balances, by product, in bn ECU

Source: Eurostat (1993)

Table 2.12 EU import shares: internal trade

	1958	1975	1992
Machinery, transport equipment	22	29	37
Other manufactures	32	33	30
Food, beverages, tobacco	20	15	12
Chemicals	7	11	12
Fuel	10	7	3
Other raw materials	8	5	3
Miscellaneous	1	0	3

Source: Eurostat (1993)

costs of imported goods, restricting entry to export markets or distorting markets) and what measures have been adopted to move towards a single European market.

INTRA-INDUSTRY TRADE

Observations since the 1930s (see, for example, Ohlin 1933) have suggested that countries, and especially more developed nations, embark on intra-industry trade: export *and* import of what are essentially product categories belonging to the same industry (i.e. close substitutes). The UK, Italy, Germany and France, for example, all trade in different high-quality cars (Jaguars, Alfa Romeos, BMWs, top-of-the-range Citroens). Intra-industry trade reflects consumers' demand for variety or product differentiation. Although we shall, in considering Europe's trade pattern, primarily concern ourselves with the empirical aspects of intra-industry trade, it is important to note the main factors accounting for this phenomenon. They are, according to Loertscher and Wolter (1980):

- A country's stage of economic development (intra-industry trade increases as a country develops).
- Similarity in market size between trading partners (countries at about the same stage of economic development and with similarly sized markets are likely to have developed very similar industries).
- Market barriers (intra-industry trade levels will rise as the dismantling of trade barriers leads to greater market access).
- A country's industrial structure (some industries offer more scope for product differentiation; differences in countries' industrial structures will, therefore, lead to different average levels of intra-industry trade).

Intra-industry trade can be measured in a number of ways. The most frequently used measure is the index developed by Grubel and Lloyd (1975):

$$B_i = 1 - \frac{|X_i - M_i|}{X_i + M_i}$$

where X are exports, M imports, i the industry in question, $|X-M|$ the trade imbalance and B the level of intra-industry trade. The value of B varies between 0 and 1 with a value nearer 0 indicating a (relatively) low level of intra-industry trade and a value nearer 1 suggesting a (relatively) high degree of two-way trade in very similar commodities. Prior to establishing the extent to which Europe's trade is of an intra-industry nature it is important to deal with the main problems inherent in measuring intra-industry trade. First, the *intra-industry trade index* is a relative rather than an absolute measure; the index would not be affected if both exports and imports were, for example, doubled or halved. Second, the measure is sensitive to the level of aggregation adopted. What goods should be treated as similar or different goods is clearly a difficult question. At one extreme we could define an industry very narrowly by choosing goods only a particular country produces (e.g. French Muscadet, German Mosel wine, Italian Chianti). In that case our measure B would yield the very unhelpful result that no intra-industry trade has taken place. If, on the other hand, we define all agricultural produce (e.g. cheese, fruit, wine, etc.) or all manufactures (e.g. cars, hi-fi equipment, toys, etc.) as a single industry, we would, in calculating our intra-industry index B, obtain a relatively high value of intra-industry trade – a both misleading and nonsensical result. Third, any intra-industry indices for all traded products (or traded manufactures) are weighted averages; their values will depend on the relative importance of countries' exports and imports by products. Thus, a country with disproportionately high shares of exports in industries with characteristically low levels of intra-industry trade will exhibit a lower index of trade in differentiated products than a country whose exports are heavily skewed towards industries where the intra-industry indices are relatively high. The standard international trade classification (SITC) forms the basis for calculations of trade flows; data tend to be available at the '3-' or '4-digit' level.

Although the importance of intra-industry has now been recognised for some time and has, *inter alia*, played a part in investigations of European integration, data on average levels of intra-industry trade in Europe are not readily available. The CEC (1989a) has, however, published data of intra-industry indices in the USA, Japan and the EU for high-technology industries (we shall discuss these in Chapter 6

Table 2.13 Average intra-industry trade, 1970 and 1985: France, Germany, Japan and USA

	1970	1985
	All traded goods	
France	.67	.74
West Germany	.54	.63
United States	.53	.54
Japan	.26	.23
	Manufactures only	
France	.78	.82
West Germany	.60	.67
United States	.57	.61
Japan	.32	.26

Note:
Index basis: 3-digit SITC categories
Source: Lincoln (1990: 47)

when we shall deal with Europe's trade with Japan and the United States). But work carried out by Lincoln (1990) enables us to discern the trend in intra-industry trade at least in the EU's two leading traders – Germany and France – and make comparisons with two other large trading nations – the USA and Japan (*Table 2.13*). Looking at all traded goods, we can see that, taking 3-digit SITC categories intra-industry became more significant in both France and (West) Germany between 1970 and 1985. The index increased from .67 to .74 in France and from .54 to .63 in Germany over this period. At a more disaggregated level (manufactured products only), both countries exhibit even higher levels of trade in differentiated products: the indices were .78 (1970) and .82 (1985) for France; in Germany intra-industry trade in manufactures increased from .60 in 1970 to .67 in 1985. Both the USA and Japan appear to have smaller indices of intra-industry trade with Japan exhibiting a significantly lower level of trade in differentiated products than the other three members of the G-7 group of Western industrialised countries. An earlier study by Lawrence (1987), while not permitting to detect changes in trade of differentiated products over time, enables us to compare intra-industry indices across six of the Communities (*Table 2.14*): in 1980 intra-industry levels in the EU ranged from .82 in France to .61 in Italy.

TERMS OF TRADE AND COMPETITIVENESS

The *terms of trade* measure the ratio of export and import prices and, as such, provide some indication of the purchasing power of exports in

Table 2.14 Intra-industry trade indices: selected European and other countries, 1980

Country	Intra-industry index number (based on 94 industries)
France	.82
Belgium	.79
Netherlands	.78
UK	.78
Canada	.68
Sweden	.68
Germany	.66
Italy	.61
Switzerland	.61
USA	.60
Norway	.51
Finland	.49
South Korea	.48
Japan	.25
Australia	.22

Source: Lawrence (1987: 520)

terms of imports. Weighted averages tend to be calculated in arriving at terms of trade data. When a country's (or a trade bloc's) export prices rise faster than its import prices, we say that the terms of trade have improved. Improved terms of trade result in a country's real income being enhanced. When, on the other hand, import prices rise at a faster rate than export prices, we are dealing with a worsening of the terms of trade; a country has to have a higher export volume to be able to acquire the same number of imported commodities (i.e. the country experiences a lowering of its real income). The available evidence suggests that the European Union benefited from more favourable terms of trade in the 1980s. During the second half of the 1980s, for example, they improved by nearly 40 per cent (CEC 1993: 14). The overall improvement in the Union's terms of trade conceals, however, variations between major trade partners. The terms of trade with the Third World improved by much more than those with the Western industrialised world and the high-performing economies of the Far East (Japan and the four NICs). The lowering of the relative prices of primary commodities and oil in the 1980s must be regarded as a major factor accounting for the Third World experiencing worsening terms of trade with the EU; primary commodities and/or oil have represented the principal export component for the developing countries (CEC 1993: 14).

Table 2.15 EU gains in export volume market shares and price competitiveness, 1973–90

	1981/1973	1990/1982
Gains (+)/Losses (–) in market shares	+0.2	–4.0
Gains (+)/Losses (–) in price competitiveness	+2.8	–5.7

Source: CEC (1993: 13)

A country's (or trade bloc's) price *competitiveness* on the world market can be measured by calculating the difference between the growth rate of its competitors' export prices and the growth rate of its own export prices. A positive difference between the two growth rates suggests that a country or trade group has gained in price competitiveness; export prices of the country or trade group have increased less than the export prices of its competitors. A negative sign implies that the country or trade group has lost in international price competitiveness as the export prices of its competitors have increased by less than its own export prices. The Union's price competitiveness improved between 1973 and 1981 but deteriorated in the 1980s (CEC 1993: 13). The losses in the EU's price competitiveness must be seen as a major factor explaining the Union's losses in its export volume market shares. Data on export volume market shares can be obtained by calculating the difference between the growth rate of exports (for a country or trade group) and the growth of world demand measured by (weighted) world import volume. When the difference between a country's or trade group's growth rate of export volume and world demand has a negative (positive) sign, the market share of a country or trade group has decreased (increased). Data produced by Eurostat suggest that, focusing on the EU's external trade (i.e. ignoring internal exports), the direction (and size) of the changes in the EU's export volume market share correspond largely to the changes in her international price competitiveness. Between 1973 and 1981, the Communities became more competitive and increased their export volume market shares. For the period 1982–90, it was found that losses in the EU's competitiveness were accompanied by reductions in its export volume market shares. (CEC 1993: 13). The main results of the Eurostat investigation are summarised in *Table 2.15*. While the results suggest a link between price competitiveness and export volume market shares, we should, in considering them, not ignore the possibility that non-price competition also played a part in determining the EU's export market shares.

GUIDE TO FURTHER READING

CEC (1989) International Trade of the European Communities, *European Economy*, 39.

CEC (1991) *Europe: World Partner. The External Relations of the European Community*, Brussels, CEC.

CEC (1993) The European Community as a World Trade Partner, *European Economy*, 52.

Eurostat (1993) *External Trade and Balance of Payments, Statistical Yearbook*, Recapitulation 1958–1992, Luxembourg, OOPEC.

GATT (1992) *International Trade 90–91*, Geneva, GATT.

GATT (1993) *International Trade Statistics*, Geneva, GATT.

ECE (1992) *Economic Survey of Europe in 1991–1992*, Geneva, United Nations.

ECE (1993) *Economic Bulletin for Europe*, 45, Geneva, United Nations.

3
THE SINGLE MARKET

INTRODUCTION

Since the Common Market came into operation in 1958 its internal trade has, as we saw in Chapter 2, been increasing at a faster rate than its trade with third countries. In 1958, internal trade accounted for 37 per cent of the Union's total trade; by 1992 the EU's internal trade contributed as much as 61 per cent to the EU's overall trade (*Table 2.4* and *Figure 2.5*). The stroke of midnight on 1 January 1993 marked the beginning of a further trade liberalisation process – the creation of a single European market. In creating a single market ('single', 'internal', 'domestic', 'unsegmented', 'unified' or 'integrated' market will be used interchangeably in referring to the internal liberalisation process set in motion by what has generally become known as '1992') within Europe, the Commission aimed to create a fully integrated and liberalised market for goods, services and factors of production. What factors led to the creation of this single market? What barriers to internal trade had remained after tariffs and quotas had been abolished in the late

1970s? What measures did the single market consist of, and what routes to economic integration have been pursued? To what extent will '1992' affect internal trade flows and make the EU better off? Are there any further obstacles to successful integration following the removal of non-tariff barriers at the end of 1992 and, if so, what corollary economic policies would have to be pursued in an attempt to create a fully integrated European market? What are the external trade implications of the European domestic market? These are the main questions we shall address in this chapter.

THE SINGLE EUROPEAN ACT

The EU white paper *Completing the Internal Market* (CEC 1985) and the *Single European Act* (CEC 1986) can be seen as the start of a campaign to revitalise what the six original members of the European Union (Benelux countries, France, Germany, Italy) agreed to achieve by signing and implementing the 1957 Treaty of Rome – a 'common market' characterised by the uninhibited movement of goods, people, services and capital. Although the Treaty of Rome had, by 1969, led to the virtual abolition of tariffs and quotas between member states, markets continued to be segmented; non-tariff barriers added to the costs of internal trade and restricted exporters' entries to other member states. Non-European rather than European companies increasingly established themselves in the European markets. American multinational enterprises such as Ford and IBM are cases in point; they reaped benefits from economies of scale via transnational organisation of production and marketing. In *Le Défi Américain* (1967) Jean-Jacques Servant-Schreiber focused on the way American companies had started to challenge, if not threaten, the emerging European markets in the 1960s. But the analysis he applied can easily be extended to the way the Japanese began to conquer Europe in the 1970s. *Eurosclerosis* with its symptoms of comparatively high labour costs and low productivity (Posner and Sargent 1987) must be seen as the main factor accounting for Europe being less competitive than other advanced industrialised trading partners, notably Japan and the United States (CEC 1989a). As a remedy for the adverse effects Eurosclerosis and non-tariff barriers had had on the integration and liberalisation of European markets the European Commission, under pressure from industry, proposed wide-scale deregulation of industry and finance within Europe in the 1980s. This led to the Single European Act with a large number of measures designed to lay the foundation for a more, if not wholly, unified European market by 31 December 1992.

NON-TARIFF BARRIERS TO INTERNAL TRADE

In order to create an unsegmented market within Europe *all* barriers to the free flow of goods, services, capital and labour had to be eliminated. Tariffs and import quotas had virtually been abolished for intra-EU trade by the late 1970s. But other barriers had been impeding Europe's internal trade in the period up to '1992'.

In a study carried out on behalf of the European Commission, Nerb (1988) used identical questionnaires in all EU member states involving some 20,000 enterprises in an attempt to ascertain what barriers industrialists identified as inhibiting internal trade flows. His findings suggested that industrialists ranked the seriousness of different types of barriers to trade between member states (in descending order of importance) as follows:

- technical standards and regulations
- administrative barriers
- frontier formalities
- freight transport regulations
- value-added tax differences
- capital market controls
- government procurement restrictions
- implementation of Union law.

The factors that respondents to Nerb's questionnaire study perceived as inhibiting inter-state trade could be grouped differently by adopting the list of barriers which, according to the Commission's white paper (CEC 1985), had to be eliminated if European business, consumers and governments were 'to enjoy a real European home in the 1990s' (Cecchini 1988: 4). According to the Commission non-tariff barriers imposing additional costs on internal trade can be seen to be falling into three broad categories:

- physical barriers
- technical barriers
- fiscal barriers

Physical barriers are those arising from delays at frontiers for customs purposes (assessment of value-added tax or excise duties), and related administative burdens (collection of statistics, the checking of forms etc.).

Technical barriers cover any restrictions that operate within national territories such as the need to comply with particular technical regulations or norms for goods and services; discrimination against foreign suppliers in public sector purchases (public procurement); restrictions on freedom to embark on certain service transactions, notably financial and transport services; restrictions on cross-border movements of capital and establishment of subsidiaries etc.

Fiscal barriers exist because member countries impose different rates of indirect taxes (value added tax and excise duties) on goods and services and, in accordance with the 'destination' principle, goods are exempt from tax in the country of origin but are subject to tax in the country which imports the goods.

THE SINGLE MARKET PROGRAMME

The main aim of the Single European Act was to create a unified market. It would seem advisable at this stage to clarify what is meant by a 'common market' and by other terms such as 'economic and monetary union', 'customs union' and 'free trade area' – concepts that tend to be used in discussions of economic integration.

- A *free trade area* is an arrangement resulting in the member countries, while retaining independence over their external trade policies, agreeing to abolish all barriers to trade among themselves.
- A *customs union*, like a free trade area, implies that there are no barriers to internal trade. Members of a customs union are, however, no longer pursuing independent trade policies in dealing with the countries outside the customs union; their external trade reflects a common and coordinated trade policy.
- A *common market* is a customs union which, in addition to free trade of goods and services, is also characterised by the uninhibited movement of the production factors capital and labour.
- An *economic and monetary union* meets all the criteria of a common market; it would, however, also require both a common currency and common or harmonised monetary and fiscal policies for all its member countries.

It would follow that, although the media had, in discussing the EU, tended to refer to it as a common market, it had really been operating like a customs union between 1958 and 1992 as the movement of labour and capital had not been entirely uninhibited during this period. In fact, the large array of non-tariff barriers that existed in the period between 1958 (when the Common Market came into operation) and 1992 was a clear indication that the member states were, during this period, in the process of completing rather than having already achieved a customs union.

The Commission's programme for completing the European internal market – the white paper (CEC 1985) – initially contained 300 directives (or European laws) designed to abolish cost increasing, entry restricting and market distorting barriers to internal trade. Some twenty of these directives were subsequently deleted from the initial list. The Commission, in what became to be known as the *Cockfield Report* (Lord Cockfield, the then commissioner for the internal market, was in charge of preparing the 1985 white paper), provided a very detailed catalogue of measures required to establish the single European market. But the initially compiled list of directives had, in fact, been far from comprehensive. Some important aspects such as, for example, the need for powers to control mergers and for harmonising corporation tax in order to reduce, if not eliminate, inter-state capital movements (Swann 1992: 17) did not feature in the single market action package. Despite these limitations the '1992' programme, implemented on 1 January 1993, formed an appropriate basis for creating a much more unified and integrated economic area than had been possible in the previous three decades. Following a Commission report concerning the implementation of the white paper (CEC 1992a), agreements to turn most of the single market rules into laws had been reached by 31 December 1992. Although it proved impossible to remove the fiscal barriers (indirect taxes have continued to differ in the member states) most, if not all, physical and technical barriers had been removed by the end of 1992. As a result:

- people, goods, capital and services have, on the whole, been able to move freely (either on the basis of harmonised or common rules or on the basis of mutual recognition of regulations and standards);
- little or no customs documentation has been necessary since January 1993 to accompany domestically produced goods moving within the Union or released for free circulation in a member state.

A detailed discussion of all the steps taken by the Commission to facilitate the completion of the internal market is outside the scope of this book (for detailed accounts see, for example, Owens and Dynes 1989; CEC 1991a; Swann 1992). What is worth noting is that, in attempting to complete the internal market, the Commission had, prior to 1992, tried alternative routes to economic integration. At the risk of oversimplifying matters, it could be argued that economic integration can be achieved by pursuing either a 'Bismarckian' or 'Jeffersonian' approach (Kay and Posner 1989). The Bismarckian approach is characterised 'by the imposition . . . of a strong central authority on the component parts' (Kay and Posner 1989: 55); the Jeffersonian route, on the other hand, consists of spreading best practice or 'competition between rules' (*ibid.* 1989: 57). It is in the area of technical barriers that the differences between the Bismarckian and Jeffersonian approaches to economic integration and liberalisation of trade can perhaps be best illustrated. Technical barriers represent impediments to internal trade if a member state insists on imported goods complying with its national production standards and regulations even though such a compliance cannot be justified in terms of environmental or consumer protection. In the 1970s, the Commission appeared, on the whole, to favour the Bismarckian approach to economic integration by trying to impose harmonisation of goods from above. This might well have led to futile attempts to find common definitions for commodities such as, for example, chocolate, icecream, jam, pasta and sausage and concomitant creations of concepts such as 'Euro-chocolate', 'Euro-icecream', Euro-jam', 'Euro-pasta' and 'Euro-sausage'. But a judgement by the European Court of Justice in 1979 – the *Cassis de Dijon* case – demonstrated that 'harmonisation' was not necessarily the optimal route to economic integration. In the *Cassis de Dijon* case Rewe Zentral AG – a German company – had planned to import the liqueur *Crême de Cassis* into Germany. It was initially prevented from doing so because the *cassis* – so the German authorities maintained – did not conform to Germany's liqueur norms because it did not contain sufficient alcohol to be regarded as *Likör* (liqueur) by German standards. However, the European Court of Justice ruled that Germany was not allowed to discriminate against the French liqueur. Rewe Zentral AG was entitled to import and sell cassis in Germany as the German authorities could not prove that it violated health and safety regulations. Since the *Cassis de Dijon* case the Commission has, in dealing with technical regulations, more often than not used the 'new approach' of mutual recognition rather than the harmonisation approach. Goods manufactured according to the producing country's standards and regulations have had to be considered as acceptable in all other member countries. Competitive rule-making resulting from the adoption of the 'new approach' clearly has the advantage of being more compatible with the notion of consumer sovereignty; consumers rather than producers or governments decide what products they would like to purchase. Mutual recognition of laws would, furthermore, seem to be consistent with deregulatory practices that member states, notably the UK, France and, to a lesser extent, Germany, have been incorporating into their economic policies since the 1980s.

'1992' AND INTERNAL TRADE

Distinguishing between different types of non-tariff barriers to trade (physical, technical and fiscal) is a useful starting point for considering the single market programme. It is, however, of greater interest to analyse the impact of the removal of non-tariff barriers than to identify their causes. In discussing the economic effects of '1992' it would seem appropriate to consider both the internal and external dimensions of the single market. The external trade implications of '1992' will be considered in the last section of this chapter. We shall focus here on '1992' and the Union's internal trade. In dealing with the alleged internal benefits of the European internal market, we shall consider both qualitative and quantitative aspects of '1992'. Our discussion of the internal effects of the domestic market will also distinguish between the microeconomic and macroeconomic impact. Although some reference will be made to the overall effects of the internal market programme, emphasis will be placed on its trade implications.

The numerous measures introduced by the single market project amounted to removing non-tariff barriers to trade. The removal of these barriers was supposed to lead to *trade creation* (more efficient producers replace less efficient producers in supplying markets) among the Communities, in order to improve the competitiveness of domestic firms and to make the EU better off. What is the theoretical basis for making these predictions? Assuming that economic theory can be used to predict that the EU will be better off as a result of the removal of non-tariff barriers, how plausible are the existing predictions and estimates?

Microeconomic effects

Let us first consider the microeconomic effects that the Commission expected to result from the creation of a European domestic market. Abolishing non-tariff barriers means that the prices at which goods and services are being traded should be less distorted and the countries affected by the removal of these barriers should experience gains in efficiency. There should, as a result, be more scope for increased specialisation. Economies should, following the law of comparative advantages, be in a position to enhance their consumption beyond their production possibilities. Consumers should benefit from the removal of non-tariff barriers because prices should be more equalised, and there should be an increase in the variety of goods on offer. In considering the impact the removal of non-tariff barriers have on producers, it is important to distinguish between short-term and long-term effects. In the short run, domestic producers are likely to experience lower profit margins as they are being exposed to competition from suppliers located in the other member states. In the long run, firms should be able to operate more efficiently. Factor mobility should increase efficiency via a better allocation of resources. Mass production should enable firms to benefit from economies of scale and to gain experience of how to produce more efficiently – the so-called learning curve effect. Finally, firms could be expected to acquire an improved capacity to innovate. The combined effects of increased competition and economies of scale – the supply side effects (a more competitive climate in industry; opening up of public procurement and lifting barriers to competition in Europe's financial services sector; greater opportunities to exploit economies of scale) should bring about a lowering of the average prices at which goods and services are being traded within the EU.

Macroeconomic effects

In considering the macroeconomic effects resulting from the internal liberalisation process associated with '1992', the Commission had attempted to predict the impact the European domestic market was likely to have on gross domestic product, prices, employment, the budget deficit and trade in Europe. As this book is concerned with trade issues we need not discuss all the aspects of the (medium- and long-term) consequences of the completion of the internal market for the EU as predicted by the Commission. It is, however, worth noting that the Commission expected '1992' to lead to growth of the Union's gross domestic product by 4.5 to 7 per cent, depending on whether or not there would be accompanying economic measures to support the single market programme (CEC 1988a: 167).

Opening up the internal market was expected to create trade among the European Communities as high-cost suppliers would be replaced by low-cost suppliers. '1992' was also expected to improve the EU's export competitiveness in external trade. In addition to predicting that '1992' would result in higher growth of the European economy, the 'cost of non-Europe' study (CEC 1988a,b) contained the following four specific trade-related predictions:

- intra-EU imports would be substituted for national goods and services;
- intra-EU imports would replace imports from outside the Union;
- the EU's terms of trade would improve (the same level of exports would buy more imports);
- the EU's balance of trade would improve.

Official estimates

The Commission did not merely predict the overall effects of the creation of an internal European market; attempts were also made to quantify the benefits resulting from '1992'. The economic impact of the removal of non-tariff barriers can be measured either in terms of the cost of their presence or the benefits of their removal (CEC 1988a: 33). In considering the estimates of the benefits of the single market, we shall present the official forecasts and then evaluate the Commission's findings.

The Commission's official estimates involved calculations of:

- short-term barrier removal effects
  - stage 1 – costs of barriers affecting trade
  - stage 2 – costs of barriers affecting all production
- long-term market integration effects
  - stage 3 – economies of scale from restructuring and increased production
  - stage 4 – competition effects on inefficiency (resulting from managerial slack) and monopoly rents.

The results of stage one of the barrier removal calculations (CEC 1988a: 182) suggested that internal imports would increase by 3.7 to 4.5 per cent and external imports would be reduced by 2.2 to 2.6 per cent; the second stage of the barrier removal calculations lead to a predicted reduction in external imports amounting to 5.7 to 7.7 per cent (CEC 1988a: 182). Combining the total barrier removal effects resulting from stages one and two meant that the Commission predicted external imports to be reduced by approximately 10 per cent. Much more significant trade effects were forecast by Smith and Venables (1988) who, instead of basing their calculations on a competitive model, tried to estimate the effects of increased competition and market integration assuming non-competitive markets. According to them abolishing internal trade barriers would have the following effects: internal imports would increase by 45 per cent; external imports would be reduced by 25 per cent; and the Union's exports would increase by 6 per cent.

Evaluation

Arguments have been advanced as to why the official estimates should be viewed as being too cautious or too optimistic. Baldwin (1989, 1992a), for example, regarded the Commission's calculations as too conservative as they tended to ignore possible positive 'knock-on' effects. Gains in output, so Baldwin argued, could bring about an increase in the EU's capital stock; he also thought it possible that the gains generated by the single market would not be of a 'one-off' nature but could increase Europe's growth rates on a more permanent basis. Most commentators have, however, been sceptical about the precise magnitude of the officially estimated effects of the single market programme. The criticism made of the Commission's calculations of the likely benefits of the single market would appear to question the following aspects of the 'cost of non-Europe' study (CEC 1988a,b):

public sector procurement; removal of non-tariff barriers; price convergence; adherence to rules; non-price competition; economies of scale.

As long as important areas of public sector procurement such as defence, telecommunications, water, energy and transport are excluded from the '1992' programme (only about 15 per cent of the telecommunications sector, for example, is open to free competition under EU directives), there is unlikely to be a significant increase in public sector procurement across borders within the EU.

In considering the likely impact of the removal of non-tariff barriers, a distinction should be made between total and partial removal of these barriers. The cost reductions generated by the removal of border controls and transport regulations may be smaller than the Commission estimated, because not all border controls and procedures administered by customs authorities were, in fact, abolished by 31 December 1992. Some non-tariff barriers connected with technical standards and regulations may, in fact, have not been removed, because cost considerations (adjusting to common standards, etc.) would have offset or outweighed the gains resulting from the removal of the barriers (Kay 1989). Yet, the various institutions that were commissioned to quantify the 'cost of non-Europe' (CEC 1988b) were, it appears, specifically asked to calculate the effects of a removal of non-tariff barriers on the premise that the single market programme, once implemented, would remove *all* non-tariff barriers.

The actual price equalisation process resulting from the single market programme may fall short of the predictions made by the Commission. Even within one member state we may find that prices for the same goods are far from equal. A study of prices for consumer electronics, for example, found that in the 1980s inter-city price differences in Germany amounted to as much as 53 per cent of the price differences within the EU (Cecchini 1988: 79; CEC 1988a: 122). In other words, price differences for the same goods and services purchased by EU citizens may well continue to exist despite the removal of internal non-tariff barriers.

The magnitude of the Cecchini gains depends, no doubt, on the extent to which member states and business cooperate in the implementation of the various directives included in the '1992' programme. The Commission's predictions were based on the assumption that business could be expected to compete rather than resort to collusions or mergers. The Commission authorities will, therefore, have to make sure that any competition rules will be enforced rigorously; and member states and business will have to obey any European Court of Justice rulings.

While it seems plausible to predict that the removal of non-tariff barriers is likely to increase internal imports as consumers tend to substitute imported for domestic products, the magnitude of this substitution process clearly depends on the strengths of consumers' preferences. If consumer have distinct preferences for imported products, then non-price rather than price competition would influence their decisions and the single market would, as a result, have less of an impact on trade.

The Commission's estimates about the gains resulting from a domestic market crucially depended on the economies of scale argument. The removal of non-tariff barriers was expected to lead to a changed economic environment in which business could reap the benefits of large-scale production. It was furthermore assumed that there would be more competition among firms and that prices would, on average, be reduced following the completion of the European internal market. Undoubtedly, the hopes the Commission had about the scope for economies of scale (CEC 1988a: 107–15) were influenced by comparisons with the US internal market. But considering that there appears to be no evidence to suggest that European plants are comparatively too small and therefore less efficient, it seems difficult to be too optimistic about the economies of scale which the removal of non-tariff barriers may generate. Any reduction in costs may, therefore, be small.

The European single market will have had to function for a number of years before it will be possible to measure the actual benefits derived from '1992' and to compare them with the potential benefits Cecchini (1988) predicted. Despite the reservations we expressed about the plausibility of some of the qualitative predictions and the quantitative aspects of the official calculations – based on the massive research sponsored by the Commission (some 40 consultants were commissioned to carry out research on the 'cost of non-Europe' and their findings were published in 16 volumes containing 27 reports (CEC 1988b)) – one would, on balance, expect the EU to derive some benefits from the measures associated with the single market project. But caution should clearly be expressed against the precise magnitudes of the benefits of '1992', especially as the calculations were carried out years before the various directives were implemented. While the EU, as a whole, may gain and internal trade may well increase at the expense of the EU's external trade, the distributional effects of the single European market are somewhat uncertain – an issue that was excluded from the Commission's investigations (for a discussion see, for example, Neven 1990; Winters 1992a: 11–12).

OBSTACLES TO SUCCESS

The existence of an internal market presupposes that, in addition to goods and services moving freely within an economic area irrespective of any national borders, we find uninhibited movement of capital and people. This raises the more general question of whether any additional obstacles would have to be overcome before we can view the European domestic market as approximating, say, the north American version of a single market. In considering any such remaining obstacles to the creation of a truly unified market within Europe, it is important to distinguish between political and economic problems that have beset the completion of a single European market.

Political problems

There are a number of political problems that would appear to be preventing '1992' from marking the creation of a truly unified European market. Political factors may undermine the operation of a single market if they affect the actual removal of technical barriers to internal trade and frontier controls.

What political factors are likely to impede the removal of technical barriers to internal trade? First, the single market programme was, from the start, far from comprehensive in producing directives for the removal of non-tariff barriers. Second, only a fraction of the 300-odd measures for creating the single market were adopted by both the Commission *and* the governments of all the member states (DTI 1993). Third, the way governments may have chosen to interpret the various directives that came into force by 1 January 1993 will crucially determine the success of the single market. Fourth, the political determination to complete the programme may be absent: governments may be reluctant to surrender their national sovereignty; they may yield to lobbying from pressure groups, especially if they face elections; they may consider the costs involved in adhering to directives as too high (Lintner 1989: 19–20). Fifth, it seems likely that the European Court of Justice will inevitably have to be involved in clarifying many of the '1992' directives and, prior to contentious issues (similar perhaps to the *Cassis de Dijon* case) being addressed, a lot of time and energy will have to be expended.

What political factors have prevented the complete removal of frontier controls in Europe's internal trade? The abolition of frontier controls was supposed to apply to goods, services, capital and people. Yet, not all frontiers disappeared on New Year's Day 1993. Britain, Denmark and Ireland envisage keeping controls on people for an indefinite period on the grounds that the principle of 'free movement of people' covers EU nationals only and that border controls are necessary to check non-EU nationals. The other member states, on the other hand, relaxed border controls significantly on 1 January 1993. Any remaining frontier controls between the countries who signed the 1985 *Schengen accord* are supposed to be lifted at a later stage. But although complete freedom of movement for citizens in the Unions has been a goal ever since the Treaty of Rome was signed, governments concerned about controlling drugs, terrorism and illegal immigration have been worried about taking steps to implement this goal.

Economic problems

Economic obstacles have been equally, if not more, important than political obstacles in hampering progress towards achieving the declared objective of '1992' – a 'Europe without frontiers'. The principal economic factors that have been impeding the creation of a completely unified market would appear to be: indirect taxes and excise duties; alternative measures of protection (restrictive practices, subsidies, etc.); absence of corollary economic policies and of a single currency.

Creating a well-integrated market requires, strictly speaking, harmonisation of *indirect taxes*. As long as rates for indirect taxes differ between countries and the 'destination' system is being applied (exports are exempted from the indirect tax in the country of origin – the exporting country – but are subject to the indirect tax at the local rate in the country of destination – the importing country), frontier controls will continue to be necessary in order to monitor internal trade. The single market programme initially envisaged an approximation of indirect taxes – VAT and excise duties – between the member states in order to reduce, if not eliminate, the costs incurred by companies and governments. But discussions of harmonising indirect taxation did not go beyond the proposal stage. As a result, different rates of VAT and excise duties have continued to be applied even after January 1993.

Application of the destination principle, although of course associated with costs of collecting VAT and excise duties in the importing country, tends to be economically 'neutral' in that it avoids trade distortion; imported and domestic goods face the same taxes in each country. Trade distortions, albeit of a minor nature, may, however, arise for three reasons. First, countries may use high VAT rates in order to discriminate against imports of goods if the level of domestic production of substitutes of the imported commodity is fairly small (Guieu and Bonnet 1987). Imposing low taxes on, for example, beer while taxing wine fairly heavily would be likely to boost beer sales in a country like the UK (which produces very little wine) and discriminate against imports of wine-producing countries such as France, Germany and Italy. Second, significantly different VAT rates may result in personal or parallel imports with consumers purchasing a good from a country which charges a relatively low pre-tax price for the good but levies a relatively high rate of VAT on this good. Denmark, for example, imposes considerably higher taxes on the sales of cars than the other member states; its pre-tax car prices are also among the lowest in Europe (BEUC 1992a). In the absence of trade barriers there would, therefore, be scope for personal imports. Third, trade may be distorted because 'member states differ in their allocation of goods to zero-, standard – and higher-rate brackets' (Pelkmans and Winters 1988: 41).

Faced with the need to remove non-tariff barriers governments or business may resort to the use of *alternative means of protection* such as restrictive practices and subsidies.

The adoption of *restricted practices* may contribute to market segmentation. Examples of segmented markets in the EU's internal trade abound. Pharmaceutical markets, for example, have continued to be one of the most fragmented markets with large price differences between high-priced countries like Denmark, Germany, and the Netherlands and low-priced countries like Greece, Italy, Portugal and Spain (Economists' Advisory Group 1988; Klepper 1992). The BEUC's price surveys established considerable price variations for goods such as compact cameras, camcorders, CD players, car tyres, toys, compact discs (BEUC 1992b). In illustrating how restrictive practices have served to create obstacles to establishing a single European market, we shall discuss the car market. This market represents a particularly appropriate illustration of an 'uncommon' market. The fragmentation of the European car market has received widespread publicity since the 1980s; it has been well documented; and cars are one of the most traded manufactured goods.

A number of recent studies (BEUC 1992a; MMC 1992) clearly demonstrated the extent to which the *EU car market* has remained fragmented. This fragmentation has manifested itself in two distinctive features. First, car prices in the member states still vary enormously with (pre-tax) price disparities typically in excess of 40 per cent (BEUC 1992a). Second, consumers who would have liked to purchase a car from a lower price country have been facing major and, at times, insurmountable difficulties in personally importing a car. Manufacturers and dealers, it would appear, have been able to form 'informal cartels' which have enabled them to practise price discrimination – selling identical cars at different prices with the price differentials reflecting different elasticities of demand rather than cost differences (IFS 1982). What barriers have been set up to separate the markets? What attempts have been made to remove these barriers? What chances are there for the European car market to become less fragmented in the future?

Barriers between the car markets in the member states have been created by governments, the car manufacturers and the Commission. According to EU law, consumers should have the freedom to buy cars in any member state. In practice, consumers who want to import a car from another member state have had to contend with a considerable amount of bureaucracy. Forms have to be completed, special registration procedures have to be followed and national rules on technical standards have to be met. Not only may it be difficult to register a car imported from another member state; it may also create problems in selling a personally imported car at a later stage. The Consumer Association drew attention to the car price differentials within Europe more than a decade ago and tried to encourage parallel imports in order to narrow the price gaps by issuing a kit *How to import your car* for residents of the UK in the early 1980s. This kit on shopping for cars in Europe is no longer available as UK residents, faced with the difficulties with which personal imports are associated, appear to have become less rather than more inclined to buy right-hand drive cars in other member states. Why? Difficult registration procedures may play a part in explaining this phenomenon. But the principal factor accounting for the segmentation of the European car market must be sought in the exclusive dealership system that characterises car sales in the Union. For, in marked contrast to the system in operation in the United States, European car dealers exclusively sell the cars of a particular manufacturer. This selective dealership system has resulted in restrictive practices and has impeded cross-border sales of cars. Manufacturers' guarantees are not automatically honoured for cars which customers personally bought 'abroad'. EU competition law does not allow exclusive dealerships. But adoption of a special regulation in 1985 – the so-called block exemption – has enabled the European car industry to continue with this system. This 'block exemption' may, it appears, only be withdrawn if the selective dealership system can be shown to lead to cross-border price differences of more than 12 per cent; dealers are also required to make it genuinely possible for customers from other member states to purchase cars and import them into their countries. Despite the 1985 ruling, car prices across the Union have differed by more than 12 per cent (BEUC 1992a; MMC 1992). Some car dealers, while not refusing to sell right-hand drive models of cars, have tended to add disproportionately high charges for selling a right-hand rather than a left-hand drive model. The Commission was, however, not in a position to withdraw the exemption clause as there was no proof that the selective dealership system had 'caused' the significant price differences. As a result, the system was allowed to continue. However, car manufacturers were urged by the Commission to facilitate cross border purchases of cars and enable customers to make more informed purchasing decisions by publishing price lists for each model in each member state on a regular basis.

What then are the chances of the EU car market opening up as all European markets are supposed to? As long as the Commission tolerates the exclusive dealership system and personal imports of cars from one member state into another are associated with bureaucratic rules and regulations, the EU car market is bound to remain fragmented. The price differences could, admittedly, be narrowed if the Commission were prepared to prosecute car dealers who decline either to sell cars to, say, UK buyers or add excessive charges for supplying a right-hand drive model. But a single European car market will only emerge once the selective dealership system has become illegal, markets become more transparent to the consumers and dealers sell cars of more than one manufacturer.

Apart from resorting to restrictive practices to curb internal trade flows, member states may respond to the removal of non-tariff barriers by subsidising industries in order to make them more competitive. Article 92 of the Treaty of Rome specifies that, prior to member states providing state aid for industrial projects, the Commission must approve the payment of any such *subsidies*. In practice, governments, more often than not, appear either to submit schemes for approval after providing funds or to omit notifying the Commission altogether. Since the 1980s the Commission has produced regular reports on state aid in the Union with the first survey covering the years 1981–86 (CEC 1989b) and the most recent survey providing information on the extent of state aid for 1988–90 (CEC 1992b). According to the survey published in 1992, the annual averages of state aids were fairly similar for the years 1986–88 and 1988–90 (93 and 89 billion ECUs respectively). But it appeared that the 'big four' (Britain, France, Germany and Italy) accounted for a growing share of state aid in manufacturing: their share of other manufacturing subsidy grew from 75 per cent in 1986–88 to 80 per cent in 1988–90 (CEC 1992b).

Our discussion of the European car market suggests that removing non-tariff barriers is clearly but one condition for achieving market integration. Successful economic integration also requires the pursuit of appropriately chosen *corollary economic policies*. In the case of the car market effective competition policy measures should be able to break up the informal cartel agreements that have contributed to, if not caused, market segmentation and price discrimination. There are two other important areas where complementary economic policies are called for if the objectives of the single market programme are to be attained. First, there is a need to develop a common transport policy. A more efficient, less expensive and faster transport system is necessary in order to facilitate increased internal trade. Second, steps will have to be taken to provide the basis for generating the long-term supply side effects of '1992' that the Commission has been hoping for. Europe's high technology sector has been lagging behind the United States and Japan (CEC 1989a). Europe's car industry has also not been very competitive; Japan's exports to Europe have had to be curtailed by trade restrictions in order to reduce car imports from Japan to the 'agreed' market share of 11 per cent. While it seems clear that an industrial policy is needed (N'Guyen and Owen 1992), there is no agreement as to what form this industrial policy should take. One possible course of action would be to protect both the car and the high-technology industries by adopting a 'strategic trade policy' (via providing aid in the short run) in order to make them more competitive in the long run. Investment in human capital (via improving the standard of technical education in Europe) would be a further way of tackling the problem of Europe's lack of competitiveness in the long term.

A *single currency* as envisaged, for example, in the Maastricht Treaty is doubtless a prerequisite for a single European market. As long as member states use different currencies the gains from market integration will inevitably be more limited in magnitude. The use of different currencies imposes heavy transaction costs on to industry with a concomitant reduction in internal trade flows. Absence of a common currency would also tend to be associated with risks of doing cross-border business.

The US experience

The American version of the European domestic market clearly has the advantage over the European internal market of being based on one currency and one language – ingredients that inevitably make for a higher degree of market integration. But we should bear in mind that even the American single market has been characterised by a number of non-tariff barriers which have had adverse effects on US internal trade (Pelkmans 1988). For example, entry into the road haulage business is subject to restrictions in some 43 states; some 20 states have so-called preference laws which allow them to discriminate in favour of local tenders; the insurance market is fragmented in that insurance companies tend to be state controlled with the state fixing prices; there are interstate differences in excise duties and sales tax.

EXTERNAL TRADE IMPLICATIONS

The 1992 programme was concerned with European domestic issues and, as such, it clearly focused on internal rather than external liberalisation of trade. The white paper (CEC 1985) in fact marginalised, if not ignored, the external implications of '1992'. Considering the importance of the EU in world trade (in 1992 the Union accounted for nearly two fifths of world trade (*Table 2.1*)) the external repercussions of an internal European market must clearly be taken into account. The single market is bound to have an impact on the EU's internal *and* external trade. Trade flows with the Union's main trading partners are likely to be particularly affected. The Commission's calculations suggested that a reduction of external imports of about 10 per cent would result from the completion of the internal market (CEC 1988a: 181–2).

From an analytical viewpoint, '1992' is likely to have an impact on the EU's external trade links for a number of reasons. First, the magnitude of its external trade flows depends on the growth of the EU's economy as its imports from the rest of the world vary with the level of its total income. Second, given today's interdependence of the global world economy, external trade will be influenced by the interaction between internal and external liberalisation processes accompanying the completion of the single market. Third, and this is arguably the most important point, what determines the direction and magnitude of the EU's trade flows with third countries is the extent to which the EU will adopt and be exposed to protectionism in their external economic relations.

A positive or optimistic view of the external effects of '1992' would be to suggest that the rest of the world would, on balance, benefit from the completion of a single European market. Although the internal trade liberalisation process will undoubtedly result in internal trade gaining at the expense of the EU's external trade, the effects of this trend would have to be balanced against the opportunities created by '1992'. Assuming that the Commission's estimates about the impact of the removal of trade barriers and the supply side effects prove to be correct and the Union, as a result, increases its growth rate (an additional growth of 4.5 to 7 per cent was expected to result from '1992' (CEC 1988a: 167)), then foreign competitors supplying goods for which there is a high income elasticity within the EU will benefit by exporting more to the EU. Third countries might also be able to take advantage of scale economies offered by the opportunities to sell on an enlarged European market.

Furthermore, if it can be demonstrated that competition from abroad (rather than competitive pressure from within the EU) contributes to a strengthening of Europe's competitive position (Jacquemin and Sapir 1991: 166), as two empirical studies (Jacquemin and Sapir 1990; Neven and Roeller 1990) appear to suggest, then, if internal is combined with external trade liberalisation, the actual gains from the completion of the single market would be maximised. Finally, if the Commission's external trade policy relinquishes protectionist measures such as quantitative restrictions, 'rules of origin' regulations, barriers resulting from 'reciprocity' agreements and 'anti-dumping' actions, then additional trade for the rest of the world would be created. Such an abandonment of protectionism would be consistent with the philosophy underlying the single market concept: 'the logic of the EDM (European domestic market) to promote competitiveness and efficiency implies not only a common trade policy, but that protectionism should be minimised' (Pelkmans and Winters 1988: 101).

A negative or pessimistic view of the external repercussions of '1992', on the other hand, would lead to a very different scenario. If the EU economy, despite the single market programme, grew at a slower rate than the Commission's estimates suggest, then not even those third country firms supplying products for which demand is fairly income elastic within the EU would benefit from the operation of a European internal market. If, in the absence of external trade liberalisation, European producers are not exposed to competitive pressure from external producers and the competition among the domestic producers is insufficient to bring about the desired supply side effects, then the actual gains would fall short of the potential advantages of a single market. Finally, if protectionist measures continue to be used by the EU, *trade diversion* (less efficient producers from within the EU will have access to the domestic markets rather than more efficient producers from the rest of the world) is likely to be the predominant outcome for third countries in trade links with the Union.

According to the Commission, what impact would '1992' have on the rest of the world? The 'cost of non-Europe' project (CEC 1988a,b), in addition to attempting to calculate the global trade diversion effects, also estimated the trade effects on a sectoral basis. According to the Commission's calculations (CEC 1988a: 181–2) which covered more than thirty sectors, trade diversion effects were expected in most sectors; particularly large reductions in external imports were predicted for credit and insurance, electricity, gas, water, ores and metals, and communications. In nine sectors (notably agricultural and food products, and some service sectors) the effects of '1992' were expected to be nil. In two sectors (coal and coke) the Commission actually predicted an increase in the EU's external trade (it was assumed that eliminating trade barriers for coal and coke would reduce the cost of domestic *and* external production of these two products). Since the Commission's calculations excluded the new Mediterranean members the trade diversion effects are likely to be underestimates.

The Commission's study on the 'cost of non-Europe' (CEC 1988a,b) does not explicitly deal with the effects of '1992' on its principal trading partners. The question of third country effects has, however, been addressed in a number of independent studies from which some, albeit tentative, conclusions may be drawn. Davenport and Page (1991) concluded that developing countries would not, on the whole, be adversely affected by the single European Market. But the analysis was based on the assumption that there would be no change in the EU's trade policy towards developing countries and that '1992' would, in fact, generate the magnitude of economic growth predicted by the Commission. The impact of the single market on the Nordic EFTA countries, according to Norman (1989, 1991), would be of considerable significance in that they will lose their comparative trade advantages in most goods except simple forestry and metal products. In the absence of changes in trade policy such as moves towards more protectionism, Hufbauer (1990) suggested that the United States would gain marginally from the single European market. To our knowledge, no studies have been undertaken about the likely global effects '1992' on the EU's trade with Japan. A sectoral study dealing with motor vehicles led Smith (1989) to suggest that the single European market would result in an overall reduction in the Union's car imports from Japan. However, as Winters (1992a: 10) stresses, 'the critical issue is not barriers to intra-EC trade, but the treatment of restrictions against Japan after 1992'. Abolishing quantitative restrictions in the trade of motor vehicles between Japan and the EU (currently envisaged as from 1999) would be likely to double, if not treble, Japan's share in the European car market.

GUIDE TO FURTHER READING

Borner, S. (1992) (ed.) *The European Community After 1992*, London, Macmillan.
Cecchini, P. (1988) *The European Challenge: 1992 – The Benefits of a Single Market*, Aldershot, Wildwood House.
CEC (1988) 'The Economics of 1992', *European Economy*, 35.
— (1991) *Opening up the Internal Market*, Brussels.
Davis, E. *et al.* (1989) *1992: Myths and Realities*, London, London Business School.
Emerson, M. (1989) *The Economics of 1992*, Oxford, Oxford University Press.
Helm, D. (1993) (ed.) 'European Internal Market', *Oxford Review of Economic Policy*, 9 (1).
Jacquemin, A. and Sapir, A. (1990) (eds) *The European Internal Market*, Oxford, Oxford University Press.
Owen, R. and Dynes, M. (1992) *The Times Guide to the Single European Market*, London, Times Books.
Pelkmans, J. and Winters, L.A. (1988) *Europe's Domestic Market*, London, Routledge.
Swann, D. (1992) (ed.) *The Single European Market and Beyond – A Study of the Wider Implications of the Single European Act*, London, Routledge.
Winters, L.A. (1992) (ed.) *Trade Flows and Trade Policy after 1992*, Cambridge, Cambridge University Press.

4
TRADE POLICIES

INTRODUCTION

In this chapter we shall discuss the trade policy of the European Communities. In dealing with Europe's trade policies we shall cover several aspects. First, we shall outline the objectives of the Communities' trade policy. Second, we shall describe the framework within which European trade policies have been conducted. Third, we shall describe the instruments employed by the European Communities to pursue their trade policy objectives. Fourth, we shall consider the trade agreements entered into by the EU and what system of preferences has been offered to third countries. Fifth, we shall analyse the impact of Europe's trade policies. In conclusion, we shall discuss a particular aspect of EU trade policies – their welfare implications.

EUROPE'S TRADE POLICY OBJECTIVES

The broad features of the European Communities' approach to international trade are covered by articles 110 to 116 of the Treaty of

Rome. Article 110 of the 1958 Treaty expresses the Communities' trade policy objectives as follows:

By establishing a customs union between themselves Member States aim to contribute, in the common interest, to the harmonious development of world trade, the progressive *abolition of restrictions on international trade* [our emphasis] and the lowering of customs barriers. The *common commercial policy* (our emphasis) shall take into account the favourable effect which the abolition of customs duties between Member States may have on the increase in the competitive strength of undertakings in those States.

According to Article 110 the Communities' trade policy objectives are twofold. The EU is, first of all, committed to a liberal approach to trade – it supports a free multilateral trading system in the world (as established by GATT) with the most efficient producers supplying markets (trade creation). A logical outcome of supporting free multilateral trade would be to avoid protection of trade in whatever form. But Article 110 also embodies a second principal policy objective: the formation of a customs union resulting in a common market which discriminates against third countries. The establishment of customs unions and free trade areas is not against GATT rules; the General Agreement makes provision for the creation of trading blocs such as the EU. But although GATT sees the purpose of a customs union or free trade area 'to facilitate trade between the constituent territories and not to raise barriers to the trade of other contracting parties with such territories' (GATT Article XXIV), customs unions, while not illegal under GATT rules, are clearly against the spirit of free multilateral trade. Their existence amounts to a departure from, if not derogation of, the fundamental most-favoured nation (MFN) clause to be found in Article I of GATT which stipulates that in international trade transactions:

any advantage, favour, privilege or immunity granted by any contracting party to any product originating in or destined for any other country shall be accorded immediately and unconditionally to the like product originating in or destined for the territories of all contracting parties.

A further objective of the Communities' external trade policy is to aid the development and industrialisation efforts of countries of the Third World, especially the non-European countries and territories which for historical reasons have special relations with member states (Article 131 of the Treaty of Rome), and, more recently, the European transition economies – the CEECs. In pursuing the aim of contributing to the economic development of countries of the Third World the EU has, for example, introduced a General System of Preferences (GSP). In order to facilitate trade with the CEECs, new association agreements – the so called 'Europe Agreements' – were signed.

FRAMEWORK

According to the Treaty of Rome all important policy decisions are taken by the Council of Ministers. But, except for some limited cases, the Council can only decide if and when there is a Commission proposal (Article 113 of the EEC Treaty). Only the Commission can, therefore, initiate common policies. Any Commission proposal goes through a decision-making process with member states. This decision-making process is coordinated by the Committee of Permanent Representatives (COREPER). Consultations also take place with the European Parliament, which plays an advisory role, and, if deemed appropriate, with the Economic and Social Committee. The consultative process may lead to modifications of any proposals made by the Commission. Apart from special cases a simple or qualified majority vote is necessary for the Council to take a decision. All trade policy measures can be decided on the basis of majority voting.

Because of the differential progress member states have made in the process of integration 'there is no single mechanism of formulating, coordinating and implementing the broad range of trade-related policies in the EC' (GATT 1991, I: 51). Trade policy competences may be conferred on the European Commission; alternatively they may be shared between the Commission and member states. It should be recognised that the Communities speak with a single voice in (bilateral or multilateral) trade negotiations with the rest of the world. Article 113 of the Treaty of Rome made provisions for transferring the competence to negotiate tariffs and other trade policies from the individual member states to the Commission. Within the GATT system the EU has a special status in that it signed a number of international trade agreements despite the fact that the individual member countries and not the EU are the contracting parties to the General Agreement. The Communities also occupy a unique position within the Organisation for Economic Cooperation and Development (OECD) which has, *inter alia*, played an important role in the field of export credits/control of export credit subsidies; the Commission regularly speaks on behalf of the EU even though the Union is not a member of the OECD.

A centrepiece of the creation of the Treaty of Rome was the establishment of a *common commercial policy* (CCP) towards third countries described in Article 113 of the EEC Treaty. Article 113 reflects common trade principles throughout the member states: a *common external tariff* (CET); common trade agreement with the rest of the world; and the uniform application of trade policy instruments on both the export and import sides.

What is the legal basis for the Communities' trade policy? The Treaty of Rome is restricted to defining the broad orientation and setting the general rules of the Communities' commercial policy. It does not contain any specific rules for the conduct of policies in specific trade policy areas. A comprehensive summary of the Communities' regulations affecting trade would be beyond the scope of this book (for a detailed treatment see, for example, GATT 1991, I: 46-50). A short outline of the major features of Communities' trade legislation is, however, necessary to enable us to understand the framework within which the common trade policy regime operates. Prior to outlining the principal features of EU trade legislation, it is essential to throw light on the hierarchy of EU legal instruments. Article 189 of the EEC Treaty establishes the following hierarchy of legislation governing the Communities' policies: (GATT 1993b, I: 31).

- *Regulations* are directly applicable and binding in their entirety in all member states; they need no enabling legislation.
- *Directives* are binding, with regard to the specified results, on the member states to which they are addressed; in order to become legally effective, national implementing legislation is necessary.
- *Decisions* are binding in their entirety on the member states or on the private or legal persons to whom they are addressed.
- *Recommendations* and opinions have no binding effect.

Imports are covered by six regulations; common rules for exports are laid down in one regulation.

Council Regulation No. 2886/89 covers what represents the centrepiece of the CCP, namely the common customs tariff (CCT) levied on imports into the Communities. The CCT consists of more than 9,000 tariff lines with either conventional tariff rates (applicable to all imports from countries which qualify for MFN treatment) or autonomous levies (applicable to items such as a wide range of food products for which no conventional rates exist).

Council Regulation No. 288/82 deals with imports from all sources apart from state-trading countries. The starting point for this regulation is unrestricted access to the Communities' markets. But the regulation allows for a number of exceptions to the principle of unrestricted imports. The Commission may introduce and maintain surveillance measures; it may also decide to impose quantitative restrictions on imports from the rest of the world. Such protectionist measures may be introduced if imports 'cause or threaten to cause injury' and 'if the Community's interests so require' (Articles 15 and 16 of Regulation No. 288/82 which follow fairly closely the wording of Article XIX: 1(a) of the GATT). In practice, the Commission has tended to interpret the Communities' interest in terms of the impact of growing imports on production and employment in the industries most affected by import penetration.

Regulations No. 1765/82 and No. 3420/83 govern the imports from state-trading countries. They specify, *inter alia*, surveillance procedures and other appropriate measures in the event of surging imports. With the declining number of state-trading countries it will, in future, probably not be necessary for the Commission to have separate regulations for this group of countries, especially as the measures specified in Regulations No. 1765/62 and No. 3420/83 are, in fact, very similar to those described in Regulation No. 288/82.

Regulation No. 2641/84 describes the so-called 'New Commercial Policy Instrument' (NCPI) which was introduced in response to unilateral US actions against the EU (see, for example, Schoneveld 1992). The new commercial policy instrument essentially provides the EU with a mechanism for counteraction in the case of 'illicit' commercial practices affecting either the Communities' imports or exports from the EU to the rest of the world; broadly speaking, it corresponds to Section 301 of the US Trade Act (see Chapter 6).

Regulation No. 2603/69 provides common rules for exports. Like Regulation 288/82 it considers free trade as of paramount importance, but it enables the Commission to introduce export authorisation schemes if and when there is a shortage of essential commodities. It also entitles the Commission to limit exports from certain regions within and to specific destinations outside the Communities.

In addition to these general regulations, the Commission may also, in dealing with particular trade situations, draw on a large number of specific regulations. Dumping, subsidisation and trade-related policies in areas such as public procurement and standardisation, may be trade issues where the Commission may want to act or counteract.

POLICY MEASURES

The Communities have recourse to a large number of trade policy instruments influencing their trade flows with the rest of the world. A comprehensive discussion of the Communities' trade policy measures would involve us in dealing with measures affecting imports (tariffs, import levies and charges; quantitative restrictions; import controls and prohibitions; emergency trade measures; anti-dumping measures; countervailing actions; government procurement; standards and technical requirements; countertrade; rules of origin); measures affecting exports (export promotion; export finance and insurance; export subsidies; export controls and restrictions); and measures affecting production and trade (competition policy; subsidies; taxation policies). We shall be selective in our discussion and focus on what appear to be the Communities' major trade policy instruments (for a more detailed analysis of all the trade policy measures adopted by the EU see, for example, GATT 1993b, I: 64-126). The trade policy instruments we have selected for treatment are the following: tariffs; quantitative restrictions; subsidies; and import surveillance measures.

Adopting a common external tariff has required the Communities to harmonise the sometimes widely differing tariff levels of the member states. Some 10 per cent of some 9,000 tariff lines allow duty-free access to the Communities' markets. The Council may, in response to a Commission proposal, arrange for *tariffs* to be suspended (Article 28 of the EEC Treaty) in order to enable domestic producers better access to components, semi-finished goods and raw material which are not available in the Communities or cannot be supplied in sufficient quantities. In 1991, tariff revenues accruing to the Communities' budget amounted to 12.8 billion ECU and contributed more than one fifth to the Communities' budget (GATT 1993b, I: 66). With relatively few exceptions (wine and spirits and coal are subject to specific duties), the CET has relied very heavily on *ad valorem* duties. Tariff protection levels for selected sectors are given in *Table 4.1*. Taking a weighted average, the 1988 (i.e. pre-Uruguay Round) tariff levels were 5.6 per cent for all imports of industrial products (excluding petroleum) from third countries (GATT 1993b, I: 258); tariffs for agricultural commodities have been higher and less evenly spread than tariffs for industrial products.

Import levies (which are tantamount to tariffs) have played a major role in the common agricultural policy (CAP). The variable levy system used by the CAP aims to offset external producers' price advantages by setting import threshold prices above the internal prices. The magnitude of the levy for the import of a particular agricultural good tends to be calculated as the difference between the import threshold price established for the good in question and the lowest price external producers offer to sell the produce on the Communities' markets. Levies effectively restrict exports from third countries because the domestic prices are, on the whole, lower than the threshold prices.

GATT bans the use of *quantitative restrictions* as a trade policy measure (Article XI). But Article XIX permits the use of quantitative restrictions under particular circumstances; emergency action on imports of particular products may be taken if 'any product is being imported . . . in such quantities as to cause or threaten serious injury to domestic producers'. The Communities have, however, taken very few actions under Article XIX and those that have been taken have related to agricultural goods. Restrictions on imports into the Communities have, to a large extent, been remnants of individual member states' trade regimes from before the enactment of the Treaty of Rome. As a result, many EU restrictions have been levied at member-state level and not by the Communities as a group. At the end of the 1980s, the Communities restricted imports of more than 120 industrial products

Table 4.1 European Communities: tariff protection by sector, 1988* (selected industries with above average protection levels)

Sector	Average tariffs Simple	Weighted	Tariff range
	(in %)		
Textiles and clothing	10.1	7.6	0–17.0
Fabrics	10.9	10.8	3–17.0
Clothing and clothing accessories	13.0	13.2	0–14.0
Ores and metals	5.1	2.6	0–17.0
Iron and steel	5.4	5.5	0–10.0
Non-ferrous metal products	6.2	5.9	0–10.0
Metal manufacturers	5.4	6.0	0–17.0
Chemicals	7.3	6.7	0–17.6
Plastics	9.3	9.9	0–16.0
Non-electric machinery	4.1	4.4	0–12.0
Electric machines and apparatus	5.8	8.3	0–15.0
Telecommunications apparatus	7.2	8.8	0–14.0
Electrical equipment and parts	7.2	10.6	0–15.0
Transport equipment	7.0	7.3	0–22.0
Motor vehicles	9.5	9.4	4.4–22.0
Footwear and travel goods	10.4	11.1	4.6–20.0
Footwear	11.7	13.5	11.7–13.5
Foodstuffs	14.5	9.8	0–30.0
Fruit, prepared or preserved	22.8	19.0	0–30.0
Vegetables, prepared or preserved	17.6	18.7	0–24.0
Coffee, tea and maté	11.8	5.2	0–18.0
Spices	8.5	9.1	0–25.0
Beverages and spirits	21.5	14.3	0–24.0
Fish, shellfish and products	12.2	10.3	0–30.0
Tobacco	26.4	9.4	26.0–117.0
Manufactured tobacco	66.6	30.9	26.0–117.0
All industrial products	6.4	5.6	

Note:
* The data provided in this table refer to the pre-Uruguay round situation.
As a result of the Uruguay round tariffs are, on average, expected to be lowered by about a third. At the time of writing no data were available about the post-Uruguay round tariff protection levels.

Source: GATT (1993b, I: 256–58)

with two member states – France and Italy – accounting for virtually all the quantitative restrictions. In most cases the import restrictions were imposed on suppliers from Japan and the Asian NICs. A number of measures taken in the 1990s led to a significant reduction in the number of import restrictions. Apart from import quotas third countries' access to Communities' markets has also been curbed via *voluntary export restraints* (VERs); other voluntary restraint agreements (VRAs) have, at the same time, effectively limited the Communities' share of exports of, for example, steel to third countries such as the United States. A VER is a step taken by an importing country to ensure that an exporting country restricts the volume of its exports to the importing country on a voluntary basis. Although formally it is the exporting country that decides to restrict its exports, VERs often result from the exporting country yielding to pressure from the importing country. A VER is, therefore, a bilaterally agreed measure to restrict exports on a selective basis. Motor vehicles, steel, machinery, electrical and electronic household equipment, and textiles are the major products that have been affected by export restraint arrangements. Both import restrictions and VERs were initially confined to individual member states, but are now increasingly subject to regulations introduced jointly by the Communities (VERs covering all the member states were, for example, not introduced until 1990).

Subsidies for any sector affect trade flows because they distort relative prices – products and services benefiting from financial aid programmes gain an advantage over other competitors both on the domestic and export market. It is for this reason that GATT has viewed subsidies as having adverse effects on the world trading system by creating obstacles for the achievement of the objectives of the General Agreement (Article XVI). GATT, therefore, urges any contracting party granting subsidies to notify other signatories of the 'extent and nature of the subsidisation, of the estimated effect of the subsidisation on the quantity of the affected product or products imported into or exported from its territory and of the circumstances making the subsidisation necessary'.

The European Commission regards its control over subsidies and other state aid as an integral part of its competition policy (Articles 92 and 93); EU countries, therefore, do not have the right to implement aid schemes without Commission approval. In discussing subsidies within the Communities, it is important to draw a distinction between the agricultural sector and other sectors. Subsidies for agricultural commodities are, on the whole, funded by the Communities' budget; financial support for other sectors, on the other hand, has tended to be provided by member states' budgets. The agricultural sector's share of the Communities' budget has declined since the 1970s, but continues nonetheless to absorb more than 50 per cent of the Communities' overall expenditure. Between 1981 and 1990 the shares of agriculture, coal mining, transport and manufacturing in state aid provided by the Communities amounted to 13, 18, 29 and 40 per cent respectively (CEC 1992b). State aid has declined over the years but, like the Communities' level of subsidisation for agriculture, continues to be high: it averaged 2.2 per cent of the Communities' gross domestic product between 1988 and 1990 (CEC 1992b).

We now turn to *import surveillance* – anti-dumping measures, safeguard actions and origin rules.

Dumping describes a situation in which a product is sold to purchasers abroad at a price lower than that charged for the identical product on the home market ('reverse' dumping occurs where the price charged abroad is higher than the domestic price). Dumping may occur when governments subsidise exports; or it may be unrelated to government activities (i.e. reflect commercial decisions of the private sector). Dumping can be 'sporadic' (disposal of occasional surpluses on foreign markets), 'predatory' (low prices charged abroad in order to drive out competitors and gain control over markets) or 'entry-limiting' (low prices charged abroad to establish barriers to entry). When dumping or reverse dumping persists on markets it amounts to price discrimination. Price discrimination can only be practised by firms when markets have not been fully integrated although, as we established in the previous chapter, even 'unified' markets can exhibit the characteristics of price discrimination in internal trade. Market segmentation will, however, only lead to persistent price differentials across markets if the demand elasticities on the export and domestic market are different and the leakages between the two markets are minimal.

The rules that the Communities have developed for dealing with dumped imports have been derived in accordance with Europe's international trade obligations. Article VI of the GATT condemns dumping ('by which products of one country are introduced into the commerce of another country at less than the normal value of the products') 'if it causes or threatens material injury to an established industry in the territory of a contracting party or materially retards the establishment of a domestic industry'. In cases of proven evidence of dumping, Article VI entitles an individual country (or a group of countries like the EU) to levy *anti-dumping duties* on the 'dumped' imports. The specific rules governing the Communities' anti-dumping legislation were laid down in Council Regulation No. 2423/88. Regulation 2423/88 permits the EU to take anti-dumping measures provided there is:

- evidence of dumped imports;
- industry in the Communities has been injured or threatens to be injured by the dumped imports;
- intervention is in the Communities' interest (GATT 1993b, I: 79).

Whether or not a product is being regarded as 'dumped' crucially depends on the magnitude of the so-called 'dumping margin' – the margin by which the 'normal' value of a good is greater than the price at which it is being sold on the export market. This, of course, begs the question as to what constitutes the 'normal' value of allegedly dumped products. In practice, the price in the exporter's home market (also known as the 'reference' price) has been regarded as the 'normal' value or price of an exportable. The problem of calculating the dumping margin tends to be complicated by possible ambiguities surrounding the export price used in the calculations. As Hindley (1992) points out, the technical basis for demonstrating dumping leaves the Commission scope for using specific 'tricks' to find in favour of anti-dumping complaints, especially when there is no readily available information about the reference price of a product. The latter may have to be established by referring to the comparable price of a similar product exported to other countries or determined by using computed production costs (including overheads and advertising expenses) and an appropriate profit margin. In short, the procedure for finding whether dumping takes place or not is potentially open to abuse and may lead to a situation where 'many exporters who would be acquitted of dumping by objective observers will be found to dump by the EEC' (Hindley 1992: 93).

GATT's anti-dumping code and the Communities' own legislation specify that the appropriate investigations should be completed within one year. In practice, it has proved difficult for the Commission to complete procedures dealing with dumping complaints/anti-dumping actions within twelve months. The anti-dumping measures taken by the Commission may be in the form of price undertakings (committing exporting countries not to sell in the Communities' markets at prices below an agreed price) or of definitive duties being imposed. Between January 1985 and June 1992 there were, on average, more cases of anti-dumping duties being imposed than price undertakings being given (GATT 1993b, I: 76); anti-dumping duties should, in accordance with GATT Article VI, not exceed the dumping margin. Of the 29 investigations launched in the 18 months between January 1991 and June 1992 and resulting in the Commission imposing definitive anti-dumping duties, about 50 per cent led to duties of less than the full dumping margin (GATT 1993b, I: 76, 80).

The Commission has extended its anti-dumping actions to the so-called *screwdriver plants* lest exporters circumvent anti-dumping duties by setting up assembly operations within the Communities and manufacturing products using a high proportion of imported components and parts. The Commission has, since 1991, also made use of the so-called 'absorption clause' (contained in Regulation No. 2423/88) to impose additional anti-dumping duties in cases where the original duty is found to be borne, in full or to large extent, by the exporting country. Provisional duties which are levied on the basis of preliminary findings of dumping and injury may be used for a period of four months with the possibility of a two-month extension. Definitive anti-dumping duties normally expire after five years (the so-called 'sunset clause'), although an affected industry has the opportunity to demonstrate that abolition of anti-dumping duties would cause or threaten material industry to the industry; anti-dumping investigations may, in such circumstances, be reopened.

How important are anti-dumping duties? The latest trade policy review of the European Communities carried out by GATT suggests that the EU has been making frequent use of anti-dumping actions (GATT 1993b, I). Anti-dumping measures have, arguably, been the Communities' most frequently used trade policy instrument and the EU belongs, according to GATT, to the group of the most intensive users of anti-dumping measures in the world (GATT 1991, I: 17). Between 1988 and 1992, the number of anti-dumping measures used (definitive and provisional duties; price undertakings) fluctuated between 152 in 1988 and 139 in 1990 (GATT 1993b, I: 76). That said, it should be recognised that less than one per cent of all external imports into the Communities tend to be affected by anti-dumping duties (GATT 1993b, II: 72).

Most of the preferential trade agreements that the European Communities have embarked upon also contain so-called *safeguard clauses*. For example, Article 30 of the Europe Agreements with some of the central and east European transition economies (Czech Republic, Hungary, Poland and Slovakia) allows the Communities to resort to unspecified safeguard measures in case imports from any of these countries lead to serious injury to domestic producers of like or directly competitive products or 'serious disturbance or difficulties which could bring about serious deterioriation in the economic situation of a region within the EU'. The EU's preferential trade agreements are supposed to liberalise trade flows between the Union and third countries; yet safeguard clauses, if used to curb exports to the EU, threaten to impede trade liberalisation, especially when concepts such as 'serious deterioration' and 'region' are not clearly defined.

A feature applying to virtually all the Communities' special trade agreements is the so-called local content requirement (*rules of origin*). Exports from countries covered by free trade, association or co-operation agreements into European Union states usually only qualify for concessionary treatment if the exporting country contributes at least 60 per cent of value added of a good in question. Such rules of origin are likely to discriminate against suppliers from third countries that are transition or developing economies with limited access to domestically produced components and raw materials.

Although the Communities have been aiming to pursue 'common' external trade policy they have, in fact, not as yet been reaching the stage where a harmonised trade policy approach has been achieved. A truly common foreign trade policy would have to be devoid of any restrictions by individual member states. Yet, a number of national restrictions on imports from third countries were in operation as recently as 1992. The restrictions by individual member states on extra-EU imports of motor vehicles are cases in point (see *Table 4.2*). The removal of internal barriers on 1 January 1993 led to intensive debates within the EU about the need for common and coordinated commercial and industrial policies. Over the last few years, the EU has made considerable efforts to harmonise its trade policies, but not all members have in fact dismantled national import quotas. Italy, to quote just one example, has continued to operate import quotas on commodities such as shoes and cars.

TRADE AGREEMENTS AND PREFERENCES

The Communities are signatories of the GATT and are, therefore, supposed to apply the MFN clause in all their external trade relations. Among GATT members the EU has very few trading partners (Australia, Canada, Japan, New Zealand and the United States) with whom it does not have special trade agreements. The Communities have, over the years, set up a complex set of trade links with third countries: from the creation of the EEA to the granting of preferential treatment under the Communities' GSP for exports from developing countries. In this section we propose to provide a brief outline of the types of agreements that exist between the Communities and their trading partners; for a more detailed treatment of the evolution of the agreements between the EU and its trade partners see Chapters 5 and 7 which deal with the Communities' European neighbours and the Third World respectively. An overview of the types of agreements/participants is provided in *Table 4.3*.

Free trade agreements and the European Economic Area

As from 1 January 1994 the EEA took precedence over the bilateral free trade agreements that had been in force between the European Communities and the EFTA countries since 1972 (a bilateral free trade agreement was also signed between the Communities and Israel in 1975). The significance of the formation of the EEA is that the EU and EFTA took steps to facilitate improved trade without establishing a customs union and thus formed the largest and most integrated market in the world. The EEA is characterised by the following features:

- free movement of goods, services, people and capital;
- enforcement of common rules (e.g. establishment of a system of competition rules in order to avoid market distortions);
- closer cooperation in fields such as education, environment, research and development and social policy.

Table 4.2 Restrictions by individual member states on extra-EU imports of motor vehicles, 1992

		Direct imports	
Member state – third country	Vehicle category	Measures in force	Accepted trade volume
	A	B	C
France			
Japan	Passenger cars and light commercial vehicles.	Unilateral quota. Restrictive car registration and certification.	Market share of about 3 per cent (direct plus parallel deliveries).
Republic of Korea	Import ban until spring 1992.		
Italy			
Japan	Passenger cars.	Bilateral quota	3,500 units
	Four-wheel-drive vehicles.	Bilateral quota	1,000 units
	Light commercial vehicles.	Bilateral quota	750 units
	Diesel engines.	Bilateral quota	US$280,000
	Motorcycles (<380 ccm).	Bilateral quota	2,500 units
Successor states of the Soviet Union	Passenger cars.	Unilateral quota	3,180 units
	Commercial vehicles.	Unilateral quota	96 units
	Motorcycles.	Unilateral quota	320 units
	Car parts.	Unilateral quota	
Spain			
Japan	Passenger cars, buses and commercial vehicles.	Quota	1,200 units
Japan	Motor cycles.	Quota	
Republic of Korea	All categories.	Quota	
Successor states of the Soviet Union	Four-wheel-drive vehicles.	Quota	
Portugal			
All third countries	All categories.	Quota	
United Kingdom			
Japan	Passenger cars, commercial vehicles, vehicles, four-wheel-drive vehicles.	Voluntary export restraint	11 per cent market share (direct plus parallel deliveries)

Source: GATT (1993b, I: 281–82)

Table 4.3 EU preferential trade schemes, December 1992

Type of agreement/participants	Main features
Free Trade Agreements	
European Economic Area (1992)	
EFTA countries	
Austria, Finland, Iceland, Norway, Sweden, Switzerland, Liechtenstein	Reciprocal free trade in industrial products and services; agriculture largely exempted.
Israel (1975)	
Association Agreements	
Turkey (1963), Malta (1970), Cyprus (1972)	Free access to EC markets for industrial products; customs union envisaged (Turkey 1995; Cyprus 1998; Malta 1995).
(Europe Agreement)	
Czech Republic, Slovakia, Hungary, Poland (1991), Bulgaria, Romania (1993)	Creation of a free trade area over 10 years; limited coverage in agriculture (differences between the individual agreements).
Cooperation Agreements	
Mediterranean countries (1975–76) Algeria, Egypt, Jordan Lebanon, Morocco, Syria, Tunisia	Free access for industrial products, raw materials and traditional agricultural exports (by 1995) to the EC; no reciprocal obligations.
Lomé Convention (1990) 69 developing countries (ACP)	Free access for ACP exports of industrial products and of agricultural products not covered by a common market organization under the CAP. More favourable than MFN treatment for other agricultural products. Guaranteed exports of cane sugar (1.3 million tonnes per year) for signatories to the Sugar Protocol (18 ACP countries); guarantees of continued favourable access under the Protocol on Bananas.
General System of Preferences (GSP) (1971)	
About 130 independent developing countries and 20 dependent territories	Autonomous preferences on a temporary basis (annual prolongation). Duty-free treatment for a wide range of manufactured and semi-manufactured products, subject to quantitative ceilings or a safeguard provision. Preferences for MFA textiles are contingent on the conclusion of bilateral agreements under the MFA or similar commitments *vis-à-vis* the EC (except for least developed countries). Limited preferences in the agricultural area.

Source: GATT (1993b, I: 36)

The idea behind setting up the EEA was to enable EFTA countries to participate in the benefits of the Communities' post-1992 single European market; the agreement between the EFTA countries and the Communities was signed on 2 May 1992. In order to facilitate the creation of such an enlarged and integrated European market there are to be neither tariff nor non-tariff barriers to trade (including services but excluding agricultural trade) between the countries involved. But both the Communities and the EFTA countries continued to operate their own tariffs and non-tariff measures towards third countries; they also retained any preferential arrangements they may have with trading partners in the rest of the world. Provisions exist – and this is where the 1992 agreement goes well beyond the 1973–74 agreement – for the harmonisation of EU and EFTA legislation for a large number of trade-related issues such as, for example, competition policy, government procurement, subsidisation, technical regulations. In these areas the EFTA countries accepted the *acquis communautaire*.

Association agreements

A number of association agreements were reached between the European Communities and Turkey, Malta and Cyprus. These agreements have given the three countries free access to the Communities' markets for industrial goods; customs unions are envisaged for the late 1990s.

New association agreements were signed between the Communities and the Czech Republic, Hungary, Poland and Slovakia in December 1991 and interim agreements came into force in March 1992; European agreements with Bulgaria and Romania followed in 1993. The aim of these European agreements was to create free trade areas over ten years (i.e. by the year 2002). These recent association agreements are more ambitious than the Communities' previous association agreements with Cyprus, Malta and Turkey in that they contain a declared objective of the central and east European countries becoming full members of the European Union.

Cooperation agreements

In considering the Communities' cooperation agreements, a distinction has to be drawn between preferential and non-preferential cooperation agreements.

A group of Mediterranean countries (Algeria, Egypt, Jordan, Lebanon, Morocco, Syria and Tunisia) benefit from a preferential cooperation agreement with the EU which allows them, *inter alia*, free access for industrial products and raw materials to the Communities' markets without reciprocal obligations. A preferential cooperation agreement known as the Lomé Convention also exists between the

Communities and 69 developing countries, generally referred to as the ACP group. In accordance with the Lomé Convention, the ACP countries' industrial products and agricultural produce that are not covered by a common market organisation under the CAP have free access to the EU.

A number of non-preferential cooperation agreements have been concluded with developing countries in Asia and Latin America. These agreements do not give the countries any preferential access to the Communities' markets and are, therefore, somewhat limited in scope. The Asian and Central/South American states are, however, beneficiaries of the Communities' GSP which, subject to quantitative ceilings or safeguards provisions, offers some 130 independent countries and 20 dependent territories in the Third World duty free access to the European markets for a wide range of manufactured and semi-manufactured products.

IMPACT

What have been the consequences of the Communities' trade policy? More precisely, how evenly spread have the levels of protection been across industries? How has the rest of the world been affected? What conflicts have arisen? These are the issues we shall now consider.

Trade policy across industries

The evolution of the Communities' trade policies has been characterised by 'a propensity for sector-specific solutions, resulting in large differences in the levels of protection across industries' (GATT 1991, I: 8–9). In discussing trade policy by sector, we shall deal only with those sectors of the EU economy that, for strategic reasons, appear to have been subject to 'managed trade' – agriculture; electrical and electronic products; iron and steel; textiles, clothing and footwear; and transport equipment.

Most of the *agricultural goods* produced and consumed are protected from world competition via the system of variable import levies and export refunds that constitute the core elements of the CAP. Other agricultural products not covered by the variable levy system have tended to be subject to substantial tariffs. These may consist of specific tariffs levied on, for example, wine and spirits; seasonal tariffs levied on particular fruits, vegetables and cut flowers; and alternative tariffs payable on the imports of commodities such as tobacco, apples and certain other fruits and vegetables. Additional protection of the Communities' agricultural sector arises out of subsidies and farm support schemes provided at national or regional level. The agricultural sector is the most protected sector of the EU; more than half of the Communities' budget has tended to be spent on agriculture, fisheries and food production. The degree of protectionism applied to agriculture remains high despite the fact that in May 1992 it was decided that, while preserving the basic features and mechanisms of the CAP, changes affecting the levels of price support would be implemented as from 1993–94.

The changes embodied in the farm reform package resulting from the EU Council's 1992 decision affect cereal, beef and veal but not produce such as dairy products and sugar which have been equally, if not more, protected by the price support system. Overall, the intensity of agricultural protection has had three consequences. It has led to overproduction (via high guaranteed prices); it has generated an export push (via export refunds); and it has reduced demand for imports from third countries' suppliers (via variable import levies).

The Communities' *electrical and electronic industry* has, like many European industrial sectors, been subject to strong import pressure. The degree of import penetration has, of course, varied in the member states but in 1990 external supplies, on average, amounted to 43, 26, and 17 per cent respectively of the domestic consumption of office and computing machinery, radio and telecommunication, and electrical machinery respectively (GATT 1993b, I: 280). In addition to imposing the CCT (on average about 8 per cent but amounting to 14 per cent in many cases) the Communities have sought to protect themselves against high and possibly rising levels of external imports by resorting to both informal steps and formal procedures. The 'informal' trade policy measures have consisted of monitoring exports by the exporting countries, notably Japan and South Korea, and retrospective surveillance of imports by the Communities. On a more formal level, the Communities have embarked on a number of anti-dumping measures against imports of electronic imports.

Iron and steel products are not covered by the Treaty of Rome, but by the ECSC (European Coal and Steel Community) Treaty which was signed in 1951 – several years before the Rome Treaty came into force. Both the economic conditions in the markets for steel and the trade policy measures pursued by the Communities have witnessed changes over time. High levels of production, additional supplies from the central and east European transition economies have, over the last few years, made the steel market more competitive; subsidies to European steel producers and voluntary restraint agreements with the United States had protected this industry in the 1980s. Over the last few years, subsidies have dwindled in significance, and the Communities' export restraint agreement with the United States (which limited European exports to 7 per cent of United States' consumption) expired in March

1992. The emphasis in protecting the Communities' steel sector nowadays is on import surveillance measures and anti-dumping actions. Anti-dumping actions have been used against producers from some of the CEECs. Exports of seamless steel tubes from Poland, Hungary, the Czech Republic and Slovakia have been subject to anti-dumping duties of between 10.8 and 30.4 per cent; Poland gave a price undertaking for exports of ferro-silicon in 1992 (GATT 1993b, I: 206). In trade relations between the EU and the United States anti-dumping actions have been taken since the early 1990s, and these measures have affected both imports and exports. Additional protection of the Communities's steel markets has continued to be provided by the CCT (on average 3.5 per cent on unworked steel and 5.5 per cent on semi-manufactures in 1988).

The Communities' external imports of *textiles and clothing* have been restricted by relatively high tariffs (the 1988, i.e. pre-Uruguay Round weighted tariff averaged 7.6 per cent) and import quotas negotiated as a result of bilateral restrictive agreements under MFA (the Multi-Fibre Arrangement) which led to bilateral restraint agreements with some twenty-one developing countries from Asia (Bangladesh, China, Hong Kong, India, Indonesia, the Republic of Korea, Macao, Malaysia, Pakistan, Philippines, Singapore, Sri Lanka, Thailand), America (Argentina, Brazil, Peru) and Europe (Czech Republic, Hungary, Poland, Romania, Slovakia). Access to the Communities' textiles and clothing markets from other third countries' suppliers has also been restricted under some of the preferential agreements. Under the association agreements with the countries of the Mediterranean Basin, for example, imports of certain textiles and clothing products have been monitored and, if deemed necessary, moderated on a 'voluntary' basis.

Footwear in the Communities' market, like textiles and clothing, has been vulnerable to increasing import penetration; China, for example, increased its EU market share between 1990 and 1991 from 11 to 15 per cent (GATT 1993b, I: 213). The common external tariff imposed on footwear in 1988 was significantly higher than that for textiles and clothing; taking a weighted mean the CET on footwear has averaged 13.5 per cent. There is no MFA equivalent for the footwear industry but trade has, over the last 10-15 years, been restricted as a result of unilateral quotas, voluntary self-restraints and other restraint arrangements at industry level. Prior to '1992' national restrictions played a particular role in those member states that have a major share in the Communities' footwear production (Italy, Spain and France). They have also been significant, for example, in the United Kingdom which restricted footwear imports from Eastern Europe. Winters and Brenton (1988) attempted to estimate the welfare costs resulting from rationing leather footwear supplies from these countries; their calculations would suggest that the losses to British consumers amounted to some £260 million in 1986 (appoximately 25 per cent of British consumers' total expenditure on footwear). Since 1990 the Commission has endeavoured to replace national restrictions by EU-wide arrangements. Nevertheless, some member states have continued to take unilateral actions. In March 1992 France, for example, announced restrictions on the import of leather shoes, sports shoes and slippers from China.

In discussing protectionism in the *transport equipment* sector, we shall consider motor vehicles and shipbuilding.

The EU accounts for about two fifths of the *motor vehicle* production in the world. The motor vehicle industry is yet another sensitive and strategic sector of the Communities' economy that has been subject to considerable import pressure from the high performing south east Asian economies, notably Japan. Not all member states have, however, sought protection against import penetration. The member states that have tried to protect their markets beyond the use of the CET (which averaged just under 10 per cent in 1988) have been France, Italy, Portugal, Spain and the United Kingdom. Up to 1991 imports of cars produced in Japan and, to lesser extent, in South Korea into these countries were restricted by measures such as (bilateral or unilateral) quotas, trade restraint agreements and restrictions affecting technical standardisation and vehicle registration procedures. Article 115 of the EU Treaty which deals with trade deflection was used to prevent supplies of motor vehicles from third countries via those member states whose markets were less protected (the non-producers – Denmark, Ireland, Luxembourg – and the less protectionist states – Belgium, Germany, the Netherlands).

Since July 1991 when the EU and Japan reached an agreement (the EU–Japan consensus) on Japan's access to the Communities' markets, national arrangements have been replaced by supra-national trade policy measures. The 1991 consensus was characterised by two features. First, its background considerations were the recognition that there was 'an enormous overall gap' (CEC 1992c) between the productivity of the Communities' motor vehicle industry and that of their principal competitors, especially Japan. Second, it was recognised that strategic trade policy would have to be pursued (i.e. measures would have to be taken that would enable the industry to become more competitive in the long run by adopting, for example, new production techniques). In order to enable the Communities' car producers to establish a sufficiently high degree of international competitiveness, full liberalisation of trade between the EU and Japan is postponed until 1999. In the intervening years the Communities committed themselves to discontinue all import restrictions at member state level; they also undertook not to apply Article 115 any longer to cars imported from

Japanese manufacturers. The Japanese, in turn, agreed to facilitate the structural re-adjustment process in the European car industry by monitoring their exports of cars to the Communities' markets. According to the consensus reached between the two trading blocs, exports of Japanese cars in 1999 are not to exceed 1.23 million or 8.1 per cent of the predicted EU market in that year (GATT 1993b, I: 170); in case of shortfalls in the overall level of demand for cars in the European markets Japan would be expected to reduce its supplies accordingly. Annual export supply targets would thus be negotiated between Japan and the EU, and this, according to Costello and Pelkmans (1991), would appear to formalise a practice that has existed informally since 1986.

Although tariffs offer little, if any, protection to the Communities' *shipbuilding* industry (nominal tariffs were less than 2 per cent in 1988), GATT has regarded this sector of the European economy as 'one of the most heavily supported segments of EU manufacturing industry' (GATT 1993b, I: 179) because the industry has been protected from international competition via high levels of subsidisation. In the period 1988-90, for example, subsidies to the Communities' shipbuilding industry as a whole exceeded one third of value added; higher levels of subsidisation were, during the same period, found in countries like Italy and Portugal (CEC 1992b). Considering that the Council has regarded the shipbuilding sector of 'vital interest to the Community and contributes to its economic and social development' (Council Directive No. 90/684) the EU is unlikely to take steps in the direction of abolishing subsidies to this area of the European economy unless an international agreement can be reached to reduce, if not abolish, subsidies and other trade obstacles in this industry. At OECD level such an agreement has been discussed, and the EU has contributed to the debate by proposing a multilateral elimination of subsidisation in order to move towards 'normal competition' (CEC 1992d) and a situation which allows signatories of an international agreement to take effective action against any unfair trading practices.

External effects

What impact have the Union's trade policies had on the rest of the world? We shall, in discussing the effects of the Union's trade regimes on countries outside the EU, deal with the following issues: discrimination; disputes; and long-term consequences.

Discrimination

The global impact of the Union's trade policy regime amounts to discrimination. Its discriminatory nature has three distinct roots. First, discrimination results from the EU pursuing a common commercial policy. Second, the Union's trade policies have been discriminatory in that the number, range and nature of the special trade agreements concluded by the European Union have led to a 'pyramid of preferences'. Third, as mentioned earlier in this chapter, specific trade policy measures have resulted in protectionism on a sectoral basis.

The CETs levied by the Union on imports from third countries and the non-tariff barriers they have created for exporters in the rest of the world have meant that for a large number of goods low cost supplies from third countries have been replaced by higher cost supplies from producers within the Union. The trade diversion effect has been relatively higher for products in industries in which member states have been less competitive (e.g. agriculture, electronics, motor vehicles, steel, textiles etc.).

The special trade agreements with certain groups of countries have resulted in very few countries being subject to the full CET. While all these trade or cooperation agreements have given the trade partners involved preferential access to the Union's markets, the extent of the preferences granted have differed from agreement to agreement. Among the developed or industrialised countries EFTAns have been more favoured than the CEECs. The CEECs, on the other hand, while being discriminated against in comparison with the EFTA countries, have been offered easier market access than non-European industrialised countries. Among the group of the developing economies ACP countries are more favoured than countries belonging to the Mediterranean Basin or non-associate countries of Asia and South America. The latter, however, are more discriminated against than Mediterranean countries. The implications of the 'pyramid of preferences' will be considered again in Chapters 5 to 7, which will deal with the Union's trade links with the rest of Europe, Japan/USA and the Third World respectively.

Trade has not been inhibited to the same extent for all sectors of the Union. Protectionist trade policy measures have been applied particularly in industries that have been regarded as 'sensitive' such as agriculture, electronics, motor vehicles, steel, textiles and clothing, to name the principal areas where trade has been managed. Agriculture has been Europe's most protected industry. In fact, the Communities have, while supporting the principle of free trade for industrial goods, never committed themselves to free trade for agricultural products. The CAP, which is not part of the common commercial policy, has both inhibited agricultural imports into the EU (via import levies) and promoted the export of agricultural goods (via export subsidies). All external agricultural producers have been adversely affected by the protectionist nature of the CAP. The developing countries which tend to rely heavily on agricultural goods as exportables have been deprived of access to the large European market for these products. However, developing countries such as Australia, Canada, New Zealand and the USA have similarly incurred significant costs. Not only have the European markets been relatively inaccessible to them because of the lack of liberalisation of farm trade in the Union; they have also faced unfair competition in markets of the Third World where the EU has distorted relative prices in its favour by paying export subsidies to European surplus producers of agricultural goods. Trade in agricultural produce between the EU and the rest of the world has, therefore, been diverted rather than created.

Trade disputes

The protectionist trade policies pursued by the EU (and protectionism practised by other countries for that matter) have, not surprisingly, led to frictions between the Union and its trading partners.

Over the period 1980–92, the EU was involved in 55 complaints raised under the General Agreement. The Union initiated 25 of these complaints against other countries; 30 complaints were brought against Europe (GATT 1993b, I: 214). Over two fifths of the disputes involved the EU and the United States; most of the complaints made arose out of disputes over agricultural or food products. A large number of complaints were raised under Article XXIII which, in fairly general terms, deals with 'nullification or impairment' of benefits accruing to any contracting party. Article XXIII makes provisions for consultations or establishment of panels in cases where one country's failure to meet its GATT obligations nullifies or impairs the benefits occuring to another country. It provides procedures for dealing with a wide range of complaints about alleged discrimination/protectionism, excluding, however, instances that are covered by the Subsidies Code (Article XVI) and Anti-dumping Code (Article VI).

The specific trade agreements that the EU has concluded with a number of preferential trading partners also contain procedures for dealing with disputes. With the exception of the 1992 EEA Agreement in which the *acquis communautaire* was extended to EFTA countries, none of the preferential trade agreements reached by the EU with third countries (from the 1972 EC/EFTA Agreement to the Europe Agreements with the CEECs of the early 1990s) exempt the signatories from obligations they may have under international agreements, notably the GATT.

Some of the frictions that have resulted from the barriers to trade between the Union and the rest of the world have, at times, been labelled as 'trade wars', especially when they revolved around agricultural commodities and food products. The issues that have led to these frictions have also played a significant part in the protracted

Uruguay round negotiations which started in 1986 and were finally concluded at the end of 1993 (see Chapter 8).

Long-term consequences

Most, if not all, of the external effects of the EU's trade policies that we have discussed have been short or medium term. We now propose to consider some of the long-term consequences of the Union's trade regime with third countries. Two issues are of interest in this context: the impact of Europe's external trade policy on its inward investment; and the creation of alternative trade areas or trade blocs.

Increasing trade inevitably leads to increasing globalisation of markets. If, as a result of trade restrictions, the growth of globalised markets is being inhibited, firms in an exporting country which is being adversely affected by tariffs or NTBs, may respond by exporting capital (i.e. invest in the country which has taken or is threatening to take a protectionist stance). Belderbos (1991) for example, has asserted that the European Union's trade policies have been a major factor in creating *inward investment*. In our view, such an assertion has to be viewed with caution. The Communities have admittedly been recipients of foreign direct investment over the years, and at an increasing rate. They have, however, also been a major supplier of foreign direct investment worldwide (Greenaway 1993). The precise link between protectionism and inward direct investment of the EU has as yet to be established. It is conceivable that both inward and outward direct investments of the Union merely reflect the general trend toward increasing globalisation of production (Thomsen and Nicolaides 1990; Freeman *et al.* 1991) as a market access strategy.

In 1993, the USA, Canada and Mexico established NAFTA – the North American Free Trade Agreement, which in 1992 covered a population of some 370 million (in the same year the European domestic market contained some 330 million people) and contributed 16 per cent to world exports in merchandise and 19 per cent to world exports in commercial services; the corresponding data for the EU, including internal trade flows, for the same year are 39 and 43 per cent respectively (*Tables 2.1* and *2.3*). Increased liberalisation of trade within this free trade area would create a much enlarged American market. It enables this economic zone to compete more effectively worldwide and especially against Europe and Japan. But, as in the case of the EU, the crucial question is whether NAFTA will create or divert trade.

The creation of three further *trade blocs* are foreseeable. First, serious economic cooperation could be sought by APEC (Asia–Pacific Economic Cooperation) covering trade between Japan, America and the countries that in 1967 founded ASEAN, the Association of South-

East Asian Nations – Brunei, Indonesia, Malaysia, Philippines, Singapore and Thailand. Second, an East Asian Economic Group or Free Trade Association could be formed embracing the markets in Japan, the East Asian NICs and the ASEAN countries. Third, the establishment of a potentially large trade bloc cannot be ruled out once Hong Kong becomes part of the People's Republic of China – a Chinese Economic Area (CEA) comprising Hong Kong, Taiwan and the People's Republic of China.

WELFARE IMPLICATIONS

What are the welfare implications of the trade policies pursued by the EU? We shall, in considering this question, adopt a *partial equilibrium approach* and make use of a basic technique – the so-called welfare triangle analysis. Based on demand and supply functions, it provides a useful approach for analysing the impact of trade policies. We assume that most readers will be familiar with the concepts used in the geometry of welfare triangle analysis (i.e. consumer's surplus, producer's surplus, net surplus). For the benefit of those readers for whom these concepts are new we shall briefly explain these terms and apply them to illustrate the gains from trade.

Following this digression we shall consider the welfare losses that are likely to result from some key trade policy measures employed by the EU: tariffs; non-tariff barriers; subsidies; and import quotas/VERs. In order to keep our analysis of the welfare effects of trade policy measures as simple as possible we shall ignore complications such as the existence of imperfect competition and large open economies that can influence the terms of trade.

Consumer's surplus, producer's surplus, net surplus

The concept of *consumer's surplus* can best be explained by referring to the notion of a demand curve for a particular good or service (*Figure 4.1*). The demand curve shows the maximum price a consumer is willing to pay for an additional unit of a product. The consumer's willingness to pay a particular price can be viewed as an indication of the marginal benefit the consumer is deriving from the consumption of the good. The total benefit accruing to the consumer – the consumer's surplus – is equivalent to the sum of all the marginal benefits and can geometrically be measured by the area under the demand curve; in *Figure 4.1* the triangle ABP thus measures the consumer's surplus. The economic meaning of consumer's surplus is that it measures the difference between the sum a consumer is willing to pay (area ABCO) and the amount of money the consumer actually has to pay for

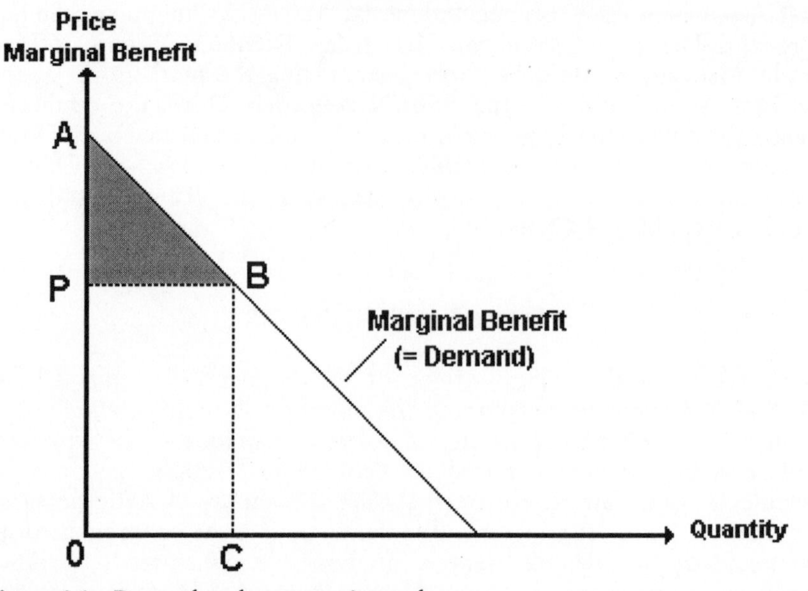

Figure 4.1 Demand and consumer's surplus

acquiring OC units of the good (area OCBP), that is, triangle ABP. If we consider more than one consumer, we would refer to the difference between the total benefits derived by the consumers from consumption and the total expenditures they incur in purchasing the good (or service) as *consumers' surplus.*

Under perfectly competitive market conditions the *producer's surplus* can be defined as the difference between the revenue received by a producer in selling a particular good (or service) and the total costs of production incurred in producing the good (or service) in question. *Figure 4.2* illustrates how the producer's surplus (or economic rent) can be measured. If we assume that the marginal costs of production are rising then, given a particular output level OC, the area under the marginal cost curve (OCBD) represents the sum of all the marginal costs or the total costs of production. The area OCBP, on the other hand, would be a measure of the producer's total revenue. The excess of total revenue over total costs – triangle DBP – is the producer's surplus. If we consider more than one producer, aggregation would yield the *producers' surplus.*

By adding up the consumer's and producer's surplus (or the consumers' and producers' surpluses) we obtain a measure of the *net surplus* (or net welfare) for society. In *Figure 4.3* the net welfare accruing to society amounts to the area ABD (i.e the consumers' surplus (ABP) plus the producers' surplus (DBP)).

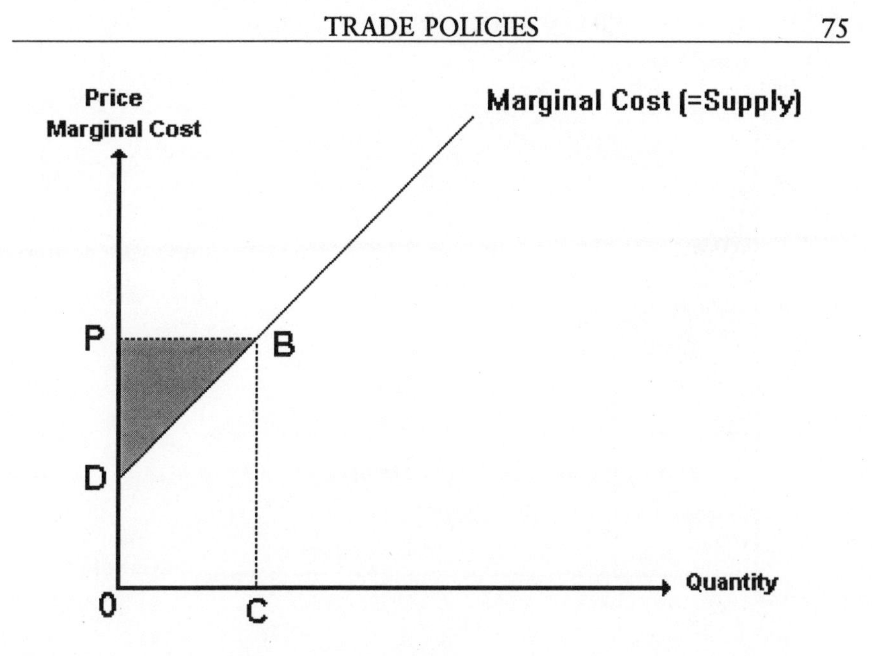

Figure 4.2 Supply and producer's surplus

Free trade and the law of comparative advantages

In the absence of trade, domestic supply and demand conditions determine price and output of any product. Under free trade, the relative prices of goods and services tend to be equalised. World prices would reflect the terms of trade and would decide how much a country produces and consumes. If a country has a comparative advantage in producing a commodity its domestic supply would, at the world price, exceed domestic demand (i.e. the country would export to bridge the gap). If, on the other hand, the country has a comparative disadvantage, the country's demand would, at the world price, be higher than its domestic supply (i.e. goods would be imported to close the gap between domestic demand and supply). *Figure 4.4* illustrates the welfare effects for the latter case. Prior to a country (say country X) trading with the rest of the world, it would produce and consume the quantity Q_2 of a product (say Y) at the price P_3 (*Figure 4.4a*). As the rest of the world can produce the good Y at the lower price P_1 free trade would lead to the price of Y being equalised with the terms of trade established between country X and the rest of the world leading to a world price of, say, P_2 (*Figure 4.4b*). At the (new) world price (P_2) country X would meet part of its home demand by importing the quantity Q_3Q_1 of good Y from the rest of the world. (Q_3Q_1, country

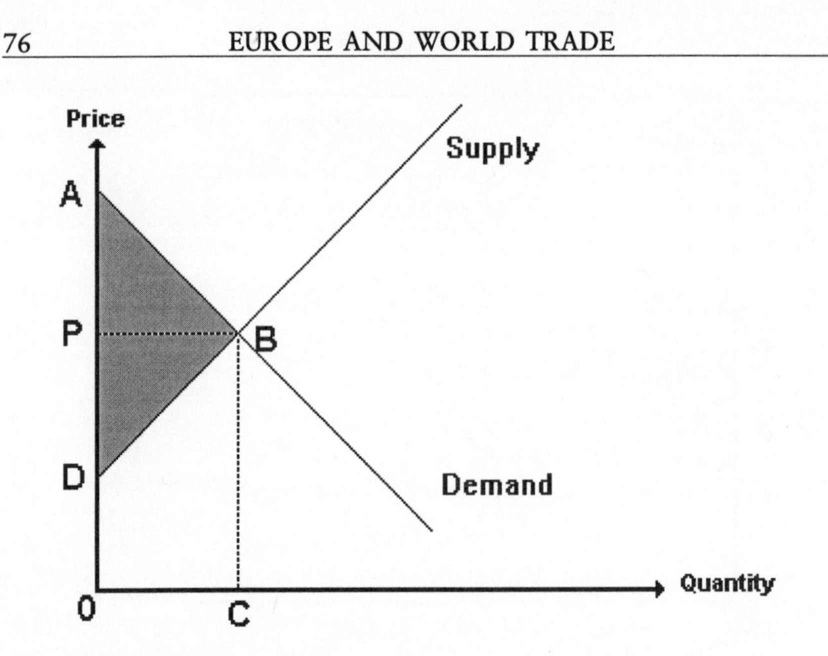

Figure 4.3 Net surplus (welfare)

X's imports (*Figure 4.4a*) equal Q_5Q_4, the rest of the world's exports (*Figure 4.4b*)). As a result of free trade, producers in country X would see their surplus reduced to the extent of area A; the country's consumers, on the other hand, would gain in consumers' surplus (A+B). In the rest of the world consumers would lose out as their surplus would be reduced to the extent of area C; the producers in the rest of the world, on the other hand, would gain to the extent of (C+D). It could then be asserted that both country X and the rest of the world benefit from free trade. Country X's net welfare gain is equivalent to the area B; the welfare gain accruing to the rest of the world will be area D.

Tariffs

Tariffs, import levies and anti-dumping duties imposed on imports into the Union can, for analytical purposes, be treated alike. In order to keep the analysis simple we shall, in considering the welfare implications of tariffs, assume that we are dealing with a situation where the tariff-imposing country is a small open rather than a large open economy (i.e. an economy that has no influence over the world prices of traded goods (fixed terms of trade)). The geometry of trade protection via tariffs is illustrated in *Figure 4.5* where D_d depicts the domestic demand, S_d the domestic supply, and S_w the world supply.

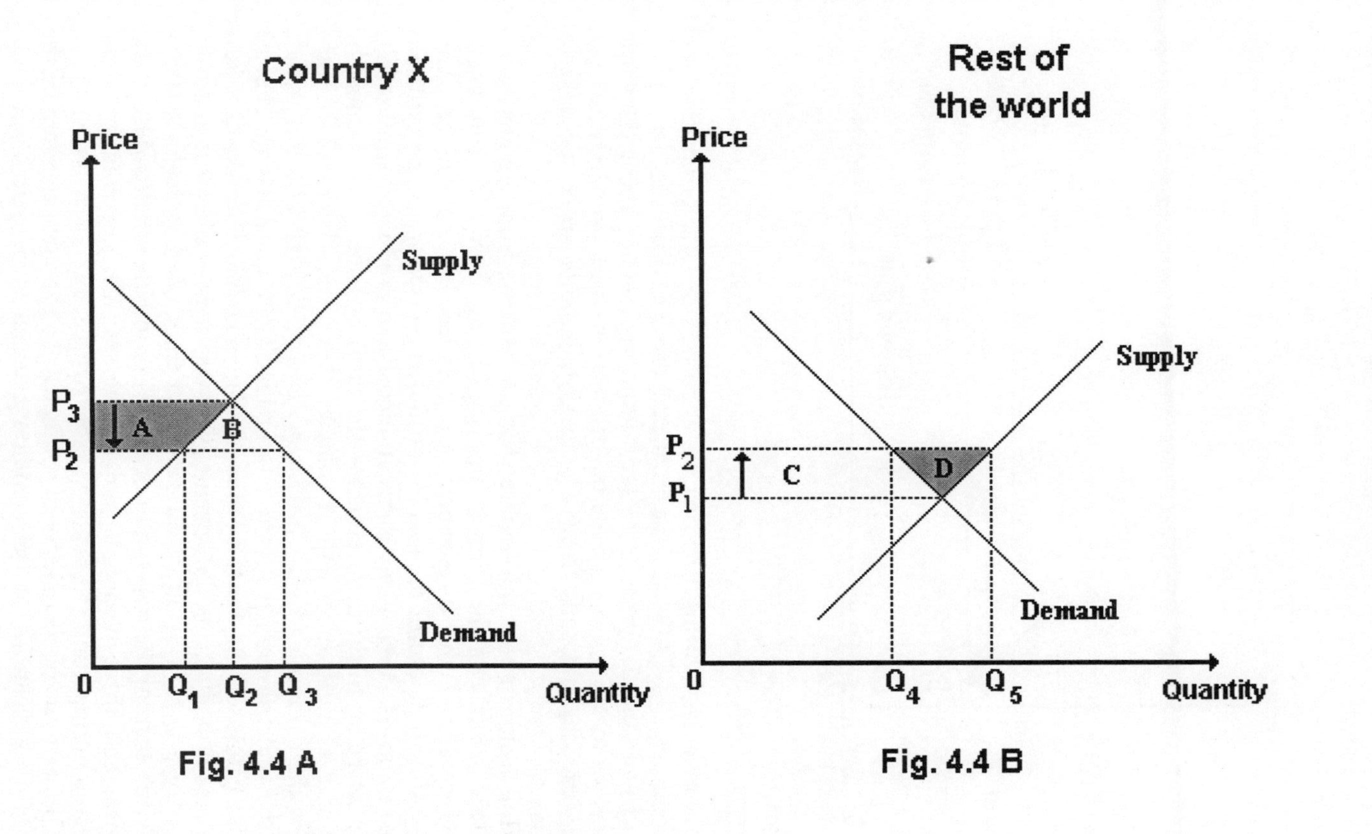

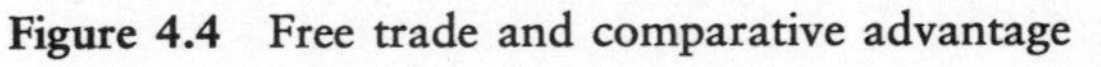
Figure 4.4 Free trade and comparative advantage

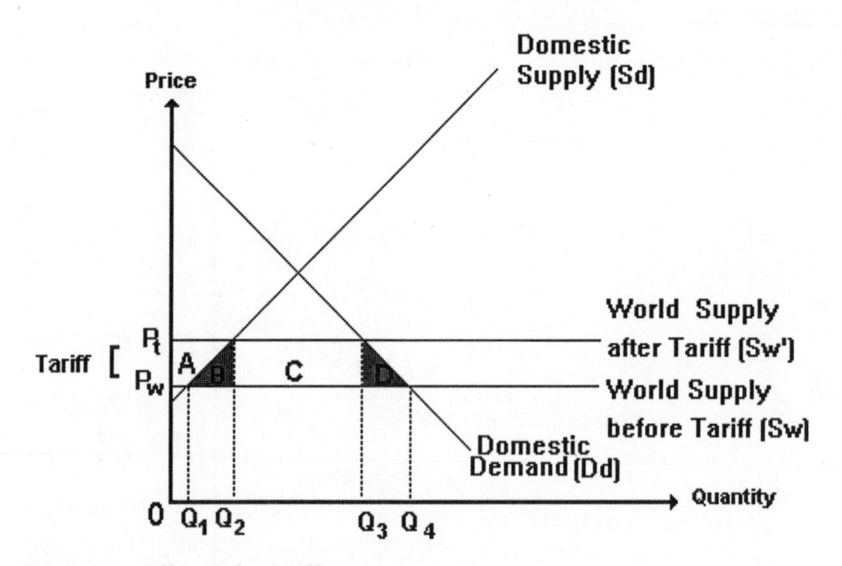

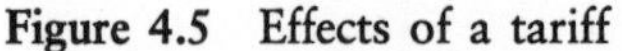
Figure 4.5 Effects of a tariff

Prior to a tariff being imposed on imports, domestic production will amount to Q_1; Q_4Q_1 will be imported to meet domestic demand. A tariff will raise the price in the tariff-imposing country above the world price (from P_w to P_t). Domestic production rises (from Q_1 to Q_2); domestic demand falls (from Q_4 to Q_3); imports are reduced (from Q_4Q_1 to Q_3Q_2).

Conclusions about the welfare changes resulting from the imposition of the tariff can be drawn by considering how the consumers, producers and the government are affected by the change. Area (A+B+C+D) measures the loss in consumers' surplus once the tariff has been imposed. Area A represents an increase in producers' surplus. The gain accruing to the government – the tariff revenue – is measured by the area C (tariff times import volume). Area A has been redistributed from the consumers to the producers; area C measures the magnitude of the redistribution from the consumers to the government. The net welfare loss of the tariff is thus (B+D); it is called *deadweight loss* because nobody gains the benefits the consumers in the tariff-imposing country lose as a result of the restricted trade. Further welfare effects may result from the imposition of tariffs (or import levies/anti-dumping duties) and these would depend on the way the government in the tariff-imposing country spends the tariff revenue.

Our analysis of the impact of tariffs can be extended to examine the welfare implications of the common external tariff that has characterised the trade policies of the European Union. The CET established by the EU has led to a preferential or discriminatory tariff regime and this may, as an interpretation of *Figure 4.6* shows, increase *or* reduce the EU's net welfare position.

Figure 4.6 depicts the domestic supply and demand curve for one member of the union U_1. Pu_2 is the price at which U_1 is in a position to import from another member of the customs union (U_2). Supply of imports from the rest of the world is also assumed to be perfectly elastic (at world price P_w). Prior to the formation of the customs union, the world price P_w will determine U_1's output; it will produce Q_1 and import Q_6Q_1 from the rest of the world. A non-discriminatory tariff (equal to P_tP_w) would increase the domestic price in U_1 to P_t. Domestic output in U_1 would be increased to Q_3; imports from the rest of the world would now be reduced to Q_4Q_3.

If U_1 and U_2 now form a customs union the tariff (P_tP_w) will only be charged on imports into U_1 from the rest of the world (i.e. countries which have been excluded from the customs union). U_1 will now be able to purchase from the cheapest suppliers within the customs union. The freeing of trade, therefore, results in trade creation between U_1 and U_2. We should, however, recognise that while consumers in U_1 can, with the formation of the customs union, buy the good at lower prices than was possible under the non-discriminatory tariff, trade will continue to be distorted. Consumers in U_1 will be confronted by a tariff-inclusive price of goods in the rest of the world and a tariff-free price of goods from the other customs union member U_2. In other words, the customs union will prevent consumers from acquiring goods from the lowest cost producers outside the customs union; trade diversion will be the consequence.

A closer examination of *Figure 4.6* shows that the net welfare effect of the creation of a customs union are far from certain. The introduction of the discriminatory tariff system leads to an increase in consumers' surplus amounting to (A+B+C+D) as consumers in U_1 will be able to purchase the good at Pu_2 rather P_t. Area A represents a loss to the producers in U_1; (C+E) is the loss in tariff revenue. The net welfare change (B+D−E) could be positive, zero or negative. The formation of a customs union can, therefore, result in net welfare gains, no change or welfare losses for a member state of the union. In the situation depicted in *Figure 4.6* (B+D) is larger than E; there has been a net welfare gain for customs union member U_1. More generally speaking, if internal imports take place at prices that are reasonably competitive worldwide then the customs union is likely to generate net welfare gains. If, on the other hand, internal supplies come from (customs union) producers that operate at relatively high costs, then the trade diversion effects are likely to outweigh the trade creation effects (i.e. a net welfare loss resulting from the customs union is probable).

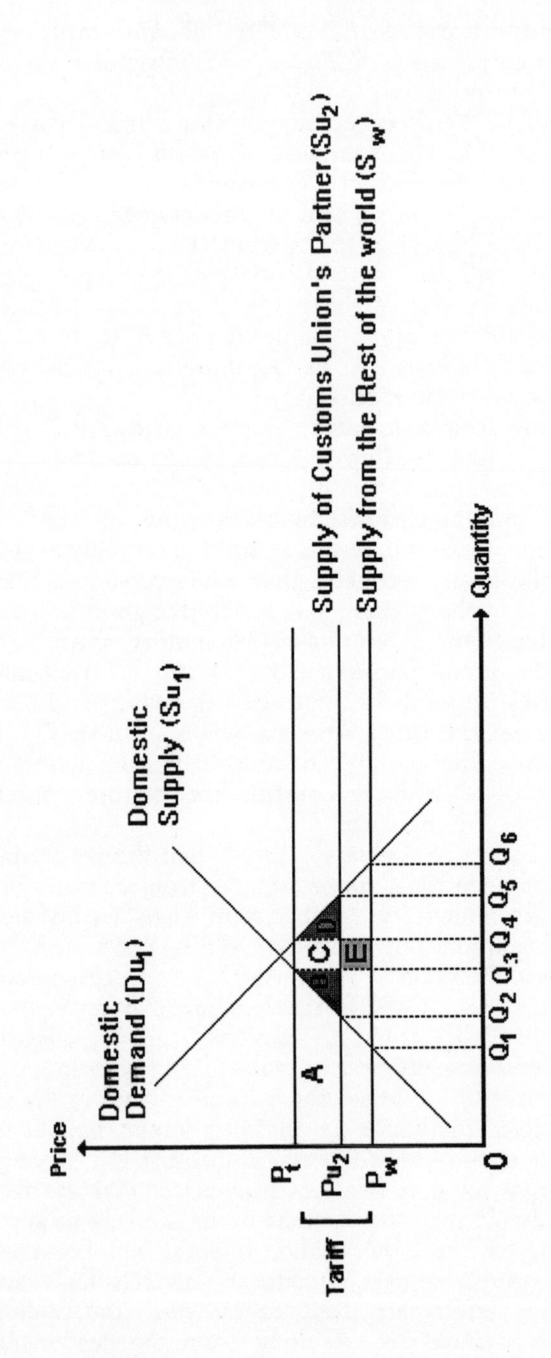

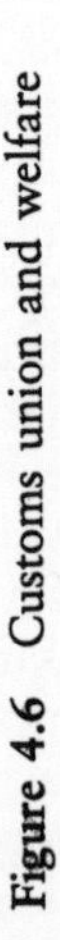

Figure 4.6 Customs union and welfare

Non-tariff barriers

Figure 4.5, although initially designed to show the effects of a tariff, can also be used to show the welfare costs of non-tariff barriers in the form of regulations that inhibit trade such as cumbersome customs documentation, unnecessary duplication of testing procedure, etc. NTBs, like tariffs, have the effect of raising the entry prices of imported products. Suppose NTBs increase the real costs of imports from P_w to P_t. The consumers' surplus would then be reduced by (A+B+C+D). Producers' surplus would rise by the area A. In contrast to the tariff case we considered earlier, the government would not now collect any revenue. Other things being equal, total welfare loss would be greater than if tariffs were imposed on imports; the social loss would amount to (B+C+D).

Subsidies

There are two types of subsidies that characterise the EU's trade policy – production subsidies and export subsidies. We shall discuss their welfare consequences in turn.

Figure 4.7 illustrates the impact that *production subsidies* are likely to have on the country which pays a subsidy to domestic producers in, say, the form of a fixed amount of money per unit of production. Prior to the production of a good being subsidised in a country, the domestic industry would produce Q_1; Q_3Q_1 of domestic demand would be met via imports at the world price P_w. A unit subsidy would result in the supply curve shifting to the right, say from Sd to Sd′. The production subsidy would, therefore, increase domestic production from Q_1 to Q_2. The immediate net welfare cost to the country would be measured by B (additional welfare losses may of course arise because the government will have to finance the subsidies via, for example, increased taxation). For, although the loss to the government which pays the subsidies would amount to (A+B), the area A represents a gain to the domestic producers.

What would be the welfare implications of *export subsidies* schemes? At the world price P_w (*Figure 4.8*) the country is competitive up to output level Q_3. Q_2 units are being sold on the domestic market; Q_3Q_2 is the volume of exports to third countries. With an export subsidy ($P_w'P_w$) being paid to the home producers, exporters would raise their export volume up to the point where the price charged to the domestic consumers reaches the level of the world price plus the export subsidy (P_w'). Consumers in the exporting country would, as a result of this export subsidy scheme, have their consumers' surplus reduced by (A+B); the government would incur additional government expenditure amounting to (B+C+D) – the cost of the export subsidy; the producers'

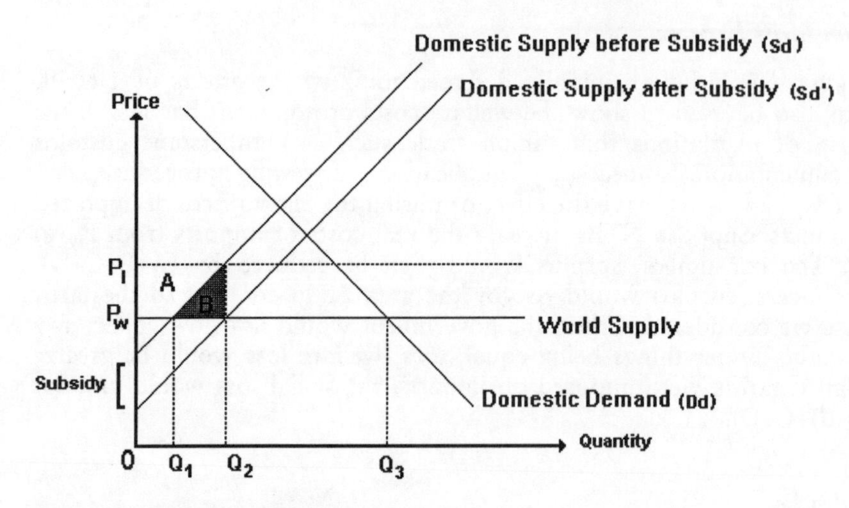

Figure 4.7 Effects of a production subsidy

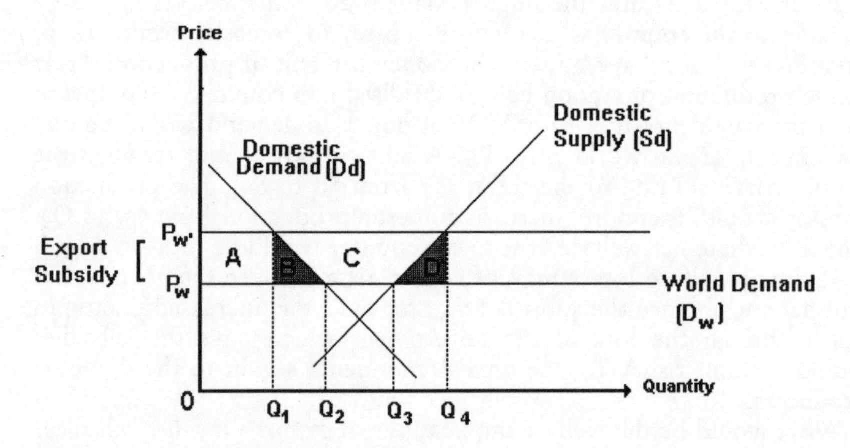

Figure 4.8 Effects of an export subsidy

surplus would be raised by (A+B+C). The triangles B and D would thus represent the net welfare loss to the country operating the export subsidy system. As in the case of the production subsidy scheme, further welfare losses are likely to be generated because the government of the country paying subsidies to exporters would have to finance the subsidies.

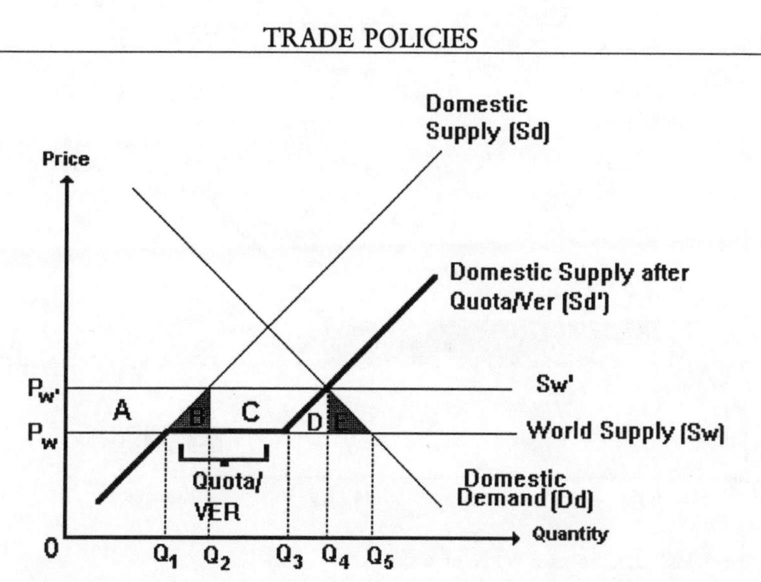

Figure 4.9 Effects of an import quota/VER

Import quotas and VERs

Import quotas and voluntary export restrains (VERs) differ as trade policy measures in that import quotas are imposed by the importing country while VERs are measures taken by the exporting country designed to limit the export volume on a 'voluntary' basis. The welfare losses that may result from subjecting imports to quotas and VERs also differ in magnitude, as we shall demonstrate.

The effects of an *import quota* may be shown with the aid of *Figure 4.9*. Under free trade domestic producers would contribute Q_1 units to domestic demand with imports bridging the gap between total demand and home production (Q_5Q_1). A quota on imports would restrict the number of units that can be imported to, say, Q_3Q_1; the total supply curve can be depicted by the bold line Sd′ (Sd plus quota). Price will now be Pw′, domestic output Q_2 and imports will be reduced to Q_4Q_2 (equal to Q_3Q_1). The effect of the import quota is to cause domestic consumers to pay a higher price for the product affected by the import quota; consumers' surplus will be reduced by (A+B+C+D+E). The net welfare loss is, of course, smaller than this area. It is equivalent to (B+E). A represents an increase in producers' surplus; (C+D) will be appropriated by the importers via increased profits (unless the Union reaps the benefits by auctioning off import licences).

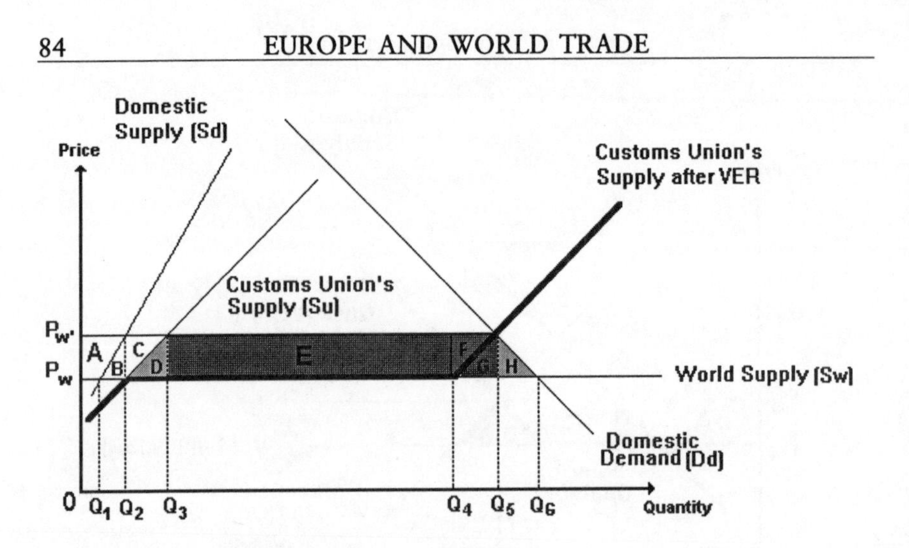

Figure 4.10 Effects of a VER in a customs union

If, instead of considering an import quota equivalent to Q_1Q_3, we assume that the external supplier voluntarily restricts exports by the same magnitude (i.e. also by Q_1Q_3), the welfare implications would be different: area (C+D) will now accrue (via higher profits) to the exporters rather than the importers.

The effects of a VER on a member of a customs union such as the one formed by the European Union are illustrated in *Figure 4.10.* In the absence of any trade restrictions the price for a particular good (on the world market and within the union) would be P_w. The union member would produce Q_1; Q_6Q_1 would be imported with the partner country (or partner countries) supplying Q_2Q_1 and the rest of the world bridging the gap between domestic demand and the Union's aggregate supply (Q_6Q_2). Once a VER of, say, Q_4Q_2 is imposed on imports from suppliers outside the union, the price within the importing country rises to P_w'. At this higher price the union member increases its production to Q_2, consumers reduce their demand to Q_5 and overall imports will be reduced to Q_5Q_3 (equal to Q_4Q_2). Internal imports will, however, be increased from Q_2Q_1 to Q_3Q_2; imports from lower cost suppliers from outside the union will be substituted by more expensive supplies from within the union (trade diversion). Consumers' loss within the union state amounts to (A+B+C+D+E+F+G+H); producers' surpluses will increase by A in the importing country and by (B+C) for internal exporters respectively. Economic rents amounting to (E+F+G) will accrue to external exporters. The VER will thus reduce welfare in the importing union state by (B+C+D+E+F+G+H); the net welfare loss for the union, as a whole, will be (D+E+F+G+H). The third country participating in the VER agreement will earn additional profits equivalent to (E+F+G); and the welfare loss for the world, as a whole, therefore amounts to (D+H). Again our analysis shows that the rent income, which under a quota system accrues to the importer, benefits the exporting country. This partly explains why the high performing east Asian countries (Japan and the NICs), in trading with the EU, have tended to prefer VERs to import quotas.

Problems of using welfare triangles

As we have shown, welfare triangles can be used to throw light on the welfare implications of free trade, customs unions and protectionist measures. As with many theoretical approaches, we must be aware of the limitations of this analysis. Some of the shortcomings of welfare triangle analysis exist regardless of what issues it is being applied to. Some other problems arise only when welfare triangles are applied to trade questions.

General problems in using welfare triangles arise for two reasons. First, triangle analysis tends to ignore distributional questions (see, for example, Mishan 1976). The notion of consumers' surplus (or producers' surplus) is only meaningful if we can aggregate (i.e. weigh consumers' (or producers') gains or losses equally). Comparing gains or losses experienced by consumers, producers and the government requires the difficult, if not impossible, task of making interpersonal welfare comparisons. Second, we are only in a position to measure consumer's surplus by measuring the area under a demand curve provided there is no or only a negligible income effect resulting from a price change (see, for example, Winch 1971).

Using welfare triangles for analysing the welfare implications of trade protection is open to criticism for a number of reasons. First, we have, in all our models, assumed the existence of perfect rather than imperfect competition. A more sophisticated analysis of the welfare effects of the EU's trade policies would require us to differentiate between perfect and imperfect competition; we would have to draw a distinction between the case of a small open economy with fixed terms of trade (i.e. unable to affect export and/or import prices) and the case of a large open economy with variable terms of trade (i.e. in a position to alter its terms of trade by varying its trade volumes). Second, the way the EU chooses to finance subsidies or spend revenues received from tariffs, import levies or anti-dumping duties is also likely to have welfare implications.

Despite these limitations, welfare triangle analysis offers an appropriate and widely used framework for considering the welfare effects of trade policies.

GUIDE TO FURTHER READING

CEC (1993) The European Economy as a World Trade Partner, *European Economy*, 52, Luxembourg, OOPEC.

The Economist (1990) Survey of World Trade, 22 September.

Eversley, J. (1990) Textiles and Clothes, *International Trade and the Consumer*, Working Paper 2, London, NCC.

Eversley, J. (1990) Shoes: The Cost of Neglecting Consumers' Interests, *International Trade and the Consumer*, Working Paper 3, London, NCC.

GATT (1991) *Trade Policy Review: European Communities*, Geneva, GATT.

— (1993) *Trade Policy Review: European Communities*, Geneva, GATT.

Grimwade, N. (1990) Consumer Electronics and the EC's Anti-dumping Policy, *International Trade and the Consumer*, Working Paper 1, London, NCC.

Hindley, B. (1992) Trade Policy of the European Community, in P. Minsford (ed.) *The Cost of Europe*, Manchester and New York, Manchester University Press.

Hine, R.C. (1985) *The Political Economy of European Trade*, Brighton, Wheatsheaf.

Holmes, P. (1991) Trade and Competition Policy: The Consumer Interest, *International Trade and the Consumer*, Working Paper 5, London, NCC.

OECD (1985) *The Costs and Benefits of Protection*, Paris, OECD.

Rhys, G. and Bridge, J. (1990) Cars – The Cost of Trade Restrictions to Consumers, *International Trade and the Consumer*, Working Paper 4, London, NCC.

5
THE EU AND ITS EUROPEAN NEIGHBOURS

INTRODUCTION

In this chapter we shall consider the trade links between the European Union and the rest of Europe. The European economies outside the Communities represent major trading partners for the EU. In 1992, a quarter of the EU's external exports reached EFTA countries (*Table 2.4*). The CEECs' share of the Union's exports to third countries has so far been much smaller. In 1992, it amounted to 5 per cent for CEECs(4) – the Czech Republic, Hungary, Poland and Slovakia – but, as we shall see later, Central and Eastern Europe is likely to emerge as a growing export market for EU producers. Europe outside the EU has been equally important as a supplier of goods; in 1992, 23 per cent of all EU imports came from EFTA countries (*Table 2.5*). If we include the CEECs(4) as a source of EU imports we find that more than a quarter of the EU's external imports came from producers in the rest of Europe. Once the Central and East European Economies have completed the transition phases they have been going through since the political and concomitant economic upheavals of the late 1980s this part of Europe is likely to gain in significance as an import source for members of the EU.

Our discussion of the EU's trade relations with its European neighbours will fall into three parts. We shall first deal with EU–EFTA trade and the creation of the EEA. In part two we shall focus on the past, present and future role of Central and Eastern Europe as trade partners for Western Europe. The final part of this chapter on trade within a more broadly defined Europe will address the question of enlargement of the EU.

EFTA AND THE EEA

History

EFTA was founded in 1960 – two years after the establishment of the Common Market (EUR 6) when seven other West European countries (Austria, Denmark, Norway, Portugal, Sweden, Switzerland and the UK) signed the so-called Stockholm Convention. Unlike the six Communities who aimed at achieving close economic integration, the seven EFTAns formed, as the very name suggests, a loose free trade area. Of the original founding members only two (Norway and Switzerland) have stayed within EFTA; the five others left EFTA and joined the EU as full members: Denmark and the UK in 1972; Portugal in 1986; and Austria and Sweden in 1995. Other countries, however, joined EFTA: Iceland became an EFTAn in 1970; Finland had acquired associate membership status in 1961 joined in 1986; and Liechtenstein, although associated with EFTA from the early 1960s through its customs union with Switzerland, became a full member in its own right in 1991. Within six years of EFTA being founded trade liberalisation between EFTA member states had, to a large extent, been completed. Following negotiations with the Union countries, bilateral agreements between the EU and each of the association countries were reached with the aim of eliminating tariffs on mutual trade in non-agricultural goods. The agreements were put into effect on 1 January 1973; by 1977 tariffs and import duties had been virtually removed on imports of industrial goods from Common Market countries to EFTA economies and from EFTA producers to EU member states. In response to numerous calls (Luxembourg Declaration of April 1984 and Jacques Delors in a speech on 17 January 1989) for the creation of a more unified and dynamic economic space within Europe, successful negotiations took place between the EU and five of the EFTA countries (Switzerland and Liechtenstein rejected the scheme). An agreement was signed in 1992 laying the foundation for the creation of a European Economic Area that would extend to EFTA countries the benefits of the European domestic market. The EEA was supposed to be put in place on 1 January 1993, the date of the beginning of the Single European Market. In the event the EEA of the seventeen did not come into being until January 1994; parts of the deal between the EU and EFTA had to be renegotiated after a ruling by the European Court of Justice in Luxembourg had declared that the EEA agreement was incompatible with EU treaties. By January 1995, EFTA consisted of merely four members – Iceland, Liechtenstein, Norway and Switzerland. The three other EFTA states – two of the 'Nordic' states (Finland, Sweden) and Austria joined the EU.

Aims and characteristics

The principal objective pursued by EFTA and its members has been to generate free trade in industrial goods amongst themselves.

Tariff-free movements of non-agricultural products within EFTA could take place by the end of 1966. By July 1990, tariffs or import duties had also been removed from intra-EFTA trade in fish and other marine products. But because of the significance of EFTA's external trade with the EU (which is in fact more important than EFTA's internal trade) EFTA has, since its inception, pursued a second main objective – to achieve a free trade area embracing both the EU and EFTA. The aim of creating an enlarged domestic market within Western Europe was reached via the implementation of the 1972 Free Trade Agreements between the EU and the EFTA countries in July 1977 (which resulted in the removal of tariffs on trade in industrial products), and later, via the creation of the EEA in January 1994 (which extended to the EFTA countries the four fundamental freedoms of the EU – uninhibited movement of goods, services, people and capital). EFTA, as a free trade area, consists of independent member states who, while facilitating free trade amongst themselves, impose their own tariff levels and non-tariff measures on external trade. They do not, like members of a customs union such as the EU, adopt a common commercial policy in their trade links with third countries.

As a free trade area EFTA differs from the EU in its management and administration. EFTA is an inter-governmental organisation with a council as its key institution. There is no powerful body equivalent to the European Commission, and the EFTA secretariat in Geneva incurs relatively low expenditure and employs but a comparatively small number of staff (about 150). Up to January 1994 when the EEA started to exist a joint committee consisting of representatives of the EU and the relevant EFTA country was responsible for the administration of each of the various free trade agreements reached in the early 1970s.

Significance of EU–EFTA trade

As pointed out earlier (Chapter 2), the commercial links between EFTA and the EU have been very close: EFTA and the EU have been each other's largest trade partners and, as *Table 5.1* illustrates, the EU has emerged as the major export market and import source for EFTA countries.

Table 5.1 EFTA–EU trade, excluding EU-internal trade, 1990

	%
Share of total EFTA imports from the EU	60.8
Share of total EFTA exports to the EU	57.9
Share of total EU exports to EFTA	26.5
Share of total EU imports from EFTA	23.5

Sources: Eurostat (1993); EFTA (1994)

It is worth noting that, while trade between EU countries increased (*Table 2.4* and *2.5*) over time, internal EFTA trade has not been very significant and has in fact decreased over the years. In 1990, for example, internal exports represented 13 per cent of EFTA's total exports; in 1972 they had amounted to 18 per cent (Eurostat 1993; EFTA 1994). While the two trading blocs are mutually interdependent, the EFTA countries are more dependent on the EU than EU countries on EFTAns. EFTA's high degree of trade interdependence with the EU is no doubt attributable to the very privileged position the EFTA countries have been able to enjoy as a result of the Free Trade Agreements relating to industrial goods concluded in 1972 and put into force by 1977.

Problems

Although trade between EFTA and the EU was largely liberalised with the abolition of import duties on non-agricultural products, certain market access issues in EU–EFTA trade links have given cause for concern. Some, although by no means all these problems, have been solved. The 1972 Free Trade Agreements between the EU and EFTA countries were restricted to industrial goods. Most of the EU–EFTA trade in non-industrial products continued to be affected by tariffs or import duties; not even the creation of the EEA as of 1 January 1994 extended the principle of free movement of goods to agricultural produce and trade in fish and fish products.

As we found in Chapter 2, export and import flows between EFTA and the EU have tended to be unequal in magnitude. EFTA countries, as a group, have until the early 1990s consistently been in deficit in trading with the EU (*Table 2.8*). EFTA countries do not pursue a common external trade policy. Policies for trade imbalances are the responsibilities of individual EFTA countries; safeguard arrangements permit EFTA countries that are adversely affected by balance of trade problems to use special protective measures. EFTA countries (except for Norway which always had a surplus in its EU trade) have at times voiced concern about their trade deficits with the Union. But the EU has in fact (with the exception of non-industrial goods) largely liberalised EU–EFTA trade.

In trading with the EU, EFTA countries have, to a certain extent, been 'free loaders rather than free traders' (*Economist* 1989b: 50) in that they have been unequal partners in the bilateral free trade agreements. EFTA-produced goods have had unrestricted access to EU markets and EFTAns have been in a position to purchase subsidised EU agricultural products without having to contribute to the Union's CAP and regional development programmes. EFTA as a free trade area consists of independent member states with each country pursuing its own external trade policy including individual tariff levels or import levies. This situation is likely to lead to situations whereby products could be imported from a country outside EFTA into an EFTA country with a low import duty only to be re-exported within the tariff-free zone to another EFTA country with a high import duty. Rules of origin, therefore, had to be introduced to prevent *trade deflection*. These origin rules had to be extended to EFTA–EU trade flows once the bilateral trade agreements between the EFTA countries and the EU had been implemented. (Provisions for the application of origin rules will also have to be made to avoid trade deflection developing within the EEA because of the recently formed trade partnerships between EFTA countries and the CEECs and the 'Europe Agreements' between the CEECs and the EU.) The non-tariff barriers we discussed in detail in Chapter 3 are relevant for both EU-internal trade and EU trade with third countries including the EFTAns. The establishment on 1 January 1993 of the single European market inevitably would have threatened the EFTA countries' privileged position as EU trade partners had EFTA and the EU not agreed to create the EEA.

The European Economic Area

The EEA extended the single market of the EU to five of the seven EFTA countries, thus creating the largest multilateral trade zone in the world – the large single market in Western Europe which governments in the 1950s had unsuccessfully attempted to negotiate. Taking 1992 data, the EFTA–EU domestic market embraces a population of over 372 million and accounts for nearly half the world's merchandise exports if we include EU internal trade (*Table 2.1*). The EEA is a significantly larger trading region than its American counterpart NAFTA. In 1992, for instance, the seventeen EEA countries, while being equal in population size to the three NAFTA countries, exported three times as much as the NAFTA group and the value of their imports was more than twice as high as that of the NAFTAns (GATT 1993a: 3).

The document containing the EEA agreement is about 1,000 pages in length. General EEA provisions are covered in 29 articles with the rest of the document consisting of annexes and protocols. Probably the two most important features of the EEA agreement are that the five EFTA countries agreed not only to adopt all existing EU legislation (the *acquis communautaire*) but also to comply with future EU legislative steps.

In order to achieve free movement of goods within the EEA all remaining trade barriers have been abolished. Two general principles are of particular importance for internal EEA flows. First, the EU's *cassis de Dijon* principle was, as from the beginning of January 1994, also applied to EU–EFTA trade. Once a product has obtained technical approval in one EEA country, it may be sold in any EEA market. Second, common origin rules are being applied in deciding what goods qualify for 'preferential products' status. In order to move freely between EEA countries products must contain raw material orginating from an EEA country and/or have had value added within the EEA. Products will not be accorded preferential status if they contain a high proportion of raw material and/or components originating from one or more countries outside the EEA; such products are not allowed to move freely between EEA countries. Since the EEA came into effect the principle of 'full cumulation' has been applied; every stage of production within the EEA counts when goods are being defined as EEA or non-EEA products (cumulative origin). While cumulation between EU and EFTA countries had become possible after 1973 when the free trade agreements between individual EFTA countries and the trade bloc of the Union came into force, full cumulation between countries of the two trading zones had previously not been achieved.

In addition to incorporating measures designed to guarantee the other three freedoms – free movement of services, of capital and of persons to all citizens of EEA countries, further integration of EU and EFTA countries has, within the negotiations leading to the EFA agreement, been pursued via 'flanking and horizontal policies'. Cooperation in areas such as education, the environment, research and development, and statistics has been extended; company law, consumer policy and protection, social policy, and tourism have been added to the fields of cooperation between the EU and EFTA.

New institutions were created, both for the EFTA side, for EU–EFTA relations and in order to provide underpinning for the 1992 EEA agreement. At EEA level there exists an EEA council and a joint committee. The EEA council consists of the ministers who are members of the EU council, members of the European Commission and a member of government from each of the five EFTA countries. The EEA council's function is to act as the most powerful political body in the EEA; it lays down general guidelines for the EEA's joint committee which has the responsibility for the operation of the EEA. It is made up of high officials from both EU and EFTA partner countries. In addition, two advisory bodies have been created at EEA level: a joint parliamentary committee and a consultative committee. EFTA established two new institutions (a surveillance authority and a court) and a new committee (the standing committee) to ensure the implementation of the EEA agreement in EFTA countries. The EFTA surveillance authority consists of five members (one from each of the five EFTAns that joined the EEA) and is responsible for the implementation of EEA decisions and the adherence to competition rules by economic agents in EFTA countries. The EFTA surveillance authority reaches decisions on the basis of majority voting. Although an independent body, it cooperates with its counterpart in the EU – the Commission of the European Communities.

The EFTA court has the judicial control over the proper functioning of the EEA agreement such as the handling of disputes over EEA rules between the surveillance authority and an EFTA country, and an EFTA country's appeal against decisions taken by the surveillance authority. The new EFTA standing committee provides a forum for EFTA states to consult and to agree on positions to take in meetings for the joint EEA Committee. The EEA agreement resulted also in the EFTA secretariat's role being affected, which, as a result of servicing the EEA joint committee and the EEA council (as well as the EFTA standing committee), has now become involved in the development of new *acquis communautaire* – new EU legal acts (decisions and directives).

The fact that the EFTA countries, in signing the EEA agreement, had decided to fulfil certain conditions set by the EU (adoption of existing and future rules of the Union; budgetary contributions towards regional and social policies) suggests that the EFTA countries expected to gain more from the pan-EEA competition than the EU anticipated to benefit from extending the European domestic market to the EFTAns. The reason why the EU countries are likely to derive but small benefits from extending '1992' to the five EFTA countries which committed themselves to EEA membership is due to the fact that the EU markets are significantly larger than the markets in the EFTA countries. Increased integration of the relatively small EFTA markets with the relatively large EU markets is likely to lead to more competition and greater economic efficiency in EFTA countries. Adding the relatively small size EFTA markets to the already large size EU markets is, on the other hand, less likely to contribute towards the degree of competitiveness in EU countries. Misallocation of resources and, therefore, higher costs are generally more frequently to be found in small rather than large markets. If EFTA countries had not agreed to the formation of the EEA, competitiveness in EFTA countries would have suffered. Lagging behind the EU's competitiveness would have meant that the EFTA countries would have encountered more problems in selling in their own markets. In EU markets and in markets located in third countries EFTA's share of (internal and external) exports would have been adversely affected; the degree of import penetration of EFTA countries' markets would have further increased. The available empirical evidence supports the view that EFTA has more to gain from its participation in European integration than the EU (Krugman 1988). Both in manufacturing industries (Norman 1989; Haaland and Norman 1992; Henrikson 1992) and, to an even larger extent, the financial services sectors (Gardener and Teppett 1992) it was found that EFTA countries will gain from market integration although the benefits of the EEA are likely to accrue disproportionately to EFTA members. The potential gains for the EU should, however, not be overlooked. While the five EFTA members of the EEA are individually small, they represent, taken as a group, a far from insignificant export market for the EU within the enlarged West European market created by the EEA. It should also be noted that small benefits accruing to EU countries collectively may well conceal important positive effects at either regional or industry level. Above average benefits from the EU and EFTA forming the EEA may be derived from increased border trade between, for example, Southern Germany/Northern Italy and Austria or Northern Germany/Denmark and the Nordic EFTA countries. At industry level, the European market for cars is bound to be affected by Sweden; Norway, as a major source of energy supplies, is likely to have an impact on Europe's energy market.

The formation of the EEA must, in light of three of the EFTA members joining the EU on 1 January 1995 as full members, be viewed as an interim arrangement and the decline, if not the end, of EFTA. Joining the EU will have the significant consequence of the three new members adopting the EU's common trade policy. Adjusting their external tariffs to the EU's CET will not create any problems for the Nordic EFTA countries as their external tariffs have in fact been lower than the CET of the EU (Hamilton 1991). Adopting the EU's anti-dumping measures, countervailing duty measures and bilateral quantitative restrictions on imports into the European Union's economy is, however, bound to be less painless for the three new members as such trade policy measures were, on the whole, not pursued by EFTA countries. While operating inside the EU would enable EFTA – the Union's most significant external import source – to evade the EU's restrictions on the import of iron and steel, restrictions on exports of, say, electronic goods from third countries may force the new members to adopt a more protectionist stance in trade (CEPR 1992). The EU's competition policy is also likely to have a liberalising impact on the three countries who left EFTA at the end of 1994 to join the EU and this will have indirect effects on intra-EU trade. Competition has tended to be less intense in EFTA markets than in the European Union; and prices in EFTA countries have, on average, been higher than in EU markets (Wieser 1989). But while price differentials may persist, they are likely to become smaller within the enlarged EU.

CENTRAL AND EASTERN EUROPE

Trade between Western Europe and the Central and East European Countries has been characterised by major changes over time and more changes in the trade relations between the 'new' and the 'old' Europe can be expected to take place in the future. We shall deal with the trade links between Western Europe and the CEECs in four separate, yet interlinked sections. We shall first discuss East–West trade in the period before the CEECs changed from command and state trading economies to market economies. This will be followed by an assessment of the shifts in trade relations between the EU and the Central and East European transition economies between the late 1980s and now. Third, we shall consider market access issues resulting from trade between the 'old' and the 'new' European countries in the late 1990s (and the next millenium). Finally, we shall assess the CEECs' future trade potential as an import source and export market for the EU.

State trading phase

The incorporation of Central and Eastern Europe into the centrally planned and state trading Eastern Bloc at the end of the Second World War significantly affected the CEECs' involvement in world trade. For the political separation of Europe into 'West' and 'East' disrupted natural and previously established trade flows between the CEECs and Western Europe. Baldwin (1992b), using League of Nations' data for the year 1928 and IMF data for the year 1991, found that 'before the War the CEECs' trading performance was on par with West Europe's' (Baldwin 1992b: 10). In the sixty years between the late 1920s and the late 1980s the CEECs' shares of total European exports declined significantly and in 1991 accounted for only a fraction of what they had been in 1928 (*ibid*. 1992: 10). Czechoslovakia, in particular, saw its role of a leading industrial European country disappear.

Not only was the volume of the CEECs' trade lower in 1991 than in 1928; the political division of Europe also affected the direction of their trade. Trade between Western Europe and the CEECs became less

important; trade between the CEECs and the Soviet Union and the rest of the world gained in significance (Baldwin 1992b: 11). The shift of the CEECs' trade links towards the Soviet Union was largely due to the Council for Mutual Economic Assistance (CMEA), also known as Comecon. Comecon was founded in 1949; it ceased to exist in 1991 and embraced the CEECs plus the republics of the (former) Soviet Union. The aim of Comecon was to promote the economic development of the Eastern Bloc via cooperation, more intensive trade relations between CMEA countries and joint bulk buying from Western capitalist countries.

It was not until the early 1970s that contacts were established between the European Union and Comecon. Although a number of meetings between the Comecon secretariat and the European Commission took place, little progress was made until Gorbachev came to power in 1986. Prior to 1986 Comecon had, at the request of the Soviet Union, insisted on acting on behalf of all its members even though it did not have the authority to negotiate trade issues for the member countries of this organisation of European and Soviet state trading countries. The European Union, while prepared to work with Comecon, was only willing to negotiate trade agreements with Comecon countries on an individual basis. Following the signing of a joint declaration by Comecon and EU delegates in June 1988 to agree on mutual recognition of the two organisations (neither the EU nor Comecon had previously recognised the legitimacy of the other), a number of trade agreements were signed between the CEECs and the Union. Although these so-called first generation trade agreements opened the way for a new era of trade links between the EU and the CEECs, they were too limited in scope to bring about increased East–West trade flows in Europe. By 1990, exports from the EU to Comecon countries still accounted for only a small fraction of their external trade; and the Comecon countries provided but an insignificant source of all imports into EU markets.

Trade between Western and Eastern Europe remained relatively small up to 1990, and this for a number of reasons. First, the economic reforms that were introduced in Comecon countries were too limited or required more time to work for bringing about trade liberalisation; trade between Western and Eastern Europe was up to the late 1980s characterised by centrally fixed prices and foreign trade monopolies (Nello 1991: 4). Second, Central and East Europe's chronic shortage of hard foreign currency to meet import bills was far from conducive to increasing East–West trade flows. Third, the mechanisms used by the Communities in trading with the CEECs – anti-dumping measures, quantitative restrictions safeguard measures, tariffs and voluntary export restraint agreements – inhibited the CEECs' access to the West European markets.

Table 5.2 Trade of Visegrad countries, by main trading partners, 1988 and 1992, in %

	Czechoslovakia		Hungary		Poland	
	1988	1992	1988	1992	1988	1992
Total exports to:						
EU	20	50	22	50	27	58
E. Europe/former USSR	51	25	45	19	43	15
Total imports from:						
EU	22	42	25	43	27	53
E. Europe/former USSR	50	31	44	24	43	17

Source: ECE (1993: 120)

Transition

The process of transformation in Central and Eastern Europe since 1989 has, *inter alia*, been accompanied by major shifts in the trade patterns of the CEECs. The principal shifts in the CEECs' trade patterns have been as follows:

- a decline in internal trade among the CEECs (and with the successor states of the USSR);
- an increase in the CEECs' merchandise trade with EU – states (and EFTA countries).

Table 5.2 summarises the exports from and imports into the CEECs that formed the Central European Free Trade Area (CEFTA) also known as the Visegrad Group (Czech Republic, Hungary, Poland and Slovakia) on 1 April 1993.

The demise of Comecon is likely to have played a significant role in bringing about the drastic shift in the composition of the CEECs' export destinations and import sources. For the abolition of Comecon amounted to a dismantling of its system of artificial preferences for mutual trade among Comecon countries: 'trade at administered CMEA prices expressed in non-convertible monetary units was replaced by trade at world prices expressed in convertible currencies, which put an end to the discrimination against non CMEA Markets' (ECE 1993: 121). The effects of abolishing Comecon could be compared to the changes in the direction of trade flows one would expect to result from the dissolution of a customs union that had led to trade diversion.

Whether EU trade policy contributed to the change in the territorial composition of the Visegrad countries' foreign trade is far from certain. The Union admittedly took steps to liberalise East–West trade within

Europe but, as we shall show further on in this chapter, the EU's trade liberalisation policies towards the East have been somewhat limited.

The European Union granted the CEECs more access to their market between 1988 and 1990 by offering them MFN treatment and GSP status, and by signing trade and cooperation agreements. The trade concessions were further enhanced when the EU concluded association agreements with Czechoslovakia, Hungary and Poland in March 1992 (separate agreements were signed by the Union with the Czech Republic and Slovakia in October 1993). The objective of the trade part of these Europe agreements which contain five core features (free movements of goods; movements of workers, establishment, and the supply of services; payments, competition and the approximations of laws; economic cooperation; financial cooperation) is to promote increased trade between the Union and the four CEECs by establishing a free trade area (comprising the EU and the Visegrad countries) over a period of ten years. Trade liberalisation is expected to be achieved in stages and with gradually increasing coverage of goods. The principal stages of trade liberalisation envisaged are as follows (Winters 1992b: 19–20):

- Most products from the CEECs will be able to enter EU markets free of tariffs and quantitative restrictions within one year of the agreements being put into force.
- Tariffs will be lowered for specified metal products over a four year period.
- Tariffs will continue to be levied on certain 'sensitive' products such as chemicals, footwear, furniture, glass, leather goods, steel products and vehicles for up to five years.
- Import duties on coal are expected to be removed in four years and quantitative restrictions on the Visegrad countries' exports of coal to most of the EU countries (Germany and Spain were exempted from this aspect of trade liberalisation) will cease one year after the implementation of the accords.
- Import duties on textiles and clothing will be phased out over six years and quantitative restrictions on exports of textile and clothing will be abolished after five years.
- While duties on the CEECs' exports of iron and steel will be removed over six years, quantitative restrictions on this category of products were abolished with the Europe accords coming into force.

Market access issues

How liberalising are the EU–Visegrad countries association agreements? In answering this question, it is important to consider two aspects: the effective liberalisation as measured by the relative importance of the CEECs' exports to the EU; and any contingent protection against EU imports from the Visegrad countries permitted under the agreements, i.e. protection directly depending 'upon the behaviour or performance of exporting . . . industries' (Hindley 1993: 3) in the form of anti-dumping actions, countervailing duties, rules of origin; safeguard clauses etc. The effective liberalisation of the CEECs' access to EU markets resulting from reduced standard protection (in the form of import duties and quantitative restrictions) would appear to be more apparent than real, and this for two reasons. First, the 'list of items in the "slow" liberalisation schedule is precisely the set of goods which CHP [Czechoslovakia, Hungary, Poland; explanation of abbreviation added] currently export with most success' (Winters 1992b: 20). Second, the Europe agreements exclude free trade in agriculture (special arrangements permit the CEECs to raise their exports of certain products such as, for instance, dairy goods, fruit, meat, and vegetables by ten per cent annually). In 1989, exports of sensitive products – food and agriculture, textiles and clothing, and iron and steel – accounted for some 42 per cent of the Visegrad countries' exports to the EU. (CEC 1991b; Mobius and Schumacher 1990, cited by Winters 1992b: 29). The figure is arguably an under-estimate of the relative importance of these sensitive industries for the composition of the CEECs' exports to the EU as the data do not accurately reflect the role these products would have played in the CEECs' export performance under unrestricted trade. The trade restrictions contained in the Europe Agreements would thus appear to discriminate against the very products in which the Visegrad countries may have a comparative advantage. The restrictive nature of the European association accords (designed to lead to a pan-European free trade area) is in marked contrast to the NAFTA accord which has given Mexico free access for agriculture, steel and textiles to the US and Canadian markets.

The Europe agreements include a range of contingency measures to which the EU countries can resort. The principal opportunities for restricting trade between the CEECs and the EU are: anti-dumping actions, safeguard clauses, and origin rules.

Anti-dumping actions (or the threat of anti-dumping actions) represent a loophole in the EU's programme of liberalising European East–West trade. The European Union's anti-dumping actions are unlikely to be objective; accusations of exporting countries practising dumping are likely to be supported by disputable 'evidence' (see Messerlin 1989; Hindley 1992). Iron and steel, and chemicals are product categories most likely to be subject to anti-dumping actions by the EU. They represent potential exportables for the CEECs; and they fall into the category of sensitive products, the imports of which EU states have viewed as threats to their domestic industries.

Safeguard clauses have been used less frequently than anti-dumping actions when the EU has sought contingent rather than standard protection against imports from the CEECs (Winters 1992b: 21), but their possible use undermines the agreed liberalisation programme, especially as the kind of measures to which the EU may resort to safeguard domestic producers or regions have not been clearly defined.

Although rules of origin would appear to be less discretionary measures of protection against imports, they too can offer contingent rather than standard protection. Exports from third countries can normally only enter the EU provided the 60 per cent local content requirement is being met, that is imports must not account for more than 40 per cent of the value of a good exported to the EU. While the value of materials or components imported from the EU does not affect the value added of an exportable, application or non-application of a cumulation rule would decide whether or not trade is being facilitated or restricted. Such a cumulation rule is, for example, laid down in protocol 4 of the EEA accord which permits unlimited cumulation with market forces deciding where, within the EEA, producers of exportables purchase their supplies. The EEA system of cumulative origin has so far not been extended to trade between the CEECs and the EEA. Goods from CEECs are, at present, not subject to duties when entering the EU provided that the domestic producer has added at least 60 per cent to the value of the goods. The goods may, however, not be able to enter the EU duty free if the producer obtained supplies of inputs from another CEEC or an EFTA country. In short, the absence of 'Pan-European cumulation' (Lindström 1994: 3) inhibits the CEECs' exports to the EU and makes the Europe agreements less advantageous. Consumers in the EU pay higher prices than under free trade; and producers in the CEECs will see their exports reduced below the free trade level.

Trade potential

After decades of operating as state trading economies the CEECs have had but a few years of participating in world trade as market economies. As our foregoing discussion has demonstrated, the period 1989–94, while exhibiting trends towards more intensive East–West trade links, has not been free of restrictions. It could, therefore, be argued that at present a discrepancy exists between Central and Eastern Europe's actual and potential trade volume, especially since, as mentioned earlier in this chapter, the CEECs were in fact major trading nations in the 1920s. A number of recent studies suggest that Central and Eastern Europe has an enormous trading potential. Most of these investigations base their predictions of the CEECs' potential exports on the *gravity model*, developed by Linnemann (1966) in order to model the aggregate trade flows of economies. The gravity model, while simple and lacking in theoretical foundations (see, for example, Deardorff 1984), appears to be yielding robust predictions and has been widely used (see e.g. Bergstrand 1985; Rosati 1992; Winters and Hamilton 1992; Baldwin 1993; Winters and Wang 1994). A detailed discussion of the gravity model would go beyond the scope of this text, but it is essential that we are aware of its basic features. Trade flows, so gravity models assume, are primarily determined by the following factors: the costs of doing business, the exporter's supply and the importer's demand. A country's imports depend on the size of its gross national product (the higher the GNP, the higher the imports) and the size of the population (the larger the population, the higher the degree of self-sufficiency, i.e. the lower the imports). Exports are a function of a country's GNP (the larger a country's GNP, the larger its export potential) and of its openness, measured by the share of total output being exported (this 'openness ratio' is expected to vary inversely with the population size). The costs of doing across-border business depend on natural trade obstacles (transport costs resulting from the physical distance between sellers and buyers; transaction costs) and artificial trade barriers (trade costs resulting from the commercial policies pursued by the trading countries). Assuming that trade flows in the whole of Europe are influenced by the same factors as trade in Western Europe and assuming that the same level of protectionism applies to the trade of both the CEECs and the EU, all the gravity model based projections suggest that the CEECs' trade would be higher than their actually recorded trade flows.

Some of the results obtained in the study by Winters and Wang (1994) are summarised in *Table 5.3*. Potential exports from two EU states (Germany and the UK) were estimated to be 2.5 (for Germany) and 7.7 (for the UK) times actual exports; comparative figures for two other main world exporters outside the EU (Japan and the USA) were found to be 5.9 and 17.6 respectively. It would be wrong to infer that Germany is benefiting less from liberalisation than the other three countries. In absolute terms Germany is by far the largest gainer and the low 'multiplier' effect is attributable to the already high trade volume it has established with the CEECs. Potential imports by the four countries listed in *Table 5.3* from the CEECs were found to be 3.4 (Germany), 5.9 (UK), 12.1 (USA) and 14.0 (Japan) times actual imports in 1992. Estimates of large trading potentials of the CEECs were also estimated by Van Bergeijk and Oldersma (1990) and Baldwin (1993). Van Bergeijk and Oldersma (1990), who used a gravity model covering 49 countries (including 6 CEECs), estimated East–West trade flows would have been eight times higher in 1985 if the CEECs had been integrated into the world trading system at that time. Focusing on EFTA countries, Baldwin established 'that EFTA countries' exports to

Table 5.3 CEECs: trade potential

	Germany	UK	USA	Japan
	Exports to CEECs			
Potential minus actual 1992 exports (in US$ mio)	18,136	7,236	3,880	17,886
Difference as multiple of actual exports in 1992	2.5	7.7	17.6	5.9
	Imports from CEECs			
Potential minus actual 1992 imports (in US$ mio)	16,804	7,069	3,674	15,454
Difference as multiple of actual imports in 1992	3.4	5.9	12.1	14.0

Source: Winters and Wang (1994: 24)

the CEECs would have been between three times greater (for Austria) and eleven times greater (for Norway) than they actually were in 1989' (Baldwin 1993: 15).

A different technique for estimating the CEECs' potential role in world trade was used by Collins and Rodrik (1991) who also found that the CEECs' actual trade volume falls short of the role they could be playing in world trade. The approach used by Collins and Roderik (1991) was a pragmatic one and, like the gravity model, not based on coherent economic reasoning; they derived their predictions of 1988 trade flows on a set of well-established empirical regularities and a number of plausible conjectures. These included, *inter alia*, reference to the CEECs' trade shares in 1928.

EU ENLARGEMENT

The evolution of the European Union since 1958 has been characterised by both an absorption of new member countries (*widening*) and increased economic (and political) integration of existing member states (*deepening*). The relative significance of the two processes – widening and deepening – has varied over the three decades of the EU's existence. 'Deepening' was clearly of paramount importance for the original Six between 1958 and the late 1960s. During this period the foundations for a customs union were laid; the dismantling of tariff barriers and the adoption of a common external tariff resulted in more intensive internal trade. 'Widening' of the Union came to the forefront in the early 1970s when Denmark, Ireland and the UK joined, thus increasing the membership to nine.

Enlargement of the EU inevitably meant that while efforts to consolidate, if not intensify, economic (and political) integration continued, problems resulting from incorporating the three new member countries absorbed a lot of effort and time. The 1980s, while leading to a further enlargement of the EU (the Union changed from EUR 9 to EUR 10 in 1981 when Greece joined; the EUR 12 was established a few years later when Portugal and Spain became full members) with its concomitant adjustment problems for both the existing and new members, were nevertheless characterised by efforts to bring about a more integrated European domestic market. These efforts implied acceptance of the *acquis communautaire*, participation in the EU's common policies (CAP, competition policy, industrial policy, regional policy, social policy, etc.), and culminated in the preparation and establishment of the single market. Implementing '1992' has taken time and will continue to require inputs from both the Commission and the Union member states in future years. Deepening of the Union is, therefore, likely to remain a key issue on the EU's agenda. That said, there is no doubt that the question of enlargement has, especially over the last few years, again become much more prominent in the evolution of the European Union. An increasing number of other European countries have been seeking membership of the EU.

A number of factors have generated this increased interest in participating in Europe's internal market. First, the end of the Cold War between the East and the West has meant that the EU has now become politically more acceptable to neutral or quasi-neutral European countries (some EFTA countries had not wished to join the Union for that reason). Second, the 'new' Europe, that is the Central and East European countries and the successor states of the Soviet Union have become politically and economically independent; their main trade is no longer tied to other members of the former Comecon. Third, and this is arguably the most important reason for other European countries to wish to become full EU members, it is the likely economic benefits of EU-membership that have persuaded a large and increasing number of European and adjacent countries to apply for EU membership or express an interest in joining the EU.

We shall, by way of concluding this chapter, briefly discuss the political feasibility and economic desirability of enlargement. In treating these questions, it would appear appropriate to divide applicants into three groups: EFTA countries, Mediterranean states, and ex-CMEA transition economies. Prior to dealing with this group of actual or potential applicants for EU membership, it will be useful to make an important general observation about the distribution of the gains arising from the enlargement of a customs union such as the EU (we assume here that there are net gains, i.e. the trade creation effects outweigh the trade diversion effects).

Integrating a small and a large economy normally results in the small area gaining comparatively more than the large area (Baldwin 1994: 161). The integration of two areas of different size will create more opportunities for producers and consumers in the small area than in the large one as there will be more scope for specialisation in the small economy than in the large economy. There will be more pressure on competition in the small area; and there will be more scope for taking advantage of economies of scale in the small area as a result of successful market integration. For the EFTA group, or at least three of its members, joining the EU became a reality on 1 January 1995 when Austria, Finland and Sweden acquired full membership status. Implementing this North–East enlargement of the Union is unlikely to create major problems. The three new members are rich; they are unlikely to call on the Union's structural funds and are bound to be net contributors to the EU's budget. Their economies are comparatively small and already fairly well integrated with the EU (duty-free trade of industrial merchandise between EFTA countries and the Union has existed for more than twenty years; with the recent creation of the EEA the EFTAns started to adopt the *acquis communautaire* and participated fully in the single European market). Both their relative wealth and the fact that their agricultural sectors are (with the exception of Sweden's more liberalised approach) also protected would suggest that farmers in the EU in general and in the four least wealthy Communities (Greece, Ireland, Portugal, Spain) in particular will not feel threatened by this accession. Additional trade creation can be expected to result from this EU enlargement as the structure of the new entrants' goods and services traded with existing EU members is competitive or overlapping rather than complementary or dissimilar. Harmonising external tariffs would also be conducive to creating trade because tariff harmonisation between EUR 12 and the three new members would be relatively easy. Some trade diversion effects are, on the other hand, likely to take place because Sweden, for instance, unlike the rest of the EU, has no non-tariff measures on imported goods such as household appliances, consumer electronics, cars, motorcycles, footwear, textiles etc. Overall, the welfare effects of Austria, Finland and Sweden joining the EU can be expected to be positive.

The question of enlarging the EU by adding the three Mediterranean states of Cyprus, Malta and Turkey poses some economic and political problems. All three have had association agreements with the EU and all three have formally submitted applications for full membership. Turkey's application is the most controversial and disputed one. It has raised the question of the boundaries of Europe (i.e. whether Turkey belongs to Europe), and it has been connected with human rights issues (i.e. whether Turkey's record in this area warrants membership of a union of democratically governed countries). Its application has been effectively blocked by Greece in protest over Turkey's invasion of Cyprus and subsequent political division of that island. Economically, there would seem to be few, if any, advantages for the EU to add Turkey to its membership list. While adding to the size of the single market in terms of population (some 50 million people), allowing Turkey to join would mean admitting a country that is even poorer than Portugal (currently the EU's poorest member state). It would increase calls on the EU's agricultural and structural budgets. Turkey's industries (with the exception of the textiles and clothing sectors) would also find it difficult to compete within an enlarged and integrated European market. Considering the EU's political reservations (plus Greece's veto) and the economic burden Turkey's membership would impose on the existing Communities, it seems unlikely that serious consideration will be given to Turkey's application before the next millenium. Offering Cyprus and Malta full EU membership would not appear to create major economic difficulties. Both are small, yet relatively open economies that could easily be absorbed into the EU's domestic market. The application of Cyprus has, however, understandably created political problems as it was submitted in respect of the whole island. No decision has yet been taken as to whether and when Malta will join the EU.

An Eastern enlargement of the EU presents a much more complex question than the North–East enlargement discussed earlier. The ex-Comecon countries intent on becoming EU members in the future include a very heterogeneous group of countries: Central and East European Countries (the Czech Republic, Slovakia, Poland, Hungary, Romania, Albania, Bulgaria, and possibly the successor states of the former Yugoslavia); the three Baltic States (Estonia, Latvia, Lithuania); and some other successor states of the former USSR. While an Eastern enlargement of the EU is bound to take place it is likely to take some considerable time, probably at least ten years. In the first instance, it may extend only to a part of Central and Eastern Europe, notably the CEECs with whom the EU signed Europe agreements in the early 1990s. It is easy to understand why it will take many years before the EU will admit (some) CEECs to the EU. From the CEECs' perspective an early accession would not be desirable as they need a few years to undergo the necessary transition to market economies. An Eastern enlargement would be connected with significant, if not unaffordable, increases in EU expenditure. A recent study estimated that admitting Visegraders would increase the EU budget by as much as 74 per cent (Baldwin 1994: 170). The four CEECs would draw for many years on the EU's structural funds as many of their regions' incomes would for a long time be below the EU averages. Being more agricultural than most of the EU states, they would also draw heavily on the EU's agricultural budget. That said, there would of course be economic gains accruing to members of the EU. The economic power of the EU in the world trading system would be increased; expanding to the four Visegrad countries alone would increase the EU's population from 372 to 436 million people. Comparative advantage type gains would be derived by both the acceding CEECs and the EU. But the gains can be expected to be larger for the CEECs (the smaller area) than for the larger area covered by the EU states.

The existing trade agreements within Europe are of a piecemeal nature and lack coherence. The individual agreements between the EU and the European Mediterranean countries, the Union and EFTA, the EU and the CEECs, between the CEECs, and EFTA and the CEECs are not interlinked. In order to move further towards a pan-European economic integration a more coherent framework for structuring European trade agreements and phasing market integration is called for (Baldwin 1994).

GUIDE TO FURTHER READING

Baldwin, R.E. (1994) *Towards an Integrated Europe*, London, CEPR.

Blanchet, T. *et al.* (1994) *The EEA Agreement: A Guide to Issues Affecting the Free Movement of Goods*, Oxford, Clarendon Press.

CEC (1990) *The European Community and its Eastern Neighbours*, Luxembourg, OOPEC.

— (1993) EC Trade with Central and Eastern Europe, in the European Economy as a World Trade Partner, *European Economy*, 52: 27–45, Luxembourg, OOPEC.

CEPR (1992) *Is Bigger Better? The Economics of EC Enlargement*, Monitoring European Integration 3, London, CEPR.

EFTA (1993) *What is EFTA*? Geneva, EFTA.

EFTA and the New Europe (1990) The European Community, *Journal of Common Market Studies*, Special Issue, xxviii (4).

Lintner, V. (1994) The Economics of EU Enlargement, *Economics*, II, 1, 5: 17–22.

Rollo, J. and Smith, A. (1993) The Political Economy of Eastern European Trade with the European Community: Why So Sensitive?, *Economic Policy*, 16: 139–81.

Wallace, H. and Wessels, W. (1989) Towards a New Partnership: the EC and EFTA in the Wider Western Europe, *Occasional Paper*, 28, Geneva, EFTA.

Winters, L.A. and Wang, Z.K. (1994) *Eastern Europe's International Trade*, Manchester and New York, Manchester University Press.

6
TRADE WITH JAPAN AND THE UNITED STATES

INTRODUCTION

Japan and the USA belong to the leading exporters and importers in world trade, and this applies to both merchandise trade and trade in commercial services.

In 1992, the top three participants in world merchandise trade (exports plus imports) were the USA (13 per cent), Germany (11 per cent including internal EU trade) and Japan (7 per cent) (GATT 1993a: 3). Once we consider the EU as one trading entity the EU replaces the USA as the main player in world trade (even after excluding EU intra-trade) with a share of world trade of 21 per cent; the USA (18 per cent) and Japan (10 per cent) rank second and third among the world's principal traders (GATT 1993a: 4). In trading in commercial services (exports plus imports), the USA was the most important country in 1992 (15 per cent); Japan, although not as dominant as in merchandise trade belonged to the top four trading countries (behind the USA, France and Germany) with a share of 8 per cent (GATT 1993a: 5).

Neither Japan nor the USA constitute the EU's most important merchandise export market or import source when we treat particular countries such as the EFTA countries as a group. Exports from the EU to Japan and the USA combined amount to less than EU exports to EFTA. In 1992, 22 per cent of the EU's exports were destined for the US and Japanese markets; EFTA absorbed one quarter of the EU's external exports (*Table 2.4*). EFTA provided nearly a quarter of all EU imports in 1992; the corresponding figures for the USA and Japan were 18 and 11 per cent respectively (*Table 2.5*). As individual countries, however, Japan and the USA are very important to the EU as trading partners. In 1992, some 17 per cent of EU exports were destined for the US market; the corresponding figure for Japan, while much lower (5 per cent), was more than double the figure in 1975 (*Table 2.4*). The difference between Japan's and the United States' importance as import source for the EU is less striking. In 1992, Japan's share of EU imports was 11 per cent (a significant increase since 1958 and 1975 when the shares were 1 and 4 per cent respectively); 18 per cent of all EU imports came from the USA in 1958 and 1975, and the USA contributed exactly the same share of EU imports in 1992 (*Table 2.5*).

Both the positions that Japan and the USA have established in world trade and the importance of these countries as export markets and import sources for the EU make it necessary to discuss their trade relations in a separate chapter. But there is an additional reason why a focus on trade between 'Europe' and the other two giants of the Western industrialised countries is appropriate. EU–Japan and EU–US trade relations have been characterised by a whole range of conflicts arising from allegations of protectionism and resulting in measures taken to counter alleged or actual protectionist policies. We shall first consider EU–Japan trade and then proceed to a discussion of EU–US trade links. Our discussion of the trade links between the EU and Japan will fall into three parts. We shall first cover some quantitative aspects of the trade relations between these two large world traders. This discussion will be followed by a consideration of Japan's trade policy. In the third part of our discussion of EU–Japan trade relations we shall deal with Japan's chronic trade surplus. In discussing EU–US trade relations we shall first outline some quantitative features. Following a discussion of US trade policies we shall, in the final part of this chapter, consider EU–US trade conflicts.

EU–JAPAN TRADE STATISTICS

After the EU and the USA, Japan is the world's third largest trading entity. It is also an important trade partner for the EU, especially as an import source. Over the years Japan has met import demand in the EU at an increasing rate; its share of EU imports rose from a mere 1 per cent in 1958 to 4 per cent in 1975 and reached 11 per cent in 1992 (*Table 2.5*). As an export market Japan has been less significant for the EU than as a supplier. While Japan is, after the USA, the largest import source for the EU, it ranked only fifth in 1992 as an export market next to the USA, Switzerland, Austria and Sweden although its share of EU exports has been increasing over the years (*Table 2.4*; Eurostat 1993: 8). What role does the EU play as an export market and import source for Japan? In 1992 (and 1989) the EU provided 14 per cent of Japan's imports; the main non-EU suppliers of Japan's imports are the USA and China who met 23 and 7 per cent of Japan's import demand respectively (Eurostat 1993: 110). The USA is by far the largest external market for Japan with some 28 per cent of all Japanese exports being destined for this part of the North American market; the EU represents the second largest export market for Japan with nearly one fifth of all its exports being sold in the European domestic market in 1992 (Eurostat 1993: 111). The trade relationships between Japan and the EU are such that, in quantitative terms, the economies of the two trading entities are fairly interdependent. But Japan appears to be relying on Europe for both its exports and imports; the EU, on the other hand, seems to need Japan for meeting its import demand but has so far not been able to direct a sizeable proportion of its total external exports to reach Japanese customers.

Japan has been recording surpluses in its merchandise trade relations with the rest of the world for many years. Although the size of the surplus has fluctuated (it declined, for instance, in the late 1980s), there has been a trend of a widening gap between Japan's exports to and imports from the rest of the world. Japan's visible trade surplus reached a record US$ 106.7 billion in 1992 (GATT 1993a: 3) – approximately 3 per cent of Japan's GDP in that year (*Economist* 1993: 68). The United States, South-East Asia and the EU between them have over the last five years accounted for four fifths of Japan's trade surplus with the rest of the world. The US share of the world's trade deficit with Japan decreased in the late 1980s and was, with a deficit of US$ 39.5 billion in 1992 (Eurostat 1993: 110–11), smaller than in 1986. Japan's increased penetration of the markets in South-East Asia resulted in an increase in its surplus with that part of the world; it grew from about US$ 12 billion in 1986 to as much as US$ 47 billion in 1992 (*Economist* 1993: 68). The EU's trade deficit with Japan also increased over the same period. *Table 6.1* provides data about the EU's trade deficit with Japan since 1958. As can be seen from *Table 6.1* the EU's trade deficit deteriorated by 42 per cent between 1986 and 1992 (i.e. on average by 7 per cent per annum). The EU's deficit with Japan is a major element in the Union's chronic trade deficit with the world; in the 1990s the trade deficit with Japan has, on average, accounted for more than half of the EU's overall external trade deficit.

Table 6.1 The EU's trade deficit with Japan and the rest of the world, 1958–92, selected years, in mio ECU

	Japan	World
1958	–47	–2,384
1975	–3,253	–14,402
1986	–21,816	–7,370
1990	–23,503	–42,906
1991	–29,663	–70,493
1992	–31,005	–52,071

Source: Eurostat (1993: 6–7)

Classical theory of international trade predicts that a country (or a trade bloc such as the EU) would display a trade structure which reflects its comparative advantage; a country's resource endowments and technology determine in what industries and what products it has a comparative advantage in production (the so-called *Heckscher-Ohlin Theorem*). Japan is a country that is not endowed with large quantities of natural energy resources and other raw materials; it has, in fact, been the world's largest importer of fuel products/lubricants and raw materials. In 1992, Japanese imports of the former product category amounted to 23 per cent of total world imports, and its import bill for the latter product category represented 11 per cent of the world's total import expenditure. (Eurostat 1993: 96). Japan has also been the world's principal importer of food, beverages and tobacco with a share of 16 per cent (Eurostat 1993: 96). It is, in the circumstances, both plausible and consistent with classical trade theory that a country like Japan could be expected to specialise in the production of goods manufactured from imported raw materials. By specialising in high value added products Japan has been in a position to earn foreign currency in order to pay for the net imports of food, fuel products and raw materials. Japan may also have had to become a net exporter of manufactured goods in order to cover its deficit in the invisible trade balance which in 1992, for example, amounted to US$ 48 billion (GATT 1993a: 5). It is in the manufacturing industries that Japan has established and exploited its comparative advantages since the 1950s. In specialising in manufactured goods the nature of its exports has changed over the years. Textiles and radios were Japan's main export items in the 1950s; ships, steel, tape recorders and television sets were its principal export products in the 1960s. In the 1970s, motor vehicles and steel played a dominant role in its export-led growth. The years since the early 1980s have been characterised by Japan's export success in machinery (both electrical and non-electrical), office equipment,

Table 6.2 EU–Japan trade by main categories, 1992, in bn US$

	EU		
	Exports	Imports	Balance of trade
Agricultural products	3.45	0.39	+3.06
Food	3.08	0.81	+2.90
Mining products	0.69	0.21	+0.48
Total manufactures	21.86	67.94	–46.08
Chemicals	5.27	3.41	+1.86
Machinery and transport equipment	8.81	51.46	–42.65
Non-electrical machinery	2.62	7.45	–4.83
Office and telecommunication equipment	0.93	20.77	–19.84
Electrical machinery and apparatus	0.81	4.25	–3.44
Automotive products	3.71	15.49	–11.78
Other transport equipment	0.74	3.70	–2.96
Textiles and clothing	2.21	1.06	+1.15
Other consumer goods	5.71	10.01	–4.30

Source: GATT (1993a: 101)

telecommunication apparatus and, continuing from the 1970s, motor vehicles.

The EU's 1992 trade balances, by main product category, are shown in *Table 6.2*. In trading merchandise with Japan, the EU was a net exporter of agricultural and mining products. Although the EU achieved surpluses in trading chemicals and textiles/clothing, these paled into insignificance in the light of the very high trade surpluses established by Japan for other manufactures, notably office and telecommunications equipment, and automotive products.

Japan's trade pattern with the European Union, while compatible with the prediction generated by the law of comparative advantage (inter-industry trade takes place with countries specialising in those sectors of their economy where they are more competitive), is at variance with what tends to be a characteristic feature of advanced industrialisation. Advanced industrialised countries tend to have a lot of trade that is intra- rather than inter-industry trade – exports and imports of similar products such as different makes of electronic equipment or motor vehicles. As discussed earlier (Chapter 2) any measurement of the degree of intra-industry trade observed depends, of course, on how we define an industry (i.e. the degree of disaggregation adopted). Provided we use the same industrial classification system and the same level of aggregation, intra-industry measures can be used as cross-country indicators of the extent of two-way trade of differentiated products belonging to the same industrial classification category.

Table 6.3 Indices of intra-industry trade for the EU, USA and Japan, selected high-technology sectors, 1980 and 1986

	1980	1986
Pharmaceuticals		
EU	0.43	0.57
USA	0.43	0.53
Japan	0.29	0.22
Office, dataprocessing machines		
EU	0.83	0.67
USA	0.38	0.61
Japan	0.59	0.42
Telecommunications and electronic precision instruments		
EU	0.69	0.86
USA	0.42	0.62
Japan	0.67	0.63
Electronics		
EU	0.90	0.75
USA	0.94	0.83
Japan	0.14	0.21
Aerospace		
EU	0.91	0.89
USA	0.48	0.43
Japan	0.14	0.09

Source: CEC (1989a: 76)

Tables 2.13 and *2.14* contain information about intra-industry indices for Japan, and other (selected) countries. Australia and Japan, although both belonging to the group of advanced industrialised countries, are 'outliers'; their levels of intra-industry trade are significantly lower than those of the other countries listed (*Table 2.14*).

Has Japan's level of intra-industry trade changed over time? According to a study carried out by the European Commission, computed values for the intra-industry trade indices in selected high-technology sectors in the EU, the USA and Japan appear to suggest that, with the exception of the telecommunications and electronic precision instruments sector, Japan's trade pattern has continued to be significantly less of an intra-industry nature than EU and US trade flows (*Table 6.3*).

Although statistically there is no doubt that intra-industry trade plays a more important part for EU and US trade than for Japan's trade flows, we cannot infer from this observation that Japan's low engagement in intra-industry trade is 'unnatural' or an indication of the existence of closed Japanese markets. Two considerations are relevant in judging whether Japan's intra-industry trade index is lower than expected. First, a low intra-industry index may be attributable to differences in taste (Lawrence 1987). Other things being equal, similar intra-industry trade levels are only likely to exist if we can assume that people's tastes are equally distributed in different countries (Ito 1992: 306). We would not expect a lot of intra-industry trade to take place if consumers in trading nations differ in their preferences for, say, consumer durables (e.g. motor vehicles). If more Japanese consumers prefer to acquire a Honda, Nissan or Toyota to a Peugeot, Fiat, Rover or Volkswagen than European consumers prefer to buy European rather than Japanese cars, then these taste differences will be reflected in the magnitude of intra-industry indices computed for Europe and Japan. The second factor that should be considered, prior to drawing any conclusions about the existence of 'abnormally' low levels of intra-industry trade and 'closed' markets, is the proximity of other advanced industrial countries. The 'big four' in the EU all engage in trade with more or less adjacent European neighbours. Japan, on the other hand, like Australia, who also has low intra-industry trade (*Table 2.14*), does not have advanced industrial countries as neighbours.

JAPAN'S TRADE REGIME

Japan's post Second World War trade policies have undergone significant changes over the decades. At the risk of over-simplifying matters, it could be argued that the 1950s and 1960s saw Japan protect its 'infant industries' against foreign competition via tariff and non-tariff barriers, notably quotas. During the 1970s Japan relied predominantly on tariffs for protection against supply from third countries' producers. Since the 1980s Japan's tariffs have, on average, been lower than the tariffs imposed by both the EU and the USA; Japan has also reduced the number of import quotas which have, at any rate, been levied more on agricultural than manufactured products. Japan is, it would appear, committed to an open world trade system in general and the MFN principle in particular. Unlike the EU and the USA, the Japanese have not engaged in preferential trade agreements with other industrialised countries. Japan has not been prepared to participate in any customs union or free trade area; it has, however, offered tariff preferences to Third World countries.

A closer look at Japan's trade policy regime would suggest that its commitment to free and fair trade is more apparent than real. This interpretation of Japan's trade policy is justified for the simple reason that Japan differs in its openness in different industries. Like the EU (and other trading nations), Japan is more open in trading industrial goods than food and agricultural produce. Japan uses a large number of measures that directly affect imports or exports; it also makes use of measures affecting trade via production (for a detailed discussion of these measures see, for example, GATT 1993c: 55–132). The various trade policy measures that Japan employs are used more effectively and more frequently in some sectors than in others; there has also been a shift in emphasis from the use of formal trade obstacles to informal trade barriers, especially in the field of industrial goods.

Japan's *agricultural sector* has been one of the most protected in the Western industrialised world. The protectionist policies that Japan has developed can be explained by its agricultural policy objectives. They are, first, to safeguard basic food supplies, especially rice production, and, second, to maintain some parity between farmers' and non-farmers' incomes. In order to achieve these objectives Japan has used mainly non-tariff measures to assist agriculture and fishing. These measures range from administered domestic prices, exclusive state-trading rights, deficiency payments, strict health and quarantine regulations and import quotas on major agricultural products such as barley, dairy products, wheat and, above all, rice, for which the import control has been tantamount to an effective prohibition of any imports (GATT 1993c: 8).

The Japanese rice market is supplied by inefficient domestic producers who can only stay in business because they face no competition from outside and charge prices that have tended to be seven times the world market price for rice. The minimum prices set for rice have tended to be so high that they have, like Europe's CAP, generated surpluses which even some rice diversion programmes such as the Rice Paddy Agriculture Establishment Programmes of the late 1980s and early 1990s (which established area quotas and allowed paddy farmers to use land for other grain products) have not been able to eliminate (GATT 1993c: 157–58). However, protection of Japan's agricultural sector has not resulted in the achievement of food security. Japan's self-sufficiency in food has in fact declined over the years; it has been less than 50 per cent since 1987 (GATT 1993c: 133).

While Japanese agriculture continues to be protected from outside competition via formal trade obstacles, there are but few formal trade barriers on *industrial goods*. Pre-Uruguay Round tariffs have been low; the average unweighted tariff amounted to 5.2 per cent (GATT 1993c: 55). But the relatively high tariffs that have been levied to protect Japan's agricultural policies have not merely had an adverse impact on agricultural trade; they have also, like Europe's CAP, distorted domestic resource allocation. The artificially high prices of agricultural produce have acted like a tax on efficient producers of industrial goods who have had to pay higher wages and rents for the (scarce) resources they employ. In a study that attempted to quantify the costs of Japan's agricultural policy, Anderson and Tyers (1987) concluded that the welfare costs incurred represented about one per cent of Japan's GNP. Similar welfare losses have been attributed to Europe's CAP by Tyers and Anderson (1986) who estimated the internal welfare costs resulting from the CAP to be equivalent to one per cent of the EU's GDP. Vincent (1989) established that free trade in agricultural products would increase Japan's earnings of foreign currency by about 3 per cent.

Specific Japanese industries, notably treated leather, leather footwear, leather products, textiles and clothing are products that are subject to tariff quotas – quantitative import restrictions combined with tariff rates amounting to up to 60 per cent imposed on above-quota imports. Other leather products have carried up to 35 per cent levies and tariff rates for textiles and clothing have, for some items, been as high as 18 per cent (GATT 1993c: 55). The way in which Japan protects its tanneries would appear to be a particularly blatant form of protectionism and economic inefficiency. Only up to 2 per cent of the value of domestic leather production can be imported and any imports beyond this quota (which is subject to a tariff of 15–20 per cent) is penalised by a tariff set at 60 per cent. Further trade barriers result from the Japanese government's unwillingness to issue import licences for larger batches of leather (*Economist* 1992b: 78). Following bilateral talks between the European Commission and the Japanese government, a higher quota of 5 per cent will operate by 1997 but this is unlikely to give the EU states (and other developed countries) sufficient scope to take full advantage of their export potential (*Economist* 1992b: 78).

While Japan, with the exception of the products just mentioned (which are not affecting the EU's main export industries), would appear to be an open economy if we focus on 'formal' trade barriers, it is generally not perceived as having an open industrial market once 'informal' trade barriers are taken into account (Lincoln 1990). The alleged lack of access to Japanese markets tends to be attributed to a range of factors such as 'the Government's procurement practices, regulations on standards and testing requirements, customs procedures, administrative guidance, anti monopoly legislation, the distribution system, *keiretsu* and other business practices' (GATT 1993c: 10). With the exception of *keiretsu* (and other Japanese business practices) the concern expressed internationally about Japan's non-tariff barriers has, to a large extent, been over matters very similar to the factors identified as impeding market integration in the EU prior to '1992' (see Chapter 3).

The Japanese word *keiretsu* means 'business group' or 'industrial network'. The term is used to describe the way that firms are linked in industrial groupings. Business organisations in Japan may be linked in either *horizontal* or *vertical keiretsu*. Horizontal *keiretsu* (financial groups) refer to a large number of companies involved in a wide range of activities and interlinked through cross-holding of shares, intra-group financing and intra-group business. At present, there are six major horizontal *keiretsu* (Mitsui, Mitsubishi, Sumitomo, Sanwa, Fuyo, and Dai-ichizkangyo).

The driving forces behind the horizontal *keiretsu* are the Presidential Council (consisting of the presidents of the leading companies that are part of the *keiretsu*), the financial interdependence of the *keiretsu* members (via cross-holdings of shares, intra-group financing and the existence of a nucleus bank) and the *sogo shosha*, a general trading company which is responsible for the group's merchandise transactions both domestically and globally. Vertical *keiretsu* differ from horizontal *keiretsu* in two respects. First, while there are only a few horizontal *keiretsu*, vertical *keiretsu* are numerous. Second, while the firms that belong to horizontal *keiretsu* are engaged in a wide spectrum of business activities, vertical *keiretsu* are characterised by either the links between a large manufacturer and its principal suppliers (vertical subcontracting *keiretsu*) or distributors (vertical distribution *keiretsu*). It is possible for vertical *keiretsu* to be involved in both (vertical) subcontracting and (vertical) distribution operations; vertical *keiretsu* can also have connections with horizontal *keiretsu*. Distribution *keiretsu* tend to exist primarily in Japan's electrical and electronic industries; the motor vehicle industry is a sector of the Japanese economy where subcontracting *keiretsu* are typically found.

Although industrial or financial interlinkages are not unique to Japan, there is no equivalent to *keiretsu* in the rest of the Western industrialised world. This raises the question as to whether or not the business practices of the close-knit *keiretsu* impede free trade. Basic economic reasoning would suggest that buying from within an industrial group is inefficient as such transactions preclude competition. But Japanese business is conducted under a very different paradigm in that business transactions are being determined by long-term relationships within segmented markets rather than free competition within preregulated markets. Competition in that case may not be a necessary condition for firms to perform efficiently; buying from fellow group members may have distinct commercial advantages for *keiretsu* firms. While *keiretsu* may result in low levels of imports into Japan, it is far from clear whether this amounts to exclusionist trade diversion or whether the trade flows are efficient (i.e. comparative-advantage based). What evidence is there to suggest that *keiretsu* work against imports into Japan? Investigations are both relatively short in supply and inconclusive. Lincoln bases his assertion that *keiretsu* have reduced Japan's imports on *a priori* arguments: 'it is true that when no overwhelming reason exists to buy a foreign product, a group member will accede to pressure from other group members to buy their products' (Lincoln 1990: 90). Lawrence (1991a), in a study using multiple linear regression, concluded that both horizontal and vertical *keiretsu* were associated with reductions in Japan's imports, thus lending support to Lincoln's assertion of the relative closedness of Japanese markets. Saxonhouse, on the other hand, has argued that *keiretsu* ties are much weaker than is generally assumed and that 'it is hard to believe that Japan's distinctive trade structure can be explained by Japan's trading companies exercising what market power they have to protect their fellow *keiretsu* members by discriminating in their purchases against competitive imports' (Saxonhouse 1991: 41). A recent review of Japan's trade policies which considered the role of *keiretsu* and the distribution system play in influencing trade flows concluded that: 'Available evidence suggests that the restrictive impact of these arrangements may be less important than often claimed' (GATT 1993c: 10–11). Japan has defended *keiretsu* on the grounds that, while leading to different business practices from the ones that tend to be adopted in the West, they amount to a fair balance between cooperation and competition (Japanese Ministry of Foreign Affairs 1992). While the Japanese government's stance is inevitably biased, it is somewhat inconceivable that business in Japan would consistently favour internal to external transactions. Judging by the success that Japan has had in exporting manufactured goods, it is difficult to imagine situations in which Japanese manufacturers make costly 'wrong' choices (trade diverting purchases) when 'correct' choices (trade creating sourcing) would contribute towards their (national and international) competitiveness.

JAPAN'S TRADE SURPLUS

The EU, like the USA, has had a chronic negative trade balance with Japan for decades and its contribution to Japan's trade surplus with the world has been growing, especially in the 1990s. While decades ago Europeans had to meet the American challenge – *le défi americain* (Servant-Schreiber 1967), they are now facing *le défi japonais* (the Japanese challenge) in world competition. What accounts for the fact that Japanese exports to Europe (and the world) have been rising at a faster rate than its imports from both the EU and the world? Two basic macroeconomic factors may explain, in part, why, despite yen appreciations and efforts by the Japanese government to facilitate third countries' access to Japan's market, the EU–Japan trade imbalance has persisted. First, the Japanese save more than they invest; sustained reductions in savings or increases in investment, so basic macroeconomics tells us, would have been necessary to bring about a decrease in Japan's surplus. The required changes in macroeconomic variables have either not taken place or the magnitude of the changes has been insufficient to reduce let alone abolish the Japanese trade surplus. Second, although the yen has over the years appreciated against the US dollar and European currencies, these appreciations have not had the effect of reducing Japan's trade surplus. One possible explanation for the failure of yen appreciations to reduce, if not eliminate, Japan's trade surpluses could be that the rates of growth in domestic (in this case Japanese) demand rather than exchange variations determine trade balance variations. Macroeconomic factors are, by their very nature, too broad and general to explain fully Japan's persistent trade surplus. It seems more fruitful to explore some microeconomic aspects of the behaviour of Japan's trade surplus with the EU. For the persistent deficit that the EU has exhibited is likely to be due to a structural imbalance between the two trading partners.

At the microeconomic level, the long-term structural trade imbalance between the EU and Japan has been determined by export promoting and import repelling factors. Japan is now the world's fourth largest importer, buying US$ 233.2 billion worth of merchandise in 1992 (GATT 1993a: 3). In the same year it also belonged to the group of the EU's five largest export markets; it ranked only eleventh in 1980 (Eurostat 1993: 8). Japan's propensity to import appears to be low compared with European countries. In 1990, for example, its per capita imports were significantly lower than those in the 'big four' of the EU. While Germany, France, Britain and Italy had imports per head amounting to US$ 4,460, US$ 4,150, US$ 3,890 and US$ 3,160 respectively, per capita imports in Japan were, with US$ 1,900, surprisingly low (*Economist* 1992a: 69). Japan also compares unfavourably when imports as a proportion of GDP are being considered. In 1990, the merchandise imports to GDP ratio was 8 per cent in Japan (GATT 1993c: 15). In the EU economy, on the other hand, the merchandise imports (including intra-EU trade) amounted to 24 per cent in 1988 (GATT 1993b: 23). Since formal trade barriers, with the exception of agriculture, are low in Japan, informal trade barriers must have played a part in bringing about such a comparatively low propensity to import in the Japanese economy. A fruitful way to establish both the existence and the influence of non-tariff barriers is to study cross-national price differentials (Deardorff and Stern 1984). While it is difficult to find strictly comparable cross-national data, especially if and when exporters sell older models of a product on the export market and the newer product version on the home market (Saxonhouse 1991: 43–44), a number of studies suggest that Japanese products tend to be sold at higher prices at home and that goods imported into Japan are generally sold at higher prices than in the countries of origin.

In a survey of the empirical evidence (including official Japanese studies) on pricing in Japan, Lawrence demonstrated that the unique Japanese system of retailing imports via sole import distributors has meant that 'many imported products in Japan *are* subject to higher markups than other Japanese products' (Lawrence 1991b: 29). It would appear that the corporate business structure embodied by *keiretsu*, while perhaps taking comparative advantage based decisions in buying inputs, impedes imports of consumer durables through high markups, thus achieving the same import substituting effect as high tariffs. It is, of course, possible that cross-cultural differences may also have contributed towards Japan's relatively low import levels. As suggested earlier, Japan's relatively low degree of intra-industry trade may conceivably be due to preferences for goods, especially consumer durables, being distributed differently across trading partners such as Japan and the EU. The impact of such cultural factors on import behaviour is difficult, if not impossible, to measure.

While *keiretsu* appear to have resulted in Japan restraining its imports, we do not know by how much Japan's financial and industrial groupings have reduced imports. But the growth rates of Japan's exports would suggest that it might have had a considerable surplus with the EU (and the world) even if there had been no non-tariff barriers. Why have the Japanese been so successful as exporters? The answer to this question may lie in three inter-related factors. First, the Japanese have shifted the structure of their exports increasingly towards industrial products in general and complex industrial products in particular. In 1965, 21 per cent of Japan's exports consisted of primary products (unprocessed, semi-processed and highly processed); by 1986 primary products accounted for less than 3 per cent of exports. The proportion of complex industrial products in Japanese exports was 48 per cent in 1965; by 1986 it had risen to 72 per cent (CEC 1989a: 49–50). Second, Japan's exports to the EU (and the world) have been concentrated on a narrow range of products. In 1990, five product categories accounted for half of Japan's total exports: road motor vehicles (22 per cent), electrical machinery (8 per cent), non-electrical machinery (7 per cent), office machines (7 per cent) and telecommunications equipment (6 per cent). A further three categories (sound recorders, producers; instruments, apparatus; electrical power machines, switchgear) combined constituted an additional 13 per cent of Japan's total exports (GATT 1993c: 214). Over time there appears to have been a focus in export policy on new growth sectors. Third, a consideration of the EU–Japan trade balance by sector (*Table 6.2*) would suggest that it is in a narrow range of export product categories that Japan has a *revealed comparative advantage* in trading with the EU (the data in *Table 6.2* could form the basis for computing an index of revealed comparative advantage whose value can vary between plus one (with the country only exporting) and minus one (with the country only importing)).

Japan would not have been able to establish and maintain comparative advantages in (complex) industrial goods, had its key export industries not been innovative and responsive to changed circumstances. It is generally believed that the Japanese are 'imitators' rather than 'innovators'; European and US firms are supposed to be inventing and developing new products with the Japanese meticulously copying, improving and then producing better quality products in large quantities at very competitive prices. This view is at best outdated and at worst based on a myth. It was the Japanese who introduced a completely new management system decades ago – *lean production* – first practised by Toyota in the 1950s. Lean production is fundamentally different from the system of classic mass production (which has been underlying much of European and American business organisation) in that it reduces waste by not isolating the various production steps. *Just-in-time production* gives the employees who work in teams a sense of involvement and results in near-perfect products being manufactured by continuous improvement and monitoring. It is important to recognise that innovative management in Japan's manufacturing industry has not been restricted to replacing wasteful or inefficient by lean or efficient production. Japan has also been innovative in product development (*Economist* 1991: 75) via, what is known in Japan as 'product covering' (process of producing instant imitations of a rival pioneer's product) and 'product churning' (process of testing new product ideas by selling small production batches instead of testing them through market research). Japanese innovators also tend to go for parallel development by working on refined replacement versions of their original innovations in order to be able to compete against rivals' imitations. Adjustability is another factor explaining the Japanese manufacturing industry's sustained export success. The creative responsiveness of Japanese exporters to changing circumstances can be best illustrated by referring to Japanese firms going upmarket, Japanese direct investment abroad and the willingness of Japan's export-oriented business to reduce profit margins. Japan may initially have opted for the production of high-volume and low-priced industrial goods. However, partly because of advanced technology, more sophisticated consumer demand and *endaka* (Japanese for the appreciation of the yen) Japanese producers have replaced low-price and high-volume manufactures by goods that are more differentiated, have shorter lives and are less price sensitive.

The higher yen value – the yen appreciation amounted to nearly 100 per cent against the ECU (Eurostat 1993: 92) between 1980 and 1992 – has probably also contributed to Japan exporting more capital abroad by setting up plants in other countries. The type of exportables has determined the choice of location for these foreign-based plants. The cheap labour countries of South-East Asia – Indonesia, Malaysia and Thailand – were chosen for the bottom end of Japan's range of industrial goods. For technically more advanced products such as engineering components, microwave ovens and video recorders which require more technical know-how Japanese firms targeted South Korea and Taiwan. Japanese cars and sophisticated (and pricy) consumer electronics equipment have been produced by Japanese multinationals in their European or US-based affiliates. Three of Japan's major car manufacturers (Honda, Nissan and Toyota) now supply cars to European markets from UK-based plants. Finally, the Japanese appear to have succeeded in holding on to their sales by adjusting their mark-ups downwards in response to the yen rising in value against both the dollar and European currencies.

Analysing the effects of exchange variations is of course a far from straightforward issue. An appreciation of the yen against the EU currencies (the French franc, the German mark, the Italian lira, sterling, etc.) is likely to have an adverse effect on Japan's trade surplus with the EU: Japanese products become less competitive in Europe while EU goods become relatively cheaper in the EU. What is the reasoning behind this prediction? According to the *Marshall-Lerner conditions* appreciations (depreciations) of a currency against another currency will worsen (improve) the balance of trade of the country whose currency appreciates (depreciates) provided the absolute values of the demand elasticities for exports and imports add up to more than unity. Strictly speaking, the Marshall-Lerner conditions only hold if the supplies are perfectly elastic and the country whose currency has appreciated (depreciated) is initially in a balance of trade equilibrium; the elasticity conditions, are nevertheless, a reasonable guide for other situations. If, as seems likely, both the volumes exported by Japan to the EU and the quantities imported by Japan from the EU take some time to change, then the *J-curve effect* will operate; the EU–Japan trade balance will improve in Japan's favour until the volume changes have taken place. For both appreciations (and depreciations) of a currency have a volume and a value effect. The volume effect will change the quantities exported and imported while the value effect will alter the revenue resulting from exports and the expenditure incurred in importing, expressed in the domestic currency, that is the currency of the country affected by the currency appreciation (depreciation). The value effect tends to precede the volume effect. Thus, in the case of a currency appreciation, the balance of trade will initially improve because, with a fixed domestic currency value of exports, the foreign currency value of the exports will be increased. The foreign currency value of imports, on the other hand, will remain unchanged while the domestic currency value of imports will, of course, decline as a result of the appreciation.

The other factor that would influence the trade flows between the EU and Japan is whether or not Japanese firms are 'pricing to market' when the exchange rate varies (for a detailed discussion see Krugman 1987). Pricing to market in the case of a yen appreciation would mean that Japanese firms would lower their profit margins for export sales to sell at approximately the same European currency price with the mark-up for domestic sales remaining unchanged. Whether the EU–Japan trade balance becomes responsive to variations in the exchange rate then depends on the elasticities of demand in Japan and the EU states, the length of time lags involved, the ease with which Japanese multinationals change supply centres to meet EU demand and their pricing to market strategies. It is possible that the existence of less price-sensitive demand for Japanese products, the Japanese multinationals' possibility of off-shore production and their absorption of a higher yen through lower mark-ups on export sales made Japanese exporters 'currency neutral' in the 1980s and early 1990s (*Economist* 1989a: 81).

The trade relations between the EU and Japan have for some time now been characterised by conflicts and tensions. The root of these trade conflicts must be seen in the persistent trade deficit which the European Union has had with Japan. The magnitude and importance of the trade imbalance has, of course, not been the same for each member state. In Germany, for example, the trade deficit has been a specific deficit that has been more than matched by an overall surplus in trading with the world. What has been a more serious factor for the EU has been the fact that Japan has been particularly successful in exporting 'sensitive' products such as motor vehicles and consumer electronic equipment. Japan's increasing import penetration of EU markets and its low level of intra-industry trade have, not surprisingly, led Europeans to suspect the Japanese of 'dumping' industrial products on EU markets while at the same time restricting access to their own markets.

What measures have Europe and Japan taken in dealing with these trade conflicts? We shall not be able to offer a comprehensive account of all the strategies pursued by the EU and Japan in their attempts to deal with situations arising out of dumping/anti-dumping procedures and import restriction/import promotion measures (for detailed accounts of EU–Japan trade policies see GATT 1993b, 1993c). Instead we shall focus on key developments in this area of bilateral trade policy. The EU has made relatively frequent use of anti-dumping procedures, and these have been targeted at Asian suppliers including Japan and affecting, *inter alia*, audio cassettes. In addition Japanese exports of some electrical and electronic household equipment (colour

TV sets, colour TV tubes, video tape recorders) to EU markets have been subject to import surveillance by the EU. The Japanese government has, in recent years, taken certain institutional steps to promote imports, including the establishment of an import board, which may in the long run contribute towards an improvement of Japan's import-related infrastructure. It is doubtful, however, whether the work of an import board will impinge on the operation of, for example, *keiretsu*. The Japanese government has also introduced financial and tax incentive schemes in order to expand imports. Financial and tax incentives should, of course, encourage Japanese imports. The cheaper imports may, however, be counterproductive in that they may enable Japanese exporters to purchase inputs (capital and intermediate goods) at below world prices and hence indirectly subsidise Japanese exporters (GATT 1993c: 100). While Japan's import promotion policy appears to be designed to reduce its trade surplus with the EU, its strategy of setting up so-called *screwdriver* plants' in the EU clearly aims to circumvent the EU's anti-dumping duties. Japanese firms avoid having to pay anti-dumping duties provided a certain proportion of value added (between 40 and 50 per cent) is of 'local origin', i.e. has been created within the Japanese-owned affiliate in the EU.

The tension between Japan and the EU over Japan's bilateral trade surplus has, however, also led to some jointly agreed trade policies that have added elements of *managed trade* to EU–Japan trade relations. In 1990 the European Commission, after successfully persuading GATT to declare the semi-conductor agreement between the USA and Japan as an illegal quota system, concluded a bilateral trade deal with Japan's microchip producers that resulted in what amounts to price fixing. A more generally known example of EU–Japan trade being managed is the 1991 consensus between Japan and the EU in which Japan 'voluntarily' agreed to restrain her exports of motor vehicles to EU markets for the period up to the end of the millenium.

When we discussed VERs in Chapter 4 we pointed out that the artificial shortage of Japanese cars in the EU increases both prices and profits for the exporting firms. If invested in the Japanese motor vehicle exporting industry, these increased profits could further strengthen Japan's comparative advantage in car production and make the EU motor industry less rather than more competitive. Apart from passenger cars, Japan has also agreed to export restraint measures affecting EU trade for the following products: ballbearings, cotton fabrics, forklift trucks, machine tools and steel products (GATT 1993c: 118–20).

In the long run the predicted ageing of Japan's population can be expected to lead to a reduction of its personal savings ratio; its trade surplus will in that case be bound to be smaller. But in the short and medium term the EU's trade deficit with Japan (and that of the world for that matter) is unlikely to disappear. There are no signs of Japan losing its comparative advantages in (selected) industrial products. The Japanese export sector seems to be able to absorb yen appreciations and to adjust to protectionist measures taken by the EU. Moreover, some of the EU's protectionism appears to have resulted in favouring Japan's exports (VERs and the globalisation of Japanese production via screwdriver plants are cases in point). Finally, it has to be recognised that Japan differs from the EU. It has its own business culture (*keiretsu*) which excludes outsiders; and it has comparatively low levels of intra-industry trade. The Japanese government has, admittedly, tried to take measures to promote imports. But it is difficult to see how the country's low propensity to import can be raised from 'above'.

EU–US TRADE PATTERNS

The United States and the European Union continue to be each other's most significant trading partners. EFTA represents the largest trading bloc for the EU but the USA is the EU's largest individual trading nation. In 1992, 17 per cent of EU exports were destined for the US market; 18 per cent of all EU imports were made in the USA (*Tables 2.4 and 2.5*). The EU plays an even more important role as trade partner for the USA. In 1992, 23 per cent of US products were exported to the EU; the EU share in the USA's total import bill amounted to 18 per cent (IMF 1993: 405).

Transatlantic trade flows between Europe and the USA differ from EU–Japan merchandise trade in that there is no structural imbalance resulting in a persistent trade deficit for one of the trading partners. The USA, while persistently in a trade (and current account) deficit situation with the rest of the world, especially South-East Asia (Japan and the NICs) since the 1980s, has had phases of both surpluses and deficits in trading with the EU (*Table 6.4*). Up to 1983, the USA tended to have a trade surplus with the EU. After running trade surpluses with the USA between 1984 and 1988 the EU has again become a net merchandise importer in trading with the United States. Both the swings in EU–US merchandise trade balances and the magnitudes of the trade imbalances, which the statistics show, would suggest that they can be attributed to variations in the (real) exchange rates, differential rates of economic growth and cyclical stages of the levels of economic activity in Europe and America rather than one trading partner exhibiting distinctive competitive advantages.

In 1992, the EU was a net exporter to the USA in the following product categories: fuels, non-ferrous metals, iron and steel, (other) semi-manufactures, (other) non-electrical machinery, automotive

Table 6.4 The EU's trade balance with the USA, 1958–92, in mio ECU

	EU		
	Exports	Imports US	Trade balance
1958	2,726	4,252	–1,526
1960	3,480	5,290	–1,810
1965	5,273	8,613	–3,340
1970	9,773	13,425	–3,652
1975	14,058	23,391	–9,333
1983	52,202	58,654	–6,452
1984	73,701	67,112	+6,589
1985	85,523	68,942	+16,581
1986	75,151	56,643	+18,508
1987	71,899	56,213	+15,686
1988	71,809	68,349	+3,460
1989	78,020	83,660	–5,640
1990	76,561	85,182	–8,621
1991	71,199	91,941	–20,742
1992	73,917	86,776	–12,859

Source: Eurostat (1993: 4–5)

products, textiles, and clothing. The USA, on the other hand, had a trade surplus with Europe in some seven industries: food, raw materials, ores and minerals, chemicals, office and telecommunication equipment, electrical machinery and apparatus, and other transport equipment (*Table 6.5*).

The EU had the worst trade balance with the USA in the field of office and telecommunications equipment with 1992 net imports amounting to US$ 14 billion. The telecommunications industry produces goods and systems that are high-technology products. High-tech products may be defined 'as those which either directly or indirectly through process technology and advanced instrumentation, require a significantly higher level of R&D expenditure intensity than other products' (CEC 1989a: 71). What is classified as a high-tech product will, of course, vary from country to country and over time. The following industries are currently regarded as high-tech sectors: computing equipment and software, consumer electronics, defence equipment, (electronically controlled) industrial equipment, semi-conductors, and telecommunications. In the mid-1980s, high-tech products accounted for more than one fifth of the industrialised countries' trade in manufactured products and they have become increasingly more important in the trade of manufactures.

Although a detailed consideration of high-tech products and their role in trade is beyond the scope of this book (see, for example, Porter 1990; CEC 1991c; Tyson 1992), some discussion is necessary at this

Table 6.5 EU–US trade by main categories, 1992, in bn US$

	EU		
	Exports	Imports	Trade balance
Food	5.57	8.27	–2.70
Raw materials	0.66	3.82	–3.16
Ores and other minerals	0.22	1.27	–1.05
Fuels	3.98	3.48	+0.50
Non-ferrous metals	1.22	0.95	+1.27
Iron and steel	2.51	0.38	+2.13
Chemicals	11.82	12.44	–0.62
Other semi-manufactures	7.46	5.29	+2.17
Power generating machinery	6.43	5.86	+0.57
Other non-electrical machinery	11.46	8.36	+3.10
Office and telecommunication equipment	6.39	20.38	–13.99
Electrical machinery and apparatus	3.72	4.80	–1.08
Automotive products	8.18	2.75	+5.43
Textiles	1.89	1.32	+0.57
Clothing	1.60	0.81	+0.79
Other consumer goods	12.52	15.24	–2.72

Source: GATT (1993a: 101)

stage for a number of reasons. First, high-tech products represent a significant share of trade in manufactures with the United States, Europe and Japan accounting for most of the trade flows. Second, success in high-tech industries is important because it is likely, through increased productivity and technological advancement, to result in improved competitiveness. Third, the EU has become less competitive in trading high-tech products *vis-à-vis* the world and the USA. The loss of the EU's competitive position has resulted in a gradual worsening of its trade balance for this product category. The EU trade balance for high-tech products with the world moved from a surplus of 7 billion ECU in 1978 to a deficit of 23 billion ECU in 1990. The EU–US trade deficit for high-tech products deteriorated over the same period from 5 to 17 billion ECU (CEC 1993: 213). EU–US economic relations have, as a result of the US producers establishing and maintaining a competitive edge in the production of high-tech goods and systems over European manufacturers, been adversely affected by market access conflicts. Trade tensions over high-tech products have been exacerbated by the fact that the USA has emerged as both the EU's largest export market and import source. In 1989–90, nearly a quarter of all EU exports of high-tech products were destined for the American market; more than a third (35 per cent) of EU imports of high-tech products were supplied by US producers (CEC 1993: 215). For the USA the EU remains the principal export market (34 per cent) but the Union, with a share of 18 per cent, comes only a distant second after Japan (34 per cent) as external suppliers of high-tech products for the USA.

US TRADE POLICIES

What characterises US trade policies? In this section we shall highlight those core features of US trade policy that are relevant for an understanding of EU–US relations – objectives, framework and measures (for a more detailed treatment see, for example, GATT 1992a). Specific trade disputes between the USA and the EU will be considered in the next section (EU–US market access issues) of this chapter.

US trade policy *objectives* are not as clearly defined as Europe's common commercial policy. Considering that the USA was the prime mover behind the eight GATT rounds that have taken place since the end of the Second World War (see Chapter 8), US trade policy can be viewed as pursuing multilateral trade liberalisation in world trade as its goal. Such multilateral trade liberalisation includes 'extending GATT discipline to trade in agriculture, textiles, services, and intellectual property'. In practice, the direction that US trade policy has taken, especially since the 1980s, has been a mixture of multilateralism, bilateralism and unilateralism. The USA has, in its economic relations with the rest of the world, practised bilateralism by, for example, reaching voluntary restraint agreements and similar measures with third countries which have affected imports into the United States. US trade policy has also led to 'aggressive unilateralism' (Bhagwhati 1990a) with the USA at times unilaterally deciding what constitutes other unfair trading practices and/or expecting third countries to liberalise trade with the USA on a unilateral basis. Thus, like EU trade policy US trade policy has elements of free trade and protectionism. That the declared objective of US trade policy – an open trading system – appears to have been modified over time can be explained by two factors. First, the US administration has responded to pressure groups at home calling for the protection of certain domestic industries and for reducing, if not eliminating, the US trade deficit. Second, although an open trading system has remained the overall goal of US trade policy, the openness in world trade has been linked to the principles of 'level playing fields' (Ostrey 1990: 90). Failure by other countries either to reduce their trade barriers or to eliminate trade distorting export promotion strategies has provided a rationale for the US government to develop and use a trade regime that protects its domestic industries from unfair competition. By putting pressure on trading partners who import too little from the USA the intention is to liberalise the trade of these protectionist countries unilaterally.

Although over the years the USA has passed a number of **Trade Acts** (Tariff Act of 1930, Trade Expansion Act of 1962, Trade Act of 1974, Trade Agreements Act of 1979 and the Trade and Tariff Act of 1984, Food Security Act of 1985, Customs and Trade Act of 1990) that provided the administration with the legal framework to take protectionist measures, the new US trade regime of increased protectionism and aggressive unilateralism dates back to amendments of Section 301 of the 1974 Trade Act. These amendments were introduced in the 1988 Omnibus Trade and Competitiveness Act of 1988 and led to the implementation of two provisions – special 301 and super 301. What is the significance of Section 301 and its 'special' and 'super' clauses for US trade policy?

Section 301 of the 1974 Trade Act was introduced in order to promote exports to those countries who, in the opinion of the US government, had not provided sufficiently open access to US products in their markets. Between 1975 and the late 1980s, Section 301 was used to ask trading partners who imported too few of those goods and services in which the USA was deemed to have a competitive advantage to lower their trade barriers and 'voluntarily' to expand their imports from the USA. South Korea was the first US trading partner to operate a voluntary import expansion scheme when, in the mid-1980s, it agreed, under threat of retaliation, to dismantle all barriers in order to allow US firms to compete in the hitherto highly protected insurance market. Both the super 301 and special 301 clauses were introduced in the late 1980s in order to strengthen the US government's power to initiate and, if necessary, enforce voluntary import expansions in countries that had been identified as infringing principles of fair trade.

The so-called *super 301* process was used for two years only (1989–90). It differed from the basic Section 301 in that action against countries practising unfair trade was not restricted to trade distortions taking place at industry level; the US administration could also act against countries whose trade-related policies created barriers against imports from the United States. The *special 301* provision which, unlike the 'super 301' clause, has remained in force, was specially introduced in order to enable the USA to take action against distortions in US exports of intellectual property rights originating in the USA (violations of intellectual property rights of US origin affecting imports into the USA are covered by Section 337 of the Tariff Act of 1930). Application of Section 301 and its amendments can result in the USA drawing up a list of 'priority' trade partners against whom action should be taken to improve US firms' market access.

In addition to trade agreements and arrangements, the USA, like the EU, can and has made use of a large number of *measures* and strategies in order to influence its exports and imports. While the EU has had preferential trade agreements with third countries for some time, the

USA did not embark on preferential trade agreements until the mid-1980s. A free trade area agreement with Israel came into force in 1985; a US–Canada Free Trade was established in January 1989 to be replaced in January 1994 by NAFTA which extended the US–Canada Free Trade zone to include Mexico. Both the free trade arrangements between the USA and Israel and the conclusion of NAFTA which matches Europe's single market in size are likely to divert US trade from third countries including the EU.

Trade diversion effects are also likely to have resulted from the Caribbean Basin (covering 24 countries) Economic Recovery Act of 1983, the Caribbean Basin Economic Recovery Expansion Act of 1990 and the Andean Trade Preference Act of 1991 (granting trade preferences to four Andean countries – Bolivia, Colombia, Ecuador and Peru). Trade would, however, have been diverted from other developing countries rather than from Europe, and the trade diversion effects brought about by these preferential arrangements would probably have been smaller than the ones likely to be generated by NAFTA. In addition to preferential trade agreements the USA has also used MFN treatment as a trade policy instrument. For political reasons, the USA used denial of MFN treatment in 1974 as a 'stick' when the former USSR created difficulties for Jews to emigrate. More recently, in the early 1990s, East European countries were accorded MFN treatment as a 'carrot' for implementing desirable political reforms. Award or denial of MFN treatment has potentially important implications for countries seeking trade links with the USA 'as the United States retains substantial differences between MFN and non-MFN tariffs' (GATT 1992a: 5). This policy instrument is, however, likely to be less and less important as fewer countries, at least among the CEECs and the successor states to the Soviet Union, will be deemed in need of political reforms.

In considering key US trade policy measures directly affecting imports into and exports from the USA, it seems appropriate to distinguish between tariff or tax-type measures (import duties, export subsidies, and anti-dumping duties) and non-tariff measures designed to restraint imports into the USA (import quotas, and voluntary restraint arrangements) or to expand imports from the USA (Section 301 actions).

The overall levels of US *tariffs* have been fairly low; the simple averages of pre-Uruguay round tariffs amounted to 7 per cent for industrial goods (excluding petroleum) and 9 per cent for agricultural produce (GATT 1992a: 74–75). In an attempt to protect certain sectors of its economy, the USA has imposed comparatively high import duties on a number of goods. The range of tariff rates has tended to be much wider for agricultural than for industrial products. Very high import duties have been levied on only a few products. Examples of very high tariffs on agricultural goods are tobacco (up to 1,775 per cent), cocoa (up to 338 per cent), sugar and confectionery (up to 136 per cent), and beverages and spirits (up to 98 per cent). Among industrial products US tariffs have been as high as 151 per cent for watches and clocks, 62 per cent for footwear, 42 per cent for textiles (synthetic and artificial fibres), 38 per cent for glass and glassware, 27 per cent for medical and pharmaceutical products, and 25 per cent for both motor vehicles and electrical equipment and parts (GATT 1992a: 284–319).

Export subsidies in the USA have been restricted to agricultural products. The USA's principal export subsidy scheme has been the export enhancement programme which was launched in 1985. The programme covers some twelve crops and was introduced to countervail alleged 'unfair' selling practices of other countries in competitive export markets. Anti-dumping investigations by the US International Trade Commission led (provided material injury to a US industry has been established) either to arrangements (price undertakings, voluntary restraint agreements or other agreed measures) between the USA and the injuring third country or to the USA imposing definitive duties on the dumped products. Between July 1980 and June 1991 the US administration took 463 anti-dumping actions; 84 of these involved EU states (Germany, France, Spain, Belgium and the UK). In 25 of the 84 anti-dumping investigations taken against members of the Union anti-dumping duties were imposed, relatively fewer than for the total number of cases (GATT 1992b: 96).

During the 1980s iron and steel products from European and other suppliers featured most prominently in US anti-dumping investigations. Since the late 1980s, other products, notably chemicals, electrical products, machinery and textiles appear to have given the US International Trade Commission cause for investigating whether dumping has taken place, whether a US industry has been materially 'injured' by dumping and whether the imposition of anti-dumping duties is the appropriate course of action to take. It is worth noting that the share of US imports in total US imports affected by anti-dumping duty scrutiny is quite small; it amounted to less than one half of a per cent in 1988 (USITC cited in GATT 1992a: 97). US anti-dumping investigations have nonetheless been important for its trade policy. Faced by actual or possible US anti-dumping investigations, exporters appear to have been persuaded 'to voluntarily restrain their exports to the United States, or to price their goods 'defensively', or to conclude bilateral agreements with similar aims' (GATT 1992a: 13). Finger and Murray (1990), for example, established a strong correlation between the number of anti-dumping investigations and subsequently negotiated voluntary restraint agreements. Voluntary restraint agreements are, of course, non-tariff rather than tariff measures.

Non-tariff measures cover a wide range of practices – tariff quotas, import prohibitions, import quotas, import cartels, standards and technical regulations, origin rules, actions against unfair practices, measures implemented in exporting and importing countries to affect imports and exports respectively to name the main types. US trade policy has made use of all these measures to a varying degree (see GATT 1992a: IV). We shall select the most important US non-tariff measures for discussion: import quotas, voluntary export restraint arrangements, and Section 301 actions. Although the USA has made use of quotas in adopting measures that would directly affect imports to America, voluntary restraints, surveillance and similar measures have also played a significant part in influencing the import side of the US visible trade balance.

The US administration uses direct quantitative restrictions in the form of *import quotas* exclusively for agricultural products, notably for cotton, dairy products, peanuts and (certain) sugar-containing goods. Some of the quotas have been bilateral; others have been global with or without allocations by country. Import quotas on meat existed until the late 1980s and have, in part, been replaced by VRAs. A global quota on specialty steel, introduced under GATT Article XIX (Safeguard Clauses), introduced in 1983, was phased out in 1989; it was replaced by VRAs which the United States concluded with a large number of countries. Import quotas on agricultural produce have been used to a varying degree by the USA. While import quotas on certain agricultural products (some dairy products and peanuts) have been fully utilised, direct import restraints on other items such as certain dried milk, cotton and specific sugar-containing products have not always been made use of. Considerable economic costs to the American consumers have resulted from the existence of these import quotas. The removal of such binding import restraints would, for example, have reduced the price of sugar and cheese in 1989 by up to 36 and 16 per cent respectively; consumer gains would have amounted to US$ 1.1 billion for sugar and US$ 263 million for cheese (ITC 1990). Since the late 1980s fewer product categories have been affected by US import quotas. No import quotas were imposed on meat after 1988; imports of speciality steel into the USA were no longer subject to quota regulation after September 1989; and the quota on cotton comber waste was abolished in November 1990.

The imports of meat and steel into the USA have continued to be restrained via *voluntary restraint arrangements*. Australia and New Zealand volunteered to restrict their exports of beef and veal to the USA as from 1991; 28 countries (EUR 12 and 16 other US trading partners) were persuaded to extend the previously concluded VRAs on steel to cover specialty steel. The EU concluded a VRA on steel and steel products with the USA in 1982. Europe's VRA on steel, like those concluded by other countries, was suspended in March 1992. The USA has also induced some of its trading partners to restrain their exports of certain other product categories: automobiles and semi-conductors (Japan); video cassette recorders, microwave ovens, footwear, stuffed toys, pianos, leather bags, fishing rods, tarpaulin products, brassware (South Korea); textiles and clothing (ten countries excluding MFA arrangements); and Tungsten products (China). While none of these export restraints have affected EU–US trade, US requests to limit its trading partners' exports of machine tools included four EU states – Germany, Italy, Spain and the United Kingdom (GATT 1992a: 115).

Section 301 – actions (involving 'regular 301', 'super 301' and 'special 301' processes) are unusual trade policy measures in that they threaten exclusionary importers with retaliation (higher tariffs or other import barriers) unless they facilitate US producers' access to their markets. More than any other US trade policy measure they epitomise 'managed trade'. No US trading partner appears to have recourse to a similar trade policy weaponry (the nearest equivalent is perhaps the EU's NCPI mentioned in Chapter 4). The US trade representative may (or may be required to) initiate investigations against 'priority' countries that adopt unfair trade practices and thus deny exporters access to the US markets.

The super and special 301 provisions differ from the basic or regular 301 Section in that the former may be used by the trade representative to 'self-initiate' cases whereas the latter would normally be used in response to a petition from US industries. By July 1992, 82 investigations had taken place under Section 301. Over two fifths of all the Section 301 investigations involved disputes over agriculture; more than a third were concerned with manufactured goods; over a tenth arose from lack of access for services and a tenth addressed intellectual property rights (Bayard and Elliott 1992: 689). Only a small fraction of all the Section 301 processes – about one tenth – resulted in the USA taking retaliatory actions. Although Japan has, not unexpectedly, featured on the USA black list of unfair traders, the EU has been targeted by more Section 301 investigations than any other US trading partner (Bayard and Elliott 1992: 689; GATT 1992a: 124–26). While most of the Section 301 investigations directed at Japan dealt with market access issues of manufactured products, more than four fifths of all the cases against the EU centred around disputes over agricultural products. Section 301 disputes with the EU over non-agricultural issues in the early 1990s have been, for example, over alleged denial of protection of intellectual property rights, lack of access for telecommunications equipment in public procurement and reduced US exports of TV programmes. According to Bayard and Elliott (who have systematically analysed all completed Section 301 investigations since 1975), the direct trade impact of these cases has apparently been small: 'in a quarter of the cases total US exports (in a few cases imports) of the product in question (from) the targeted country had a value of less than 10 million US$. In three-quarters, the value was less than 200 million US$' (Bayard and Elliott 1992: 687).

The more significant aspect of Section 301 actions must be the deterring effect on some US trade partners. Countries who are weak and depend heavily on the USA are more likely to make trade concessions if threatened by such actions than powerful trading partners. US trading partners such as South Korea and Taiwan (which after the EU and Japan are countries most frequently affected by 301 investigations) are more likely to comply with demands for voluntary import expansion than the EU or Japan because they estimate the costs of defiance to exceed the cost of compliance.

EU–US MARKET ACCESS ISSUES

The United States encouraged moves towards European economic integration after World War II. Indeed, the USA promoted the insertion of Article XVIII into the GATT, which allowed countries to establish customs unions and free trade areas. Trade between Europe and America has nevertheless more often than not been characterised by conflicts. A number of EU–US trade disputes were formally considered by the GATT. Transatlantic trade disputes have dominated GATT litigation; both the USA and the EU have been particularly active since 1980 in bringing complaints against each other (for detailed discussions see, for example, GATT 1991, 1992a, 1993b; Woolcock 1991; Coffey 1993). The market access issues that have been of major concern to one or both trading partners are agriculture, steel, aerospace and '1992'.

Agriculture has been the most contentious market access issue in the trade relations between the EU and the United States. The USA has always been an important world exporter of agricultural produce; the EU, while initially a net importer of agricultural products, has now been a leading world producer and exporter of agricultural commodities for many years. Conflicts over agriculture between the two world trade powers have arisen for two reasons. First, both the EU and the USA have used agricultural support systems conducive to surplus production – the EU's surplus production is primarily the result of its CAP, while the American farmers benefit from a range of support systems that also lead to high prices and surpluses. Second, in trying to export their agricultural products the EU and the USA have had to compete in a declining world market. In most of the formal EU–US trade disputes the USA has acted as plaintiff and the EU has typically been in the role of defendant. The USA has been concerned about three trade-distorting aspects of the EU's agricultural policies. It has regarded the EU's variable import levy as amounting to an unfair trading practice as it artifically reduces exports from the USA and other non-EU sources to the Communities. It has also been very critical of the CAP's export refund scheme (which subsidises European farmers if they sell their products outside the EU and the world price falls short of the intervention price). The EU has been accused of 'dumping' its agricultural surpluses on the US (and other countries') traditional export markets. Furthermore, the USA has complained about the EU using non-tariff barriers to restrict agricultural imports.

In 1988–89, a hormone dispute developed following European legislation banning the use of growth-generating hormones – a ban that adversely affected American exports to Europe. In 1991, to give another example, the USA requested that a GATT panel be established to consider the legitimacy of Europe prohibiting the import of certain US meat. The importance of agriculture as a source of trade conflicts between the EU and the USA can be measured by the frequency with which agricultural issues have featured in official investigations. Nearly 'a quarter of all 301 cases have involved agricultural disputes with the EC' (Bayard and Elliott 1992: 688). Since 1961 the GATT has dealt with a considerable number of complaints from the USA against the EU (and a few from the EU against the USA), and the agricultural trade conflicts between America and Europe had a significant impact on the multilateral trade negotiations that took place during the Uruguay Round (1986–93), with the United States suggesting a number of measures (tariffs to replace all non-tariff measures; gradual and substantial reduction of tariffs; phasing out of export subsidies and farm support schemes) in order to bring to an end the long-lasting EU–US confrontation over agriculture (see Chapter 8).

In the 1980s, trade tensions developed between the European and American *steel industries*. The steel industries in both the EU and the USA had had to adjust to very changed circumstances. Demand had shifted towards less steel-intensive products; steel-saving substitution processes were introduced in, for example, the motor car industry; and new suppliers arrived on the world market. Surplus capacity problems arose in both Europe and America, and these problems were exacerbated by the world-wide recession of the early 1990s. The USA was also concerned about the trade distortions resulting from subsidies paid to and state aid provided for uneconomic European steel plants. Between 1985 and 1992, the US steel industry was protected by VRAs which limited the imports from VRA countries to about one fifth of the US market. The EU was the largest VRA exporter of steel mill products and fabricated steel products in 1989 with a share of 42 per cent of VRA exports and 31 per cent of all exports to the USA (GATT 1992a: 211). The VRAs expired at the end of March 1992 despite the fact that no international agreement banning subsidies to steel producers had been reached. The USA has, however, reserved the right to seek recourse to national laws, notably Section 301 of the 1974 Trade Act, in cases of unfair steel exports from the EU and other trade partners.

Subsidies are also at the root of conflicts that have developed between the EU and the United States over the *aerospace industry*. As a result of a large domestic market, for many years after the Second World War the USA was able to benefit from economies of scale in the production of aircraft. Combined with a high level of demand, this enabled America to establish a comparative advantage over European countries which, while operating independently, were not in a position to develop a viable aircraft industry on their own. The situation changed when Europe, in an attempt to emulate the US experience, launched the airbus programme. Airbus was initally (in 1966) developed by France (Aerospatial) and Germany (Deutsche Airbus, a subsidiary of Messerschmidt-Bölkow-Blohm); the UK (British Aerospace) and Spain (Construcciones Aeronauticas) joined the consortium at a later stage. The *European airbus* programme has been successful in that, following a development phase in the 1970s, the EU aircraft industry has been characterised by continuous growth throughout the 1980s. By the late 1980s the airbus programme had 'achieved a share of about one-third of the expanding world commercial jet market' (GATT 1991: 224). Declining defence budgets (in the USA and other world powers) have resulted in shifting demand for aircraft away from the military to the civil sector. Although the USA has continued to show a significant trade surplus in the aerospace industry (the EU's external trade in civil aircraft has been in balance in recent years), the European airbus programme has been a contentious issue in EU–US economic relations. Two aspects of the airbus programme have been of concern to the Americans: the 'dollar clause' and airbus production subsidies in general. The 'dollar clause' refers to an exchange rate guarantee scheme that formed part of an agreement between the German government and Daimler-Benz (which owns 80 per cent of Deutsche Airbus) whereby Airbus would be compensated in part for losses arising out of exchange rate movements between the dollar and the Deutschmark. The United States regarded this dollar clause as an unfair trading practice and demanded the establishment of a panel under the GATT subsidies code (Article XVIII: 1). A GATT panel was duly set up by the committee on subsidies and countervailing measures in March 1991. By July 1992, the German government and Daimler-Benz had discontinued the exchange rate guarantee scheme, thus removing one of the contentious issues between America and Europe. The second thorny issue between the USA and the EU concerned subsidies paid by the four consortium members – France, Germany, Spain and the UK – to the airbus programme. The United States argued that these production subsidies effectively amounted to unfair trade, and the GATT subsidies committee was asked to consider the complaint. The dispute was to a large extent settled in July 1992 when the EU and the USA agreed to limit state aid for civil aircraft with over 100-seat capacity. The EU and USA, in the spirit of the General Agreement, also committed themselves to establishing more transparency and to strictly limiting terms and conditions of public support in order to reduce, if not eliminate, subsidies in the (civil) aerospace sector. It remains to be seen whether the termination of the (German) exchange rate guarantee scheme and the 1992 bilateral agreement will mark the end of the friction between the EU and the USA over aircraft trade. For, while the Americans stress the market-distorting effects of subsidies, the Europeans have continued to justify the public support of airbus on grounds of competition, industrial and strategic policy. Settling the dispute is connected with problems. It is difficult, if not impossible, 'to provide comprehensive assessments of all subsidies or the subsidy equivalents of support (via state guarantees, public ownership etc.)' (GATT 1991: 224). The issue becomes even more complicated if we consider that the civil and military sectors of the aircraft industry are interlinked, thus giving scope to technological spill-over effects.

The creation of a *single European market* is the most recent and ongoing EU–US market access issue. Initial discussions of the European domestic market in the United States led to talk of 'fortress Europe' – a trading bloc, unified within, but with external barriers that were anticipated to impede exports from the United States and other countries to EU markets. Following a number of studies on the impact of '1992' on EU–US trade flows, there is now less talk of 'fortress Europe'. A comprehensive investigation carried out by the International Trade Commission, for example, led to a report suggesting that, on balance, the single European market would exhibit openness towards third countries like the United States; indeed it argued that the USA would, on the whole, benefit from '1992' (ITC 1989). That said, it should be noted that the Americans, while perhaps less apprehensive now about the trade implications of the 1992 programme than in the late 1980s, have continued to be sceptical about certain aspects of the single market programme.

In considering post-1992 transatlantic trade flows, it would appear useful to distinguish between 'insiders' (American companies already located within the EU) such as Ford and Honeywell, and 'outsiders' (American companies located within the USA but seeking to have access to EU markets). 'Insiders' are being treated as European enterprises provided they meet the minimum local content requirements which are, at the time of writing, at least 60 per cent of value added being generated in the production process inside an EU-located plant. There have, admittedly, been instances where products manufactured within the EU were not universally defined as 'European' (the Nissan

Bluebird is a case in point). But American businesses operating inside the EU should, in principle, not encounter any market access problems once local content rules are generally observed, their interpretation is the same in different EU states, and common standards are being adopted. 'Outsiders', on the other hand, depending on the product concerned, may see their market access somewhat restricted as a result of the establishment of the single market. In which particular sectors then have there been trade controversies between America and Europe resulting from '1992'? Market access disputes between the US and the EU developed after '1992' mainly over two issues – cultural goods and public procurement.

The move towards an integrated European market was, *inter alia*, accompanied by attempts to adopt a common cultural policy. Pursuit of such a common cultural policy did not cause any trade conflicts between America and Europe while it was restricted to intensifying cultural exchanges among members of the Union. Disputes did, however, arise in the 1990s when Europe attempted to impose quantitative restrictions on the import of films and TV programmes made in the USA. The Commission decreed, at the instigation of the French, that at least one half of films shown in European cinemas and of programmes shown on European TV should be produced in the EU (Coffey 1993: 85). The USA retaliated by using Section 301 to put the EU on its 'blacklist' of trading partners allegedly using unfair trading practices and thus violating its GATT obligations.

Reciprocity or rather the absence of adequate reciprocal agreements would seem to be the cause of EU–US market access issues in the area of public procurement. Reciprocity in this context simply means that the EU opens its markets to US suppliers to the same extent to which European producers have access to American markets. Public procurement is an important and sizeable market in most industrialised countries accounting for between 8 and 12 per cent of gross domestic products (Woolcock 1991: 71). The main categories covered are the public utilities energy, telecommunications, transport and water. In considering bids for public procurement, both the EU and the USA give preference to 'national' producers and contractors. Both have tended to accuse each other of 'rigging' their domestic public procurement markets by discriminating in favour of 'national' suppliers, thus keeping out goods produced outside their territories.

Telecommunications equipment, in which the USA has had a comparative advantage over the EU, has been a key sector in the transatlantic dispute over public procurement policy. The dispute between America and Europe over telecommunications equipment developed before '1992' but moved higher up on the EU–US trade agenda when the single market programme was put into action in 1993. In 1991, Europe raised a complaint against the USA under the

Government Procurement Code and asked for the establishment of a GATT panel concerning discrimination in bids for a contract for a sonar mapping system for a research ship (US National Science Foundation) in the Antarctic. Two years earlier the USA, which had deregulated its telecommunications sector and unilaterally opened her market, had identified the EU (particularly because of German purchasing practices) as embarking on unfair trading practices. The USA, while putting the EU on the 'priority watch list' (which would have entitled it to adopt measures to reduce EU suppliers' access to American markets), abstained from taking any retaliatory actions against Europe but reserved the right to find levers to make European markets more accessible for US suppliers until the completion of the Uruguay Round.

Our discussion of EU–US trade links has shown that the controversies in some areas have been such that they have resulted in damaging the EU's economic relations with the USA. Europe's CAP and the application of possible use of section 301 of the US Trade Act, in particular, have been far from conducive to establishing harmonious relations between the EU and the USA. If better trade relations between these two powerful trading partners are to be formed, Europe has to adopt a less protectionist stance in its agricultural policy. The USA, on the other hand, should consider whether it should be in a position to determine unilaterally that a trading partner such as, for example, the EU has used unfair trading practices (i.e. departed from its contractual obligations under the GATT). Both agricultural protectionism and unilateral trade measures are issues that featured prominently in the multilateral trade negotiations between 1986 and 1993 (the Uruguay Round) in which both the EU and the USA played a key role (see Chapter 8).

GUIDE TO FURTHER READING

Bhagwhati, J. and Patrick, H.T. (eds) (1990) *Aggressive Unilateralism: America's 301 Trade Policy and the World Trading System*, Ann Arbor, University of Michigan Press.

Coffey, P. (1993) *The EC and the United States*, London, Pinter.

Destler, I.M. (1992) *American Trade Politics*, Washington D.C., Institute for International Economics.

GATT (1992) *Trade Policy Review: United States*, Geneva, GATT.

— (1993) *Trade Policy Review: Japan*, Geneva, GATT.

Ishikawa, K. (1990) Japan and the Challenge of Europe, London, Pinter.

Ito, T. (1992) *The Japanese Economy*, Cambridge, Massachusetts Institute of Technology Press.

Krugman, P. (1991) *Trade with Japan: Has the Door Opened Wider*? Chicago and London, University of Chicago Press.

Lincoln, E.J. (1990) *Japan's Unequal Trade*, Washington, Brookings Institution.
Tsoukalis, L. (1986) *Europe, America and the World Economy*, Oxford, Basil Blackwell.
Turner, P. (1991) *Japan and Europe as Trading Partners: Retrospect and Prospect*, Basle, Bank for International Settlements.
Woolcock, S. (1991) *Market Access Issues in EC–US Relations: Trading Partners or Trading Blows*, London, Pinter.

7
EUROPE AND THE THIRD WORLD

INTRODUCTION

We now turn to consider the trade relations that exist between the EU and the countries of the Third World – countries that do not belong to the two major economic blocs (the Western industrialised world and the former Eastern Bloc) grouping together countries with vastly different per capita incomes and degrees of industrialisation such as the NICs, the OPEC countries and the very underdeveloped countries. The EU represents the single largest trade partner of the group of developing market economies in that the latter take a significant share of Europe's exports. This amounted to 35 per cent in 1992 and accounted for as much as 44 and 39 per cent of the Union's exports in the years 1958 and 1975 respectively (*Table 2.4*). In discussing the EU's trade links with the developing countries it is important to distinguish between countries that have been offered preferential treatment by the Union and those states that have non-preferential links with the EU.

Of the countries of the 'South' there are, at present, two large groups of countries that benefit from preferential trade agreements with the EU: the ACP countries and the economies covered by the 'global Mediterannean policy' – the Mediterranean Basin. The EU has also entered into special trade agreements with certain countries in Asia and

South America. Furthermore, like the USA and most other industrialised countries, it has been operating a system of preferences for those developing countries that are members of UNCTAD. This group of mainly Asian and Latin American Third World countries covers trading nations at very different stages of economic development, with very different levels of trade performance and with very different trade potentials. It includes very poor Third World countries (such as Bangladesh), newly industrialised and successful countries in South-East Asia and South America (such as Singapore and Brazil) and emerging trade giants (such as China).

In discussing Europe–Third World trade relations we shall adopt the following sequence. First, we shall deal with the EU's trade links with the two 'privileged' groups of developing countries – ACP and the Mediterranean Basin. This will be followed by a discussion of trade between the EU and countries benefiting from Europe's GSP scheme. Considering the importance of the NICs in world trade and the fact that not all the members of this group of countries have been GSP beneficiaries, EU–NICs trade will be treated in a separate action. Finally, we shall outline the principal problems that have arisen in Europe's trade with the 'South'.

THE ACP GROUP

ACP refers to the non-European signatories of the *Lomé* convention(s) – countries highly dependent on agriculture and with low per capita incomes. The Lomé conventions are trade and aid agreements between the European Union and ACP. Following their predecessors – the Yaoundé conventions – four Lomé conventions have been signed so far: Lomé I (1976–80), Lomé II (1981–85), Lomé III (1986–90) and Lomé IV (1991–2000). The ACP membership has increased since Yaoundé I (which was signed by 18 countries in 1964); Lomé embraces 69 ACPs (for a list of signatories see footnote 3 to *Table 2.4*).

The EU's trade with ACP has been characterised by the following features:

- Virtually all ACP exports enter the EU free of tariffs and quota restrictions.
- The Union does not insist on 'reciprocity' – a GATT principle which says that, if one country reduces its tariffs on imports from another country, it is entitled to expect the other country to reduce its tariffs too.
- Preferential treatment is being granted to ACP countries for various agricultural products (sugar, beef, rum, bananas).

- Mechanisms exist to guarantee ACPs' production levels of and export earnings from the sales of raw materials (STABEX) and mineral (SYSMIN).

STABEX attempts to stabilise ACP countries' earnings from export sales of raw materials by offering 'less poor' countries repayable advances and 'poor' countries non-repayable grants whenever an ACP country's export earnings from trading with the EU are lower than the average for previous years. SYSMIN offers a similar stabilisation for export earnings from mineral products.

ACP may have enjoyed a privileged position in trading with the EU, but they have not fared well in trading with the EU over time: their share of EU imports fell from 10 to 4 per cent between 1958 and 1992 (*Table 2.5*). A number of factors account for the relatively poor trade performance of ACP as a whole (oil-exporting countries like Tobago, Trinidad, Gabon, Congo and Nigeria fared better because they were able to take advantage of oil price rises). First, the EU has insisted that 50 per cent of value added be achieved in the developing country; this has proved an obstacle to the majority of ACP countries operating at fairly low levels of industrialisation. Second, the STABEX and SYSMIN schemes have exhibited serious defects in administrative terms; they have also been biased in favour of the relatively more advanced members of ACP. Third, the CAP has represented a barrier for exports from ACP countries to the EU. Fourth, developing countries' terms of trade have experienced a secular deterioriation because, over the 1980s, the relative price of basic commodities (the Third World countries' main exports) fell substantially compared to manufactured goods (the Third World countries' main imports from Europe and other industrialised trade partners). For some countries with strong historical links with France development assistance schemes have furthermore tended to be tied to French exports which were sold at inflated prices. Fifth, the oil crises of the 1970s generated debt repayment problems for oil-importing Third World countries.

For ACP, as a bloc, trade with the EU is very significant. In the 1980s, about two fifths of all ACP exports went to the EU; about one third of all ACP imports came from the Union. Europe represents the largest export market for the African ACP countries; the EU has tended to purchase as much as half of all African exports. Not all ACP countries, however, depend on trade with Europe. The Carribean countries, for example, tend to have more intensive trade links with North America. It is also worth noting that 50 per cent of all EU imports from the ACP group come from a small number of African member states of ACP, notably the Ivory Coast, Nigeria and Zaïre. The EU has, on the whole, not been very dependent on ACP as a trading partner, although for a few selected goods ACP countries are virtually its main suppliers (e.g. copper, coffee, aluminium, cocoa and cane sugar). On balance the EU has tended to be a net importer in trading merchandise with ACP countries. Europe's (visible) trade balance deficit averaged 4,309 million ECU per annum between 1983 and 1992 (*Table 2.8*).

THE MEDITERRANEAN BASIN

Preferential links also exist between the EU and the developing countries of the Mediterranean – the Maghreb (Algeria, Morocco and Tunisia), the Mashreq (Egypt, Syria, Lebanon and Jordan), the Northern Mediterranean countries (Turkey, Malta, Cyprus and the former Yugoslavia) and Israel. For the EU the Mediterranean Basin constitutes a major export market. In 1992, one tenth of all EU external exports were sold in developing countries of the Mediterranean (*Table 2.4*); in the same year 8 per cent of Europe's import needs were met by supplies from the Mediterranean Basin (*Table 2.5*). For most of the Mediterranean countries the EU was a significant trading partner in the 1980s. The Union absorbed more than half the exports of Cyprus, Malta, Morocco and Tunisia; for Egypt, Israel and Syria, one third (of more) of their exports were destined for EU markets (CEC 1993: 98). Exports from the EU to the Mediterranean Basin have consistently exceeded imports from this group of developing economies: between 1983 and 1992 the EU's trade surplus averaged ECU 3,929 million (*Table 2.8*).

The trade aspects of the EU's 'Global Mediterranean Policy' (originally developed in September 1972) have, broadly speaking, the following characteristics:

- Industrial goods from the Mediterranean Basin have duty-free access to the single European market.
- The EU expects some countries (Turkey, Malta and Cyprus) to offer reciprocal preferences to imports from the EU; other countries (the former Yugoslavia and the Arab states) are not required to offer reciprocity in return for their tariff free exports to the Union.
- Agricultural goods do not benefit from tariff reductions except for goods where the EU is not yet self-sufficient.

The extent of the preferences that the EU has been granting to the Mediterranean countries has been less generous than those offered to the ACP group. The rules of origin applied to ACP exports to the EU have been less restrictive than those used for EU imports from Mediterranean countries; the ACPs enjoy preferential treatment for agricultural products such as bananas resulting in the EU demand for bananas being met, in part, by supplies from relatively expensive ACP producers such as Guadeloupe, Martinique and the Canaries rather than from more efficient banana-growers in central America.

While agricultural products from the Mediterranean may enter the EU market without restrictions and/or at reduced rates of duty, the Union may, under the respective cooperation agreements, initiate VRAs in the textile sector with the Mediterranean countries. In 1978, for example, the EU persuaded its Mediterranean trading partners to subscribe to VRAs for textiles.

Although the trade arrangements between the Union and the countries of the Mediterranean Basin were designed to facilitate trade between the two groups of countries and favour exports from the Mediterranean countries, the benefits appear to have been smaller than anticipated. The Mediterranean Basin has not been able to take advantage of free access to Europe's market for its industrial goods for the simple reason that it has so far had but a negligible level of industrial production. The free access for exports of industrial goods from Mediterranean countries has also been more apparent than real. Important exportables such as clothing and textiles have been subject to quantitative restrictions. The Mediterranean countries have, as pointed out earlier, tended to incur deficits in trading merchandise with the EU.

UNCTAD AND EUROPE'S GENERALISED PREFERENCES

The special preferential arrangements that the EU has entered into with ACP and Mediterranean countries have inevitably marginalised the EU's trade links with the rest of the Third World, notably countries in Asia and Latin America. Third World countries outside the groups comprising ACP and the Mediterranean Basin have been critical of the discrimination that resulted from the preferential trade arrangements between the Union and the Mediterranean Basin and ACP countries. The growing awareness of the 'North–South' divide led to pressure being exerted by countries belonging to *UNCTAD* for the introduction of a GSP (Generalised System of Preferences) leading, it was hoped, to the abolition of selective trade preferences while at the same time granting the developing countries freer access to the markets of the Western industrialised world.

Generalised preferences were first introduced following negotiations between UNCTAD and the Western industrialised countries in 1971, and then extended in 1980. The two main systems of generalised preferences that have been in operation are the American and the European schemes, covering trade links between the US and UNCTAD and the EU and UNCTAD respectively. The principal features of the EU's GSP are as follows:

- Imports of industrial goods into Europe's single market are exempted from duties provided that the quotas (which vary from one European country to another) are adhered to and a strict 'origin rule' is being applied (the exporting country must normally have added at least 35 per cent of the value of the exported good).
- Exports in excess of agreed ceilings are subject to the full CET.
- The preferential scheme covers only a limited range of agricultural goods.

The EU's trade preferences for the GSP beneficiaries are less generous than those offered to ACP and Mediterranean countries. The rules of origin are far more restrictive. Only for certain agricultural products are there reduced or no import levies. There are also limitations on preferences for 'sensitive products' such as textiles and clothing.

The first UNCTAD conference took place in Geneva in 1964 (the 1960s had been designated as the UN development decade by the General Assembly). Since then the developing countries within UNCTAD have been referred to as the 'Group of 77'. The actual number now amounts to 128 although it should be noted that the membership has at times fluctuated. South Korea, for example, was not eligible for GSP benefits between 1988 and 1991 because it was alleged to have violated European companies' intellectual property rights. Further UNCTAD conferences were convened in New Delhi (1968), Santiago (1972), Nairobi (1976), Manila (1979), Belgrade (1983), Geneva (1987) and Cartagena (1992).

What has been the impact of the European GSP? At a theoretical level, it is important to distinguish between the trade-creating and trade-diverting effects of trade preferences. A preferential trade regime will have trade-creating effects if the lowering or removal of import levies leads to additional imports from the 'preferred' supply source at lower prices; trade diversion will result from the granting of tariff preferences if the 'preferred' supply source replaces other more efficient external producers. A study of the impact of Europe's generalised tariff preferences (Langhammer and Sapir 1987) concluded that the system, although liberal in intent, has not been conducive to creating trade. The European GSP has, it seems, led to trade, on the whole, being diverted from the less developed countries. The trade diversion effect has, in part, been due to the fact that some products have been excluded from the scheme and that the quantitative restrictions have been fairly strict. Adverse effects may also have been brought about by the complex nature of the European scheme; the European GSP allocates quotas to the importing agency rather than the exporter. The importer, instead of charging consumers the duty free price, sells the product at a full tariff price.

In considering the effects of the EU's GSP on Third World countries it is important to stress the role 'managed' trade has played, notably in the textiles sector. Europe has managed trade in textiles since the 1950s (starting with the UK), when it negotiated voluntary restraint agreements with developing countries like Hong Kong, India and Japan whose supplies posed a threat to the textiles sectors in Western Europe which were operating well below full capacity levels. Multilateral arrangements at GATT level were subsequently negotiated to replace bilateral agreements, with the first MFA being signed in 1974. The current MFA covers approximately three quarters of world trade in man-made and natural fibres. Its main feature is a restriction of textile imports into the EU from GSP-eligible countries. Although initially intended as a short-term solution to alleviate the adjustment problems of the European textile industries, the MFA has continued to exist (MFA I was replaced by MFA II in 1977, MFA III was concluded in 1981, and MFA IV was signed in 1986) and with increased rather than reduced restrictions on EU imports from the Third World. The trade restrictions of the MFA are such that they lead to inefficiency; the quantitative restrictions reallocate production away from lower cost supply sources towards higher cost suppliers. The quota restrictions thus cause welfare losses for both the EU and the Third World exporters directly affected by the MFA (for a more detailed discussion, see Faini 1992: 3–12).

What proportion of EU–Third World trade is covered by the GSP scheme? Which developing countries benefit from this preferential trade regime? In 1990, seven tenths of dutiable exports from developing countries to Europe were covered by the GSP. With more than 50 per cent of these imports being treated as 'sensitive' (no or limited/ conditional coverage by the GSP scheme), only three tenths of the dutiable imports actually received beneficiary GSP treatment (CEC 1993: 70). As far as beneficiaries are concerned, it is interesting to note that in 1990 eight Asian, Latin American and South-East Asian countries (China, India, Brazil, Thailand, Indonesia, Singapore, Malaysia and Hong Kong) accounted for a disproportionately large share of GSP benefits. While their share of dutiable trade amounted to 55 per cent, 60 per cent of total GSP benefits accrued to them. The eight top GSP beneficiaries appear to have been particularly effective in utilising GSP preferences for non-sensitive products (CEC 1993: 72). The position about GSP utilisation may, however, change when the most successful of the NICs acquire 'developed country' status, thus no longer qualifying for preferential access to EU markets. However, it is far from certain whether there is a causal link between GSP benefits and trade performance. Taiwan, for example, has become an important world player in trade despite the fact that it was specifically excluded from Europe's GSP.

EU TRADE WITH THE NICs

Although NICs have featured prominently in discussions on industrialisation, trade and the world economy for some time, the term 'NIC' has never been officially defined, and there is no agreed list of NICs. As the name suggests, a NIC means a country that is in a state of transition between a developing economy and an advanced industrial country. The following four criteria tend to be used in identifying a NIC:

- absolute and relative growth of the manufacturing sector;
- rising importance of manufactures in the composition of exports;
- international competitiveness in manufacturing as measured by an increasing share in world exports of manufactured goods;
- a growth rate of per capita GDP (in real terms) in excess of that achieved by developed countries (CEC 1988c; OECD 1979).

Whether a country is referred to as a 'developing country' or an 'NIC' would then depend on how many of the aforementioned criteria are being fulfilled and the growth rates that are being used as a yardstick. In other words, the number of countries identified as NICs may be large or small. In a statistical analysis of EU–NICs trade in the 1970s and 1980s some sixteen NICs were listed: the core or Asian NICs – Hong Kong, South Korea, Taiwan and Singapore (also known as the four 'tigers' or 'dragons'); the 'baby tiger' economies – Malaysia, Philippines and Thailand; the Mediterranean economies of the former Yugoslavia, Israel and Turkey; Argentina, Brazil and Mexico; and three potentially large world traders in Asia – China, India and Indonesia (Eurostat 1991: 5).

In examining trade between Europe and NICs, we shall focus on the four Asian NICs (Hong Kong, South Korea, Taiwan and Singapore). Although other countries such as Thailand (which has been one of the 20 leading world exporters of manufactured goods since 1989) should arguably be included in the list of the core NICs, restriction of our discussion to the 'four dragons' has the advantage of enabling us to illustrate the role of NICs in Europe's external trade since the 1960s.

The Asian NICs accounted for 12 per cent of world merchandise exports (excluding EU internal trade) in 1992, and this share compares favourably with the results achieved by the EU, the USA and Japan whose shares were 20, 16 and 12 per cent respectively (*Table* 2.2). The growing importance of the 'four tigers' as EU trade partners becomes clear when we observe their changed position as markets for and suppliers of the EU. Between 1958 and 1992, the 'four dragons' tripled their share of imports from the EU from 2 per cent to 6 per cent (*Table 2.4*): EU imports from these four NICs increased from an insignificant 1 per cent to 6 per cent over the same period (*Table 2.5*). Over the years, the four Asian 'tiger economies' have increased their share of world exports in manufactured goods, and this shift is also reflected in their composition of exports to the EU. Although the four NICs are far from homogeneous, the changes in the composition of their exports have been very similar. They have upgraded production facilities; they have shifted away from labour intensive towards more technology-based (and less labour intensive) industries. The textile and clothing industries have been replaced by plastics and electronics industries as engines of export-led growth. The EU has been a major export market and supply source for the four Asian NICs. In the 1970s and 1980s, between one eighth and one fifth of their total exports reached EU markets (Eurostat 1991: 116–17). Between one tenth and one sixth of their imports have come from Europe (*ibid.*: 114–15).

The EU has had a trade deficit with the four Asian NICs since the 1970s and the deficits have been particularly substantive over the last few years. The industrial dynamism and export success of the core NICs appear to be due to four factors: appropriate development strategy based on export promotion; establishment of foreign subsidiaries of MNEs (multinational enterprises); exploitation of competitive advantages; and adjustment to changing economic conditions. The export success of the Asian NICs has developed into a challenge to Europe (and the Western industrialised world) not dissimilar to the challenge posed by Japan (arguably the 'first NIC' of the post Second World War period). What appears to have exacerbated the trade threat posed by the dynamic Asian economies for Europe were the worsening of the economic situation after the oil shock of the mid-1970s, the reduction in the Communities' growth rates and the concomitant rising levels of unemployment.

The faster growth and, more importantly, the export success of the core NICs have led to tensions in the trade links between Europe and this part of South-East Asia. Dumping accusations/anti-dumping measures and voluntary restraint agreements have been indicative of trade conflicts between the EU and the Asian NICs. The NICs have seen their potential to penetrate EU markets reduced via VERs for the following products: footwear, umbrellas, travel bags, video tape recorders, radio and TV receivers, colour TV sets, microwave ovens, steel (GATT 1991: 102–106). EU anti-dumping cases involving the four NICs have developed over electronics products – electronic typewriters, microwave ovens, compact disc players, video cassette recorders, small-screen colour TVs and video cassette tapes (NCC 1990: 50–51). Some of the anti-dumping actions taken by the EU against Hong Kong serve as a useful illustration of the 'trade wars' that have developed between industrialised Europe and newly industrialised Asia. Up to 1987, the Commission had, for instance, taken just one (unsuccessful) anti-dumping action against Hong Kong. Since then the EU has claimed that Hong Kong has 'dumped' goods such as cotton denim cloth, photograph albums, silicon, tungsten ore, cellular telephones, television sets and cassettes. In some cases the Commission's dumping allegations were wrongly targeted. Two of the above mentioned goods – tungsten ore and silicon – had been merely trade 'throughputs'; they were exports from China via Hong Kong. It is also debatable whether countries affected by quantitative restrictions opt for dumping as the most appropriate course of action. Increasing the profitability of their export operations by selling more 'up market' goods and at higher prices would appear to be a more likely course of action. Small companies, operating in a highly competitive environment like Hong Kong, would clearly reduce their profitability even further if they 'dumped' goods abroad.

The methods used by Commission officials in dealing with estimates of the true production costs incurred by Hong Kong manufacturers may also be inappropriate. They appear to assume, to take the example of video tape production, that Hong Kong producers have the same wastage rates as Western industrialised countries. Commission officials have been seemingly unwilling to believe that Hong Kong's manufacturers can produce video tapes with a wastage rate of less than 7 per cent. They have, in considering dumping accusations, assumed 'inflated' wastage rates and thus construed 'true' (i.e. higher) production costs for Hong Kong manufacturers (Hindley 1992).

CONCLUSION

Our discussion of Third World countries has shown that this group of Europe's trade partners embraces countries at very different stages of economic development, with varying potentials as world traders and in different actual positions as world exporters and importers. While some groups have become more important as world traders and Europe's trade partners, others have lost in significance in trading with the world and Europe. In trading with the EU, some have been incurring deficits (Mediterranean Basin countries); others tend to be net exporters (ACPs, NICs) to the EU. Whereas some countries call for support from Europe (or the world) or pursue policies to promote their exports and reduce their imports, others have seen Europe respond to their export successes by accusing them of unfair trading. Some have failed to establish a base for industrialisation; others have been very dynamic in industrialising and gaining a competitive advantage as trading nations. While some have clearly remained developing countries, others have either become NICs or are about to graduate to the status of developed country. In the circumstances, any attempt to generalise about EU–Third World trade is connected with difficulties. From the conclusions that we can draw in our chapter on EU–Third World trade some conclusions apply to all countries of the 'South'; others are only relevant to some of the countries included in this heterogeneous list of developing trading nations.

What have affected all Third World countries are the trade diverting effects that have been the outcome of Europe's departure from the principles of multilateralism (trade liberalisation and non-discrimination of trade partners). The 'pyramid of privileges' that characterises the EU's trade agreements with countries of the 'South' has inevitably implied that some developing countries have more and easier access to Europe's domestic market than others. The new, non-tariff based protectionism (MFA, VRA, rules of origin, anti-dumping actions, etc.) and the CAP have led to the impediment of Third World countries' exports to Europe. The new protectionism plus the CAP measures have, however, not had the same impact on all the countries of the 'South'; Europe's protectionism has been discriminatory rather than uniform. Third World countries' exports of textiles and clothing, for example, account on average for as much as one fifth of their total exports. For many developing countries, textiles and clothing are products that contribute significantly towards putting them on the path of export-led growth. Yet, these countries' exports of textiles and clothing have been restricted by both relatively high tariffs and quota restrictions resulting from the MFA. Agriculture accounts for less of all developing countries' export earnings (about one eighth) than textiles and clothing. But for many Third World countries these exports of agricultural produce have been the principal source of their export earnings. Yet, the CAP has reduced the trade potentials of developing countries.

GUIDE TO FURTHER READING

CEC (1989) *The Europe-South Dialogue*, Luxembourg, OOPEC.

— (1989) Trade with Latin America, in International Trade of the European Community, *European Economy*, 3: 54–69.

— (1993) The Developing Countries in the 1980s, in The European Community as a World Trade Partner, *European Economy*, 52: 63–99.

Davenport, M. and Page, S. (1991) *Europe: 1992 and the* Developing World, London, Overseas Development Institute.

Eurostat (1991) *EC-NICs Trade: A Statistical Analysis*, Luxembourg, OOPEC.

Faini, R. *et al.* (1992) A Primer on the MFA, *CEPR* Discussion Paper, 716.

Hamilton, C.B. (1990) European Community External Protection and 1992: Voluntary Export Restraints Applied to Pacific Asia, *CEPR Discussion Paper*, 475.
McQueen, M. (1989) Lomé IV Negotiations, *European Access*, June.
World Bank (1992) *Global Economic Prospects and the Developing Countries*, Washington D.C., World Bank.

8
THE WORLD TRADING SYSTEM

INTRODUCTION

In previous chapters we have, on a number of occasions, referred to GATT – the General Agreement on Tariffs and Trade. In this final chapter of our book on Europe and world trade we shall discuss GATT and the world trade system in more detail. We shall, first of all, cover the history, principles and operation of the GATT. Second, we shall consider the significance of the Uruguay Round (the most recent multilateral trade negotiations round conducted by GATT) – its background and objectives, the principal agreements reached, and its likely impact. In the third part we shall consider some unresolved and new problems (agriculture, competition rules, GATT for investment, regionalism, globalisation, the environment) of the world trading system – issues that the World Trade Organisation (WTO), which replaced GATT in 1995, is likely to put on the agenda of future multilateral trade negotiations. In the final part we shall, by way of conclusion, discuss the 'protectionism versus liberalisation' issue.

THE GATT

History

The General Agreement on Tariffs and Trade is a binding contract between the majority of governments in the world (involving at present

118 independent countries) with the objective to lay the basis for a secure international trade environment and to liberalise trade. The GATT forum was established in 1947 and originated in the 1944 Bretton Woods Conference which aimed at laying the foundations of the post-war economic system for the world. The principal outcome of the Bretton Woods meeting was the establishment of the International Monetary Fund (IMF), the World Bank (WB) and the International Bank for Reconstruction and Development (IBRD). Representatives of the forty-four nations who attended this international conference recognised that a smoothly functioning world economic system would, in addition to the creation of international financial institutions, also require a multilateral trade organisation. The Geneva round of trade negotiations aimed to formulate agreed rules and regulations for an international trade organisation (ITO). Although the UN negotiations conducted in Geneva and subsequently in Havana led to considerable progress in creating the broad framework for the planned ITO (the Havana Charter of 1948), the US government under President Eisenhower failed to obtain the support of Congress for the creation of the ITO. The ITO was never founded, and GATT must be seen as an 'interim' world trade body – a 'provisional' arrangement which, alas, functioned for nearly fifty years.

Although eleven of the original twenty-three contracting parties of the GATT were developing countries, GATT was for many years, if not decades, dominated by the Western industrialised countries. With the Third World countries and the Central and Eastern European countries now accounting for more than two thirds of the GATT membership, the power within GATT has somewhat shifted away from the OECD countries to the developing and transition economies. The formation of regional economic blocs via customs unions and free trade areas has meant that some countries act as a group in GATT meetings and negotiations (i.e. with a single spokesperson). The EU represents the largest, most cohesive and most influential grouping of countries with the European Commission representing the Union at GATT meetings.

Rules and regulations

The rules and regulations governing the GATT are contained in the text of the General Agreement (July 1986 version) – a 96-page document detailing GATT's 38 Articles. The GATT Articles cover four principal areas [Appendices A (GATT: the General Agreement in outline) and B (GATT: Rules of the Road for Trade) provide further details]:

- The general MFN treatment and schedules of concessions (Articles I–II).

- Contracting parties' obligations and rights such as anti-dumping and countervailing duties, marks (rules) of origin, quantitative restrictions, subsidies (Articles III–XXIII).
- Procedural aspects (Articles XXIV–XXXV).
- Developing countries' status (Articles XXXVI–XXXVIII plus annexes A–I).

Although all the 38 GATT Articles are important it could be argued that three key principles characterise GATT's overall operation:

- *Non-discrimination*
- *Reciprocity*
- *Transparency*

According to GATT there are two aspects to *non-discrimination*: most favoured nation treatment (Article I) and national treatment (Article III). The MFN clause means that

> any advantage, favour, privilege or immunity granted by any contracting party to any product originating in or destined for any other country shall be accorded immediately and unconditionally to the like product originating in or destined for the territories of all other contracting parties (Article I).

In other words, all importers (and exporters) should be able to expect the same barriers (customs duties and charges of any kind) as importers from the 'most favoured nation').

National treatment, in GATT terms, means:

> The products of the territory of any contracting party imported into the territory of any other contracting party shall not be subject, directly or indirectly, to internal taxes or internal charges of any kind in excess of those applied, directly or indirectly, to like domestic products (Article III, Section 2).

In other words, imported goods should, once they have crossed the border, be treated like domestically produced goods.

Reciprocity, although one of GATT's three main pillars, is not explicitly referred to in any of the articles of the text of the General Agreement; rather it appears to have established itself as a prominent operating procedure. Trading nations can, on the whole, only be expected to liberalise trade by reducing tariffs provided their trading partners reciprocate (i.e. are willing to offer compensating tariff reductions).

The GATT favours *transparency* in trade barriers and there are two dimensions to the transparency principle. First, GATT supports *tariffication* – replacing non-tariff barriers such as import quotas and other quantitative import restrictions with tariffs. Second, GATT likes to see *tariff binding* implemented; countries are expected to use 'bound' tariffs whereby countries, in setting tariff rates, undertake not to raise them.

Organisation and responsibilities

How is GATT organised and what kind of work does it undertake? In organisational terms the important GATT bodies are the annual sessions of contracting parties, the Council of Representatives (which meets about nine times a year and deals with routine and urgent issues such as reports of working parties), committees (which administer GATT agreements such as the MFA and the rounds of multilateral trade negotiations), working parties (which deal, *inter alia*, with current questions such as new GATT accessions), panels (which arrive at judgements in trade disputes) and the GATT secretariat whose main function is to provide administrative support (including economic intelligence/legal advice for all 'members' and technical cooperation for developing countries) to all GATT bodies and the multilateral trade negotiations rounds.

Although meetings of GATT bodies can resort to voting (decisions normally require a simple majority except for cases where departure from specific obligations of the general agreement is being sought when a two-thirds majority would be needed), consensus rather than votes tend to determine what kind of GATT decisions are being reached. This custom and practice, while democratic, may explain why GATT's powers have been somewhat limited. Although GATT aims at international trade being conducted within a framework of 'non-discrimination', 'reciprocity' and 'transparency', it is not really in a position to impose these principles on to GATT members. All GATT has been able to do is to endeavour that trading partners reach mutually acceptable solutions to any trade conflicts.

In functional terms GATT's principal areas of responsiblities are as follows:

- To sponsor major sets of multilateral trade negotiations with the objective of bringing about trade liberalisation. There have been eight rounds of trade negotiations so far (*Table 8.1*) from the Geneva round in 1947 (which lasted less than one year) to the Uruguay round (which began in 1986 and took seven years to complete).
- To settle trade disputes. Countries may call on GATT for the settlement of trade disputes via expert panels. Most trade disputes have been settled following processes of bilateral consultation and conciliation (i.e. never involved the GATT panel system).
- To monitor national trade policies. Since 1989 GATT has used the so-called 'trade policy review mechanism' whereby trade and trade-

related policies in individual countries or in the case of the EU in a group of countries are being comprehensively examined and evaluated. The objectives of these periodic reviews of the trade policies of all contracting parties are two-fold: first, to enhance the quality of public debate surrounding trade policy issues; second, 'to encourage GATT members to follow more closely the principles of the general agreement and to live up to their obligations' (GATT 1992b: 16–17). The EU, like the other three big world traders (the USA, Japan and Canada), has been reviewed twice since 1989 (GATT 1991; GATT 1993b). The trade policies of smaller trading nations are subject to less frequent reviews: every four years in the case of sixteen large trading entities (excluding the four big world traders); every six years in the case of other contracting parties except for least-developed countries for which longer periods may be chosen to review their trade policies.

- To provide assistance to Third World countries in all aspects of GATT activities including 'trade rounds' such as the recently completed Uruguay round negotiations. GATT offers trade policy training courses in this context; it also established the International Trade Centre in 1964 (since 1968 jointly operated by GATT and UNCTAD) to help developing countries' export promotion.

Table 8.1 GATT negotiating rounds

Round	Date	No. of countries participating
Geneva I	1947	23
Annecy	1949	33
Torquay	1950	34
Geneva II	1956	22
Dillon	1960–61	45
Kennedy	1962–67	48
Tokyo	1973–79	99
Uruguay	1986–93	118

GATT rounds

What were the aims of the various GATT rounds (excluding the Uruguay round which will be treated in the next section)? What did they achieve?

The objective of all the GATT rounds was to liberalise trade. The rounds were successful in that the series of trade negotiations resulted in the average tariff on manufactured goods being reduced. Tariffs were cut from over 40 per cent in 1947 to less than 10 per cent by the mid-1970s; by the early 1990s they were only about 5 per cent. In addition to negotiating tariff cuts, the GATT rounds responded to changed circumstances, and introduced novel procedures. The pre-Dillon rounds, for example, were characterised by product-by-product negotiations which, by the 1960s, proved to be increasingly difficult to conduct because of the by then larger number of GATT members. The *Dillon round* (1960–61) negotiators decided, therefore, to adopt a formula-based tariff reduction system with exception provisos whereby tariffs for a product would be lowered by a specific percentage unless an exemption from this tariff reduction could be justified. The formula-based linear tariff-cut system was first fully used during the *Kennedy round* (1962–67). The Kennedy round further liberalised world trade by increasing the share of trade affected by tariff cuts. But a number of trading nations and groups of countries such as the European Union obtained justifiable exemptions from tariff-cutting agreements and these exceptions led to bilateralism replacing multilateralism. The short- and then long-term agreement for textiles and clothing is a case in point. Its origin dates back to the Kennedy-round years, and resulted in Europe, for example, using quotas to curtail its imports of textiles and clothing from more efficient producers, notably in developing countries. Another novel feature of the Kennedy round was the introduction of agreed procedures for anti-dumping legislation. While the provisions made in the Kennedy round did not prove to be very significant, the fact that they were on the world trade agenda was indicative of changes in commercial policy taking place. Issues other than tariffs became significant. For the first time world trade negotiators also identified questions of agriculture and non-tariff barriers as relevant items for future world trade negotiations.

The *Tokyo round* (1973–79), like the Kennedy round, reduced tariffs on industrial goods imported to the industrialised world by about one third. Trade negotiations during this GATT round were characterised by attempts to arrive at formulating rules of commercial policy at world level. The negotiations were about commercial policy in general rather than merely aspects of tariffs; non-tariff barriers had begun to replace tariff barriers in the commercial policies pursued by GATT members. The Tokyo round of international trade negotiations made some progress towards tackling problems caused by the use of non-tariff barriers. Codes were introduced to cover some areas affected by non-tariff barriers. These included a code preventing governments from discriminating against external producers via appropriately devised product standards; a code requiring governments to offer domestic foreign firms equal chances in being awarded contracts (public procurement); a code prohibiting direct export subsidies; and a code permitting the use of countervailing duties to deal with unfair competition arising from, for example, dumping. Negotiators failed, however, to make informal safeguard actions like VERs subject to

Article XIX (which was designed to offer trading nations 'emergency protection' in cases of fair but unduly strong import competition). VERs which had grown in importance thus continued to be informal safeguard actions, normally negotiated bilaterally and outside the GATT – hence the term *grey area measures*.

The other important area which, while being of some concern to the Tokyo round negotiators, was largely left untouched by the agreements reached at the conclusion of the round was trade in agricultural produce. Agriculture continued to be a highly protected sector with the protection giving rise to trade frictions among industrialised countries and between the industrialised world, notably Europe, and developing countries.

THE URUGUAY ROUND

Background and objectives

Even by the time the Tokyo round had been completed, it was clear that the General Agreement needed to be extended and revised in order to incorporate key aspects of trade such as non-tariff barriers, bilateral quantitative restrictions, emergency protection and agriculture. A further round of multinational trade negotiations was called for. The new round had to be more ambitious in terms of issues covered, especially as there was a considerable amount of unfinished business from the Tokyo round.

A preparatory committee was established in November 1985 in order to draw up an agenda for the new GATT round. Its deliberations soon revealed the difficulties in trying to get agreements over the agenda for the new multilateral trade negotiations. It was far from clear at that stage whether, for example, agriculture, services, intellectual property rights and foreign investment would be included in the global package of negotiations. The European Communities, notably France, were very reluctant to see agricultural subsidies appear on the agenda of the new round. Arguments also arose over the extent to which the interests of the 'South' would be given special consideration if not priority. The Uruguay round was finally launched in September 1986 in Punta Del Este and it was agreed to define trade flows more broadly by including areas such as services, intellectual property rights, foreign investment and agriculture. The finally agreed agenda for the Uruguay round covered far more than these four dimensions of world trade. The actual agenda of the round was structured around a large number of issues. Negotiating groups were accordingly set up to arrive at agreements over concessions that would lead to trade creation in

Table 8.2 Uruguay round: targets

Liberalisation

- Sectoral Trade Flows
  - Agriculture
  - Textiles and clothing
  - Services
- Other Trade Flows
  - Intellectual property rights
  - Investment
- Measures
  - Industrial tariffs
  - Technical barriers
  - Origin rules

System improvements

- Rules
- Functioning of the GATT system
- Settlement of disputes

those areas contracting parties had identified as requiring trade liberalisation processes.

All the main world traders pursued very specific objectives. They were prepared to make concessions in some areas if they could make progress in others. The European Union, for example, was keen on seeing restrictions removed on intellectual property rights, foreign investment and services. The EU also favoured further tariff reductions; in return it appeared to be willing to reduce protectionism in sectors such as clothing and textiles and, to a lesser extent, agriculture. The Communities also seemed prepared to resort less to safeguard measures, countervailing duties and anti-dumping duties. *Table 8.2* lists the main areas targeted by GATT for liberalisation or improvement.

It was envisaged that the Uruguay round would be completed within four years (i.e. by 1990). In the event, it took a further three years, following GATT's continued failures to meet deadlines, before a deal was struck with GATT members agreeing to submit the package of results to their governments for approval. It is tempting to view the efficacy with which the Uruguay round negotiations were conducted over seven years with scepticism. The round, despite many sessions and negotiations, did not, until very late, appear to be yielding meaningful and tangible results (the 'General Agreement to Talk and Talk' became an alternative interpretation of the acronym GATT). Considering the very complex and extremely ambitious agenda which the contracting parties had set themselves, it is, with hindsight, perhaps not altogether surprising that the completion of the Uruguay round took so much longer than any of the previous GATT rounds.

Outcome

What were the achievements of the Uruguay round? The agreements reached at its conclusion on 15 December 1993 are contained in 'The Final Act Embodying the Results of the Uruguay Round of Multilateral Trade Negotiations' (GATT 1993d) – a document of over 450 pages. A detailed consideration of the legal texts covering the results of all the negotiations of the round between September 1986 and December 1993 is beyond the scope of this book. (For a summary of the Final Act see the Appendix C). Key features of the round were highlighted in the *Financial Times* (1993); for a comprehensive guide to the new GATT see, for example, Evans and Walsh (1994)). In describing what the GATT round achieved, we shall distinguish between two stages: innovations brought about before the GATT deal was concluded in 1993; and agreements reached in 1993 resulting in changes to the world trading system once all the governments of the contracting parties had approved the package of the GATT deal.

The first outcome of the Uruguay round talks was the introduction of the so-called *Trade Policy Review Mechanism* in April 1989. Trade policy reviews, it was decided, would be carried out on a regular basis for all contracting parties. The trade policy reviews were not meant to provide the basis for the enforcement of contracting parties' obligations under GATT. Nor were they to be used for the settlement of trade disputes or for the imposition of multilateral trade policy commitments. Rather, the process of reviewing contracting parties' trade policies and practises was to study the evolution of these policies and their impact on the world trading system. A second significant interim result of the Uruguay round was achieved three years later. In November 1992, the EU and the United States reached an agreement on agricultural trade at Blair House in Washington – the so-called *Blair House Accord*. Under this agreement the two trade blocs agreed to reduce both the quantity and value of subsidised exports of agricultural produce over a six-year period.

The principal results of the Uruguay round agreements due to be implemented after the completion of the negotiations and the ratification of the final Act are set out in (*Table 8.3*).

Impact

What will be the likely impact of the Uruguay round on the world economy and Europe? There are two ways of approaching this question. First, we could try to establish the direction of change likely to result from the Uruguay round agreements. Second, it is interesting to learn about the quantitative trade and income effects likely to be attributable to the rounds's trade liberalisation programme.

Table 8.3 Uruguay round: main results

Liberalisation

Agriculture
- Tariffication of non-tariff barriers.
- Reduction of
  Domestic farm support
  (Production and export) subsidies
  Import barriers.
- Gradual opening of Japan's and South Korea's rice markets.

Textiles and clothing
- Gradual incorporation of the MFA into the GATT over ten years (1995–2005) via:
  Dismantling of quotas
  Reduction of tariffs and other trade barriers.

Services [General Agreement on Trade in Services (GATS)]
- Introduction of basic fair trade principles such as non-discrimination.
- Abolition of limitations on market access (unless incompatible with regulations established by member countries' national schedules).
- Special (restrictive) provisions for air transport, labour movement, financial services and telecommunications.
- Further negotiations, especially on financial services.

Intellectual property rights [Agreement on Trade Related Aspects of Intellectual Property Rights (TRIPS), including trade in conterfeit goods]
- Introduction of measures to protect:
  Copyrights
  Patents
  Trademarks and geographical indications.
- Third World countries allowed more years to conform to agreement.

Investment [Agreement on trade-related investment measures (TRIMs)]
- No TRIMs (attempts by any government to make the operation of a foreign company within its borders conditional) to be used.
- Publication of specific TRIMs deemed to be inconsistent with Articles III (concerning national treatment) and XI (concerning quantitative restrictions on imports).

Public procurement
- Agreement restricted to 12 signatories (Austria, Canada, EU, Finland, Hong Kong, Israel, Japan, Norway, South Korea, Sweden, Switzerland, USA).
- Tokyo round agreement extended to open more areas – services, procurement by local/regional governments and public utilities – to international competition.
- Telecommunications and aircraft (temporarily?) excluded.

Industrial tariffs
- Increase in the share of trade of goods that is tariff-bound (tariffs are not allowed to increase).
- Increase in the share of trade at zero-bound tariffs.
- Cut of tariffs by industrialised countries by, on average, one third.

continued overleaf

Table 8.3 *continued*

Technical barriers

- Improved rules to reduce trade distortion resulting from restrictive technical regulations (technical norms, testing and certification producers) via harmonised international standards.
- Exchange of information on technical regulations between member countries to create more market transparency.

Origin rules

- Attempt to avoid trade obstacles by standardising rules of origin largely thwarted by specific exclusion or origin – rules used, for example, in the EU's preferential trade agreements.

GATT system

Anti-dumping and safeguard measures

- New rules for
  Determining 'dumping'
  Establishing 'injury to industry'
  Dumping investigations.
- Introduction of time limits on the use of anti-dumping duties.
- Phasing out of grey area measures such as VERs

Subsidies

- Agreement list of 'prohibited' subsidies including those favouring exports and discriminating against the use of imported goods in domestic production but excluding agriculture, aircraft, regional aid, research and development.
- Third World countries allowed to phase out export subsidies over a longer period of time than developed countries.

Settlement of disputes

- Removal of consensus voting.
- Introduction of stricter time limits for adoption and implementation of reports.
- Streamlining of procedure with provision for appeals and binding arbitration.
- Curtailment of unilateral decisions by members to seek trade remedies outside the GATT system such as, for example, America's Super 301 clause.

World Trade Organisation (change in name of the original Multilateral Trade Organisation).

- To be operative not later than 1995.
- Permanent world trade body covering in addition goods, services and intellectual property rights.
- Single institutional framework embracing the GATT, as modified by the (multilateral trade agreements embodied in the) Uruguay round and plurilateral trade agreements.
- Supposed to operate, like its predecessor, on the basis of consensus except for dispute settlements.

Sources: GATT (1993d, 1993e, 1994a); *Financial Times* (1993: 4–5); Evans and Walsh (1994)

In *qualitative terms* the impact of the main agreements reached in the Uruguay round would appear to be quite straightforward. The general (i.e. non-sector specific) agreements concerning industrial tariffs, technical barriers, origin rules, anti-dumping, safeguards, subsidies and dispute settlement should all boost world trade by reducing existing levels of trade distortions. The introduction of a General Agreement on Trade and Services (GATS) is bound to increase world trade flows in services. The new agreements on Trade-Related Investment Measures (TRIMs) and Trade-Related Aspects of Intellectual Property Rights (TRIPs) should lead to a boost in foreign investment and technology transfer between countries.

While the Uruguay round will result in trade liberalisation in all *sectors*, there are clearly differences in the extent of the liberalisation process envisaged. One sector that is particularly worth noting in this context is agriculture, which has enjoyed a disproportionately high degree of protectionism in developed countries, and especially in the EU. The agricultural policies pursued by OECD countries in general and the EU in particular have meant that domestic markets were both protected and characterised by artificially inflated prices and concomitant high levels of output. In predicting the consequences of the agricultural component of the Uruguay round it is important to separate domestic prices from world prices. It is also useful to distinguish between developed countries and Third World economies. Developing countries and the developed world differ. In Third World countries there has, unlike in the developed world, been much less bias in favour of agricultural production. Export subsidies by both the EU and the USA have depressed world prices of agricultural products in the past. The measures envisaged by the Blair House Deal would, once implemented, lead to a significant reduction in subsidised food exports. As a result, world prices of temperate goods – grain, meat, dairy, sugar – would rise, while the domestic prices of these goods in those developed economies that heavily subsidised their agricultural sectors (such as the EU, the EFTAns and the US) will be reduced. Increased world prices would benefit those trade blocs that have tended to be net exporters of temperate goods such as Europe, North and Latin America. Developing economies that depend to a large extent on the import of temperate goods will, on the other hand, be worse off because of the higher prices they would have to pay. Developing countries that export tropical goods (cocoa, coffee, tea) would lose out because liberalisation of agricultural trade, while enhancing the Third World's production and their export potential, would lower the world prices of tropical goods (for a more detailed discussion see, for example, Evans and Walsh 1994).

Most of the *empirical studies* on the impact of the Uruguay round have concentrated on a global assessment (i.e. the overall effects of this

GATT round). In but a few investigations attempts were also made to estimate how the gains from trade liberalisation will affect particular sectors (e.g. textiles and clothing, industrial products, and services). However, with the exception of the study prepared by the GATT secretariat (GATT 1994b), all the quantitative investigations available were based on hypothetical rather than the actually agreed trade liberalisation programmes (i.e. they were conducted before the Uruguay round was completed). Although the estimates arrived at in some studies carried out before December 1993 represent good approximations of the December 1993 Uruguay round agreements (see, for example, Nguyen 1993) or led to quantitatively very similar estimates (see, for example, World Bank/OECD 1993, and OECD 1993), we decided to single out the results obtained by the GATT study (1994b) for presentation. Focusing on the official GATT estimates of the results of the Uruguay round on world trade and income would seem appropriate because it is at present the only study based on the actually agreed trade liberalisation packages. The type of computable general equilibrium model from which the GATT estimates were derived is also more general in that, in contrast to previous studies, it yielded a range of estimates (reflecting alternative assumptions made about the world economy). The GATT study does not claim to produce an accurate forecast. Nor is it 'the kind of exercise that yields "correct" estimates' (GATT 1994b: 37). Rather, the purpose of the study was to produce a range of plausible estimates.

What are the estimated *trade effects* of the Uruguay round? The range of estimates produced by GATT (1994b) are summarised in *Table 8.4*. In estimating the increase in merchandise exports resulting from the implementation of the round's market access package (liberalisation of trade in goods via tariff reductions, phasing out of the MFA, and reductions in export and production subsidies for agriculture), the GATT study made three alternative assumptions about key features of the world economy. Under version 1 of the modelling exercise it was assumed that the world economy is characterised by perfect competition and by constant returns to scale (no economies of scale). This version of the model yielded the smallest estimates of annual increases in world merchandise exports for the year 2005: 9 per cent or US$ 244 billion (1992 values). Higher increases in world exports were estimated to arise under version 2 of the model when perfect competition was assumed plus external scale economies in selected sectors (mining, clothing, chemicals, steel, non-ferrous metals, fabricated metal products, transport equipment and other manufactures). By the year 2005, trade as measured by exports is, according to this model version, expected to increase by about ten per cent or US$ 273 billion (1992 values). Trade is projected to increase by nearly a quarter (US$ 668 billion in 1992 values) as from the year 2005 if it is

Table 8.4 Uruguay round – projected increase (change in volume in %) in merchandise exports in 2005 resulting from the implementation of the market access programme: main economies and country groups (excluding intra-EU trade)

	Versions of the model			
	Version 1	Version 2	Version 3	Actual value of exports in 1992 (bn US$)
World	8.6	9.6	23.5	2,843
EU	7.3	7.8	19.4	569
EFTA	3.2	3.3	6.3	227
United States	7.5	8.2	21.7	448
Japan	7.5	8.0	18.3	340
Developing and transition economies	13.7	15.3	36.7	906
Rest of the world				353

Notes:
Version 1 Assumes constant returns to scale (no economies of scale), and perfect competition.
Version 2 Assumes increasing returns to scale in industrial sectors, and perfect competition.
Version 3 Assumes increasing returns to scale and monopolistic competition in industrial sectors.

Source: GATT (1994b: 32)

assumed (version 3) that industries are characterised by monopolistic competition rather than perfect competition and there are scale economies that are internal to each firm (resulting from individual firms' output level rather than from industry's aggregate output level).

The European Union, according to the GATT study, is expected to increase its trade by 7 per cent (under model version 1), 8 per cent (under model version 2) and 20 per cent (under model version 3). Based on 1992 actual values of exports, this would amount to increases of European trade of US$ 42 billion, US$ 44 billion and US$ 110 billion respectively if we focus on EUR 12 (once we add the three EFTA countries that joined the EU in January 1995 the projected increases in the EU's trade attributable to the Uruguay round would of course be even higher).

Trade liberalisation does not only lead to increases in trade; additional gains from less restricted trade arise because the world income will be greater than it would have been under a more protectionist world trading system. Income gains amount to production gains; they may also be considered as welfare gains (see the discussion of the welfare effects of trade policy measures in Chapter 4). As the GATT study emphasises, income effects must be distinguished from trade effects when we consider the impact of trade liberalisation measures:

It is important to be clear that a $1 billion increase in exports is *not* equivalent to a $1 billion increase in income. To produce additional exports, resources must be used which could otherwise have been used to produce goods and services for domestic residents. If those resources would have produced $900 million in such domestic goods and services, the true net income gain is the $100 million difference between the value of those 'foregone' domestic goods and services and the $1 billion in goods and services that can be purchased in the world market with the additional foreign exchange earnings (GATT 1994b: 27).

Table 8.5 Uruguay round: estimated increase in annual income in 2005 due to implementation of the market access package, main economies and country groups, in bn of 1990 US$

	Versions of the model with static specifications			Versions of the model with dynamic specifications		
	Version			Version		
	1	2	3	1	2	3
World	109	146	315	184	218	510
EU	48	59	103	79	87	164
EFTA	10	13	23	18	18	34
United States	30	36	76	49	60	122
Developing and transition economies	–2	4	70	–1	3	116
Rest of the world	23	34	43	39	50	74

Notes:
Static specification: initial increase in income does not increase savings and investment.
Dynamic specification: initial increase in income assumed to increase savings and investment with the larger capital stock in turn causing a further increase in income.
Version 1, 2, 3: as in *Table 8.4*.

Source: GATT (1994b: 34)

The estimated increases in annual income as from 2005 resulting from the Uruguay round liberalisation of trade in goods are summarised in *Table 8.5*. As can be seen the GATT model produces six alternative estimates; in addition to making alternative assumptions about returns to scale and the degree of competition (model versions 1–3 as in the study of the trade effects), the estimates produced by GATT also vary depending on whether the projections are based on 'static' or 'dynamic' specifications of the underlying model. The model with static specifications assumes that the initial increase in income resulting from more liberalised trade will have no impact on savings and investment. The 'dynamic' model, on the other hand, takes into account secondary effects; the initial increase in income due to the trade liberalisation programme will lead to higher savings and investment, and the higher investment (larger capital stock) generated will bring about a further increase in income. If the impact of the initial increase in income is ignored (static specifications), annual income gains (measured in 1990 values) for the world are estimated to range from US$ 109 billion to US$ 315 billion. Once the 'dynamic' effects are introduced into the model (a fixed proportion of the initial income gain is assumed to be saved and to result in an enlarged capital stock) much higher income or welfare gains can be expected. The reduction of international trade barriers could generate annual increases in world income of up to US$ 510 billion by the time the Uruguay round's market access programme has been fully implemented in the year 2005.

Although all main economies and country groups are expected to see their incomes rise and thus experience welfare gains, the EU appears to reap the largest gains; its annual income is estimated to rise by up to US$ 164 billion – about a third of the projected maximum increase in world income of US$ 510 billion (model version 3 with dynamic specification) by the year 2005. In fact, with other versions of the model even higher shares of the estimated global income gains would accrue to the EU. Although a number of factors contribute to explaining the differences in income gains between countries and country groups, liberalisation of two broad sectors – agriculture and textiles/clothing – may be seen as the principal factors accounting for the EU's large income gains. Nguyen (1993) found this to be the case in an earlier study of the estimated benefits of the GATT deal for ten economies/groups of countries. Like the GATT study (1994b), Nguyen identified the EU as the top gainer from the Uruguay round liberalisation programme (Nguyen 1993: 1546).

Considering how protected agriculture has been in the EU, it is not difficult to see why trade liberalisation would result in considerable net welfare gains for the EU. The reductions in agricultural subsidies would lower the prices EU farmers will receive for their products. Lower EU agricultural outputs will increase world prices as the EU is a major world supplier. While imports into the EU are likely to increase, the overall net welfare gains for the EU will be positive. Consumers will pay less for agricultural produce because these will be subject to lower tariffs and fewer non-tariff barriers. Less subsidisation of the production and export of agricultural commodities also means that fewer government resources would have to be allocated to this sector. The European Communities (and the USA) can also be expected to reap significant welfare gains from freer trade flows in the textiles and clothing sectors, notably the dismantlement of the MFA. However, once we consider the prospects for the EU on a country-by-country basis, a different picture emerges: some EU countries (Portugal and perhaps Italy) may (like some former Eastern bloc economies and some developing countries) benefit as producers of textiles and clothing rather than consumers. Nguyen estimated that liberalising trade in agricultural produce and textiles and clothing would account for as much as three quarters of the Union's overall welfare gains (Nguyen 1993: 1546).

How realistic are the estimates of the effects of the Uruguay round deal? Three points are worth making in this context. First, as mentioned earlier, the results of any modelling exercise should not be interpreted as yielding 'accurate' estimates, let alone forecasts. The structure of the world economy in the year 2005 is likely to be fundamentally different from the world economy of 1990 that formed the basis for the GATT projections. The estimates are based on the assumption that unemployment rates remain constant; changing unemployment patterns will, therefore, also have an influence on the projected trade flows and income levels. Second, valid arguments could be advanced to suggest that GATT's estimates are too optimistic. Third, there are equally plausible reasons to believe that the projected trade and income effects of the Uruguay round programme are underestimates.

The official estimates are arguably overestimates for the following reasons. Governments may not fully introduce the agreed liberalisation programme; the new anti-dumping provisions to which the WTO is supposed to be able to resort may prove to be insufficient and possibly lead to an increase in disguised protectionism (growth of VERs; establishing dumping where none exists or exaggerating its importance, etc.); and the success of the Uruguay round may be impeded because of shifts towards regional rather than global agreements to increase market access.

The GATT projections could, on the other hand, also be seen as underestimating the magnitude of the trade and income effects of the Uruguay round. Why? First, the study concentrated on merchandise trade. It has excluded the service sector which accounted for as much as one fifth of total world trade even before liberalisation measures were agreed and is expected to gain increasing importance in international trade. Second, the GATT study of the effects on trade essentially focused on static rather than dynamic gains from trade liberalisation. A more competitive and less fragmented world economy is, in addition to generating static (comparative advantage based) gains, also likely to yield dynamic (innovation based) benefits. Third, the interaction between industrial trade, agricultural trade, trade in services, TRIMs and TRIPs is likely to result in creating trade and increasing world income. Fourth, gains may be derived from the establishment of the WTO provided it can and will operate within an improved set of rules and procedures for dealing and resolving trade disputes arising from trade distortions and restrictions.

OUTLOOK

The Uruguay round was more complex and comprehensive than any of the previous multilateral trade agreements reached by the GATT. Once the deal has been ratified by all the contracting parties and, provided all the agreed changes to the world trade system will take place, the Uruguay deal should contribute towards liberalising international trade. Both industrial trade (which featured on the agenda of all previous GATT rounds) and areas such as agriculture, services, trade related investment measures, and trade-related aspects of intellectual property rights and trade in counterfeit goods (which had not been on the agenda of previous GATT rounds) should exhibit freer trade. But multilateral trade rules, dispute settlement procedures and enforcement mechanisms must all be tightened up (especially once the WTO has become operational) if trade is to be liberalised.

Although the Uruguay round agreement achieved a lot to liberalise trade, a number of issues will have to be tackled to move towards a fairer and more transparent world trading system. It is this future agenda of multilateral trade negotiations which we want to consider now. The issues that the world trading system and big world traders like Europe, Japan and the USA will have to deal with and, if possible, solve fall into two categories: unresolved problems (issues carried forward from the Uruguay round negotiations) and new areas (topics that had previously not been part of the agenda or had been marginalised in previous GATT negotiations).

Unfinished business

Although the Uruguay round deal contained some agreements about financial services, shipping, telecommunications and other service businesses, the WTO will have to resume negotiations in these areas and bring them to conclusion. Another aspect of unfinished or ongoing business of the eighth GATT round is *agriculture*. The difficulties encountered in finding a solution to agricultural problems were one of the main reasons why the Uruguay round took so many years to arrive at an agreement. Although a solution to the EU–US conflict – the unfair competition resulting from export subsidies embedded in Europe's CAP – was eventually found through the so-called *McSharry Plan* (which lowers the minimum price EU farmers will receive and provides agricultural producers with compensation payments provided they withdraw a fraction of their land – up to 15 per cent – from agricultural use), the issue of subsidised agriculture is likely to continue to feature high on the agenda of world trade negotiations. For it is doubtful whether the McSharry Plan will go far enough to avoid surplus production and concomitant dumping of agricultural produce. This applies particularly to cereal which, as a result of future technical progress, may be characterised by increases in supply. The United States may, therefore, once again see EU-subsidised exports as unfair competition on the world food markets. Further changes to the EU's CAP may, in the circumstances, have to be negotiated in future multilateral trade negotiations.

Competition rules and workers' rights

Considering that the WTO aims to make the world trading system fairer, it would seem both desirable and necessary to enlarge its domain beyond the boundaries set by the Uruguay round. *Competition Rules* should arguably form part of a world trade system. There would appear to be two main aspects to the question of competition rules in international trade: competition policy and workers' rights. Competition (or anti-trust) law tends to cover areas such as acquisitions, cartels, mergers, restrictive practices, etc. With the exception of EU competition law which is applied across the EU states, competition laws are relevant for the domestic rather than the international sphere. Yet, in order to create a framework for fairer trade, competition law and international trade law should be more closely linked, if not integrated. To bring this about would, however, be a very ambitious task for the WTO, especially as the application of any worldwide competition laws would impinge on trading nations' sovereignty. Questions of labour standards and *workers' rights* are controversial trade issues. Countries who deny their workers basic rights and decent working and living conditions could be seen as competing unfairly (i.e. practicing *social dumping*). The threat of unfair competition could, therefore, justify the use of anti-dumping measures or trade sanctions. But there are likely to be problems in establishing what constitutes 'social dumping'. Workers' rights may be determined by a country's culture and it may be difficult, if not impossible, to arrive at 'internationally recognised' workers' rights; workers' rights may furthermore be confused with basic human rights. There is also the danger of a trading nation, faced by imports from a competitive third world country, using the promotion of workers' rights to make protectionism morally respectable. Perhaps workers' rights (and human rights in general) can be more adequately protected by bodies other than the WTO such as the International Labour Organisation: 'the relevant answer may well be to use trade policy to secure gains from trade and to use other policies for objectives such as human rights' (Bhagwati 1988: 122).

Investment

In coming to an agreement on trade related investment measures (TRIMs) within the December 1993 Uruguay round GATT, members recognised that trade flows can be restricted and distorted by investment measures. The final act, therefore, rules that members shall not apply any TRIMs that are inconsistent with the provisions of Article III (which requires 'national' treatment) and Article XI (which forbids quantitative restrictions). As Third World countries opposed more ambitious plans (put forward by developed countries and designed to force governments to permit the import of foreign capital), the agreement reached was restricted to requiring national treatment and forbidding certain restrictions on the operation of MNEs' subsidiaries (local-content requirements, for example), that is, trade-related investment measures rather than foreign direct investment flows. The agreement did, however, propose that further consideration should be given at a later stage to the agreement on TRIMs being complemented with provisions on investment per se. Such complementary provisions – a *GATT for investment* – are indeed called for considering the link that inevitably exists between foreign direct investment and merchandise trade flows.

A future GATT for investment would have to follow certain broad principles. First, there should be no restrictions to international investment flows in order to facilitate optimal use of capital at a global level. Second, once foreign investment has taken place, there should not be any conditions attached to any aspects of the way foreign investment is being handled. For any conditions such as requiring foreign investors to employ domestic senior managers or limiting the payment of dividends (repatriation of profits) has the same trade restricting and trade distorting effect as tariff or non-tariff barriers. Finally, the rules applying to foreign direct investment just like the rules governing the trade of goods (and services), should be transparent to all existing and potential overseas investors.

Regionalism

Although Article XXIV of GATT which provides rules and regulations for regional integration (via formation of customs unions and creation of free trade areas) was strengthened and clarified by the final act of the Uruguay round deal, the question of regionalism and multilateralism is bound to be the subject of further world trade discussions. In pre-Uruguay round days Article XXIV could, because of a number of ambiguities, be used to sanction customs unions and free trade areas (including interim arrangements) even though, while formally GATT consistent, they were at variance with GATT's basic idea of a liberalised world trading system. The principal ambiguity lies in the interpretation of Paragraph 8 of Article XXIV which stipulates that the establishment of both a customs union and a free trade area must mean that 'duties and other restrictive regulations of commerce . . . are eliminated with respect to *substantially all the trade* [our emphasis] between the constituent territories'.

The formation of the EU was made possible because of political desirability rather than compatibility with GATT's principles of multilateral free trade. When the common market was set up by the original six nations, it was far removed from a perfect customs union; it manifestly did not cover 'substantially all the trade' originating in the constituent countries of the Union. The original EU was also an imperfect union because GATT rules had to be ignored in order to accommodate Europe's ex-colonies that were granted preferential status. Since the start of the Uruguay round talks we have witnessed a trend towards more regionalism. Some 25 preferential trade agreements have been notified to GATT since 1986. Canada, Mexico and the United States formed NAFTA in 1994. A yen bloc (a trade bloc in the Asia–Pacific region) seems an increasingly possible development.

In order to avoid regionalism becoming a threat to a liberalised multilateral trade system, the WTO should make its approval of regional blocs dependent on two conditions. First, customs unions or free trade areas should not be too restrictive; they should consider potential newcomers' membership applications favourably, 'so that these arrangements more readily serve as building blocks of, rather than stumbling blocks to, GATT-wide free trade' (Bhagwati 1991: 77). Second, more attention should be paid to the trade creation versus trade diversion issue. Economic theory does not provide an unequivocal answer to this question. A customs union may create trade among its member countries by excluding inefficient suppliers in third countries. It may, on the other hand, divert trade by favouring supplies from inefficient member states by discriminating against producers from non-union countries. It all depends on the circumstances, and the WTO provides the appropriate forum for conducting investigations into the economic desirability of customs unions, free trade areas (and any related interim agreements). The aim behind regional integration should be to support the overall conception of a world trading system by serving the interests of all trading nations, not just the signatories of a regional economic integration agreement.

Globalisation

The political and economic changes in the former Eastern bloc have confronted GATT with the task of globalisation – integrating the successor states of the Soviet Union, the CEECs and China into the new international trade institution. China alone accounts now for one fifth of the world's population; it has also become a major world trader (eleventh in the ranking of leading exporters in world merchandise in 1992). A world trade organisation without large countries such as China and the Russian Federation (ranked twenty-fourth among the world's exporters) could not be seen as a global or universal institution. That said, it is clear that the WTO will have to address a number of issues before admitting any transition economy.

The first question must be to ascertain whether the conversion from a closed socialist and centrally planned economy to a market based trading nation has gone far enough to facilitate integration into a global trading system that is essentially market oriented. While it is generally conceded that the Soviet Union's successor states and the CEECs have by now been sufficiently transformed, the same cannot be said about China whose conversion from a centrally planned system of economic organisation has only been partial. The second question that will have to be considered in negotiating WTO membership of countries of the former Eastern Bloc is the extent to which these countries are willing and in a position to uphold the fundamental GATT principles of trade liberalisation – non-discrimination and reciprocity. Finally, there is the important question of how the former centrally planned economies should be classified – as developed or developing countries. The distinction matters because, as we saw earlier, the liberalisation measures that were agreed in the Uruguay round were more extensive for the group of developed countries than for the Third World. It is debatable whether China, for example, should be counted as a developing country. The Chinese, it appears, have had no problems in competing on the world markets. They have operated outside the GATT system and yet succeeded in rising to the position of eleventh largest world exporter by 1992; they have also managed trade surpluses with both the EU and the USA over the last few years.

Trade and the environment

The relationship between trade and the environment is arguably the most important issue that the WTO and major world traders like the EU will have to address. There would appear to be three principal dimensions to the interaction between international trade and the environment. First, environmental policy is likely to affect comparative advantages; second, we may have transfrontier pollution; and third, there is the danger of over-exploitation through trade.

Unless we assume that the environmental standards are exactly the same in countries trading with one another, *environmental regulation* in the form of, for example, pollution control, 'unfairly discriminates against domestic firms when they compete with firms in a country that has lower environmental standards' (Butler 1992: 9). Suppose we have industries in two countries, A and B, that produce the same product and generate the same level of pollution with the damage to the environment being contained within national boundaries. Now assume that the government authorities in country A impose a pollution tax, while no tax is being levied on the polluting industries in country B. Trade flows between the two countries will be distorted, depending on the initial situation (we assume that trade took place prior to country A introducing an emissions tax). Country A will either see its comparative advantage reduced, if not lost, or find its comparative disadvantage increased. In general, the differential impact pollution control costs have on cost and price levels in different industries and in different countries will affect the magnitudes of differences in comparative advantage between countries.

Transfrontier pollution differs from the impact of pollution control on comparative advantage. In the case of transfrontier pollution the environmental damage is not contained within boundaries. Here we have a situation whereby the pollution *per se* is being exported or imported. Well-known contemporary examples of the use of the environment leading to damage to the environment across frontiers are ozone depletion (caused mainly by chlorofluorocarbons), acid rain (caused by sulphur dioxide emissions) and global warming (supposedly caused by excessive emissions of carbon dioxide, nitrogen oxide and methane gas). But the idea of protecting the environment against harmful imports is far from novel. The USA, for instance, prohibited the import of certain insects that could harm agricultural crops or forests in 1906.

Over-exploitation of the world's nature preserves and resources is an issue that mainly arises out of trade between developing countries and the industrialised world. There are two principal dimensions to the North–South issue of the interaction between trade and the environment. One concerns the preservation of species diversity (*biodiversity*) in the world and the need to regulate trade in 'endangered' species, notably elephants or, more precisely, elephant products such as elephant hides and ivory. The other concerns the environmental impact of *deforestation* – the reduction in rain forests which are valued on environmental grounds because of the carbon absorption service they provide (they reduce carbon dioxide in the air) and because of the biological diversity they offer. Most of the rain forest countries are located in South America, although Asian countries – Thailand for example – have also been criticised for deforestation.

Although attempts by governments to protect the environment always had consequences for international trade, it is probably fair to say that it was not until the 1960s that the interaction between international trade and the environment featured in public policy debates at national levels and internationally. For many years the debate did not lead to the adoption of widespread trade-related environmental measures (*TREMs*), but some progress was made in 1973 when a large number of countries signed the Convention on International Trade in Endangered Species (*CITES*) with the objective of protecting endangered species in wild fauna and flora against over-exploitation through international trade.

CITES has, through the issue of export permits, largely succeeded in controlling trade in endangered species. The controlled trade has, however, not been entirely free of controversy. The debate surrounding the trade in elephant hides and ivory has, in part, been about the actual need for preservation. More importantly, it has centred around financial aspects. Developing countries may need the revenue raised by the sale of elephant products to fund future preservation of elephants. It is debatable, however, whether it should be the developing countries that carry the burden of protecting an endangered species like the elephant. Future multilateral trade negotiations will, it is hoped, deal with this aspect of the trade environment issue.

In dealing with purely domestic pollution the 'polluter pays' principle (which requires that the polluter be responsible for the cost of pollution-reducing measures) tends to be applied. But, following an international conference (OECD 1976) the 'mutual compensation' principle was proposed as a starting point for an *international policy on transborder pollution*. The 'mutual compensation principle' requires the polluting country to provide an estimate of the costs of pollution abatement for various levels of pollution, while the polluted country similarly provides an estimate of the cost of treating the damage (Butler 1992: 10). The estimates form the basis for an independent agency's decision on how much the polluting and polluted country can be expected to contribute to the cost of 'clean up' or pollution control. The mutual compensation principle has, to our knowledge, not been used so far. Yet, the practical problems caused by transborder pollution will have to be addressed by the WTO in future multilateral trade talks lest trade distortions resulting from physical transborder spillovers persist.

The impact of environmental policies on production costs is but one aspect of the 'level playing field' debate in international trade. Countries with high environmental standards suffer from an unfair cost disadvantage with respect to countries with low environmental standards leading to *ecological dumping*. In order to re-establish competitiveness one or more of the following measures should be introduced:

- that the countries with lower environmental standards harmonise up to the higher standards in the importing country;
- that the imports of foreign products considered to be produced in 'environmentally dirty ways' be subjected to special duties designed to offset the 'unfair cost advantage' from the less strict standards; or

- that the domestic industries be given subsidies to cover the added costs of meeting the higher standards. (GATT 1992c: 28).

Although Article XX of the GATT deals with the environment, it does not allow members to make access to their own markets dependent on the environmental policies or practices pursued by an exporting country. The next round of multilateral trade negotiations may, therefore, have to be concerned with the competitiveness issue arising from the differential imposition of environmental standards between trading nations. Rules dealing with 'ecological dumping' are long overdue; such rules would, however, have to be sufficiently clear to avoid abuse by protectionist interests.

Our outlook has, we hope, shown that the Uruguay round, while taking multilateral trade agreements much further than any previous GATT round, constitutes merely a milestone in the development of the world trade system. More important work remains to be done in moving towards liberalised multilateral trade: 'The round will therefore have to be judged as a process being set in motion not as a termination of the process' (Bhagwati 1990b: 168).

PROTECTIONISM VERSUS LIBERALISATION

EU trade relations have contributed towards both freer world trade and increased protectionism. EU trade policies have led to more liberalisation in world trade in that the EU has played a key role in reducing tariffs worldwide. The system of trade preferences that the EU has created and the Communities' increased use of non-tariff barriers have, at the same time, resulted in discriminatory trade practices and the adoption of 'managed trade' respectively.

The apparent paradox of increased liberalisation and more protectionism of European trade may reflect conflicting forces of trade policy formulation at work. Up to the 1980s, economists virtually agreed unanimously on the desirability of free trade on the grounds that it increased nations' welfare. Conventional trade theory argued that only very large countries were in a position to gain from protectionism by adopting 'optimal' tariffs. Free trade has also been the main aim of international organisations such as the GATT and the WTO. Governments, on the other hand, have always tended to lean more towards protectionism. The 1980s saw the development of the 'new trade theory' based on notions of increasing returns to scale and imperfect competition. Since then economists have acknowledged that trade may be due to two principal factors:

- Differences in factor endowments between countries leading to specialisation (the conventional trade theory based on the law of comparative advantages).
- The inherent advantages that specialisation *per se* generates (the new theory of trade based on increasing returns).

The new theory of trade thus appears to be strengthening the case of countries adopting free trade policies. But while the new trade theory can be used to lend support to the idea that trade is a 'good thing', it can also be used to justify 'strategic trade policies'; 'subsidies may tilt competition in favour of a high return domestic industry giving it a head start and a persistent advantage' (Krugman 1989: 4). The EU has, for example, tried to justify the imposition of anti-dumping duties on South Korean video recorders on the grounds that the import penetration of the European electronics market would adversely affect the European electronics industry's competitiveness in the future. Anti-dumping actions thus appear to have been used to promote a 'strategic trade policy' or industrial policy rather than to deal with unfair trading practises. The actual level of European 'managed trade' may be difficult to quantify, but the trend towards increased protectionism is clearly discernible.

What then are the prospects for European trade liberalisation? On the positive side, the outcome of the Uruguay round may help to re-establish the GATT's or the WTO's relevance to international trade in the 1990s by reducing the levels of trade distortion. Scepticism about trade policies becoming increasingly more pro-protectionist have also been dispelled by Bhagwati (1989) who has argued that exporters have, in fact, sound reasons to oppose trade barriers. First, because trade restrictions are likely to lead to retaliation in the foreign markets domestic producers may plan to export to. Second, any trade restriction is implicitly a 'tax on exports' because they increase the price of imported inputs. Third, multinational enterprises oppose trade barriers because intra-firm trade has been gaining in significance.

At the same time, there are a number of reasons why scepticism about a pro-trade bias in world trade reasserting itself is called for. First, none of the pillars of the world trading system (Japan, the USA and the EC) have shown any sign of taking the lead in reversing the trend towards more protectionism. Second, there has been no evidence of the main causes of the current distortion of world trade – VERs, the MFA, the CAP, non-tariff barriers, subsidies and preferential trade agreements – being abolished. Third, there is a danger of bilateralism rather than multilateralism dominating world trade in the 1990s because of the trend towards customs unions and free trade areas. A corollary of bilateral approaches to trade relations is market segmentation in international trade. The market fragmentation in world trade resulting from the single European market could, for example, lead to a 'fortress Europe'. There could also be a danger of world trade being increasingly managed by the big trade blocs – Europe, Japan and North America. International market fragmentation and concomitant distortion of the world trading system could furthermore result from what Bhagwati (1989) calls 'voluntary import expansion', whereby countries such as Japan and the Asian NICs commit themselves to importing agreed volumes of particular goods from trading partners such as the USA or the EU in order to reduce their trade surpluses with them. Replacing or supplementing VERs by voluntary import expansion may divert rather then create trade because the surplus countries may import from (politically) powerful trading partners rather than (economically) efficient countries.

GUIDE TO FURTHER READING

Andersen, K. and Blackhurst, R. (eds) (1992) *The Greening of World Trade Issues*, Hemel Hempstead, Harvester Wheatsheaf.

— (eds) (1993) *Regional Integration and the Global Trading System*, Hemel Hempstead, Harvester Wheatsheaf.

Bhagwati, J. (1990) Multilateralism at Risk: The GATT Is Dead. Long Live the GATT, *World Economy*, 13: 149–169.

— (1991) *The World Trading System at Risk*, Hemel Hempstead, Harvester Wheatsheaf.

Butler, A. (1992) Environmental Protection and Free Trade; Are They Mutually Exclusive? *Federal Reserve Bank of St. Louis, Review*. May–June: 2–16.

Evans, P. and Walsh, J. (1994) *The EIU Guide to the New GATT*, London, Economist Intelligence Unit.

GATT (1992) *GATT: What It Is – What It Does*, Geneva, GATT.

— (1992) 'Trade and the Environment', *International Trade 90–91*, I: 19–47.

— (1994) *The Results of the Uruguay Round of Multilateral Trade Negotiations. Market Access for Goods and Services: Overview of the Results*, Geneva, GATT.

Haus, L.A. (1992) *Globalising the GATT:* The Soviet Union's Successor States, Eastern Europe, and the International Trading System, Washington D.C., The Brookings Institution.

Jackson, J.H. (1990) *Restructuring the GATT*, London, Pinter.

Lang, T. and Hines, C. (1993) *The New Protectionism: Protecting the Future against Free Trade*, London, Earthscan.

OECD (1993) *Assessing the Effects of the Uruguay Round*, Paris, OECD.

Swanson, T.M. (1994) *The International Regulation of Extinction*, London and Basingstoke, Macmillan.

APPENDIX A

GATT: THE GENERAL AGREEMENT IN OUTLINE

[From GATT (1992) *GATT: What It Is, What It Does*, Geneva, GATT, pp. 19–21; reproduced with permission of the Information Division, GATT, Geneva].

The General Agreement has 38 Articles. They are briefly described below.

Part One

Article I is the key article guaranteeing most-favoured-nation treatment among all members.

Article II provides for the actual tariff reductions agreed to under GATT. They are listed in annexed Schedules and thus consolidated (i.e. form part of the Agreement itself).

Part Two

The General Agreement is applied 'provisionally'. Each member is required to apply the rules in Part Two 'to the fullest extent not inconsistent with' its own legislation existing when it joined GATT.

Article III prohibits internal taxes and other internal measures that discriminate against imports.

Articles IV (cinematograph films), **V** (freedom of transit), **VI** (anti-dumping and countervailing duties, **VII** (customs valuation), **VIII** (fees and formalities), **IX** (marks of origin), and **X** (publication and administration of trade regulations) are the 'technical articles' designed to prevent or control possible substitutes for tariffs.

Articles XI to **XIV** deal with quantitative restrictions: **XI** is the general prohibition of them; **XII** specifies how they may be used for balance-of-payments reasons; **XIII** requires that they be used without discrimination, apart from exceptions specified in **XIV** (see also Article XVIII).

Article XV concerns GATT's cooperation with the International Monetary Fund.

Article XVI calls for the elimination of export subsidies.

Article XVII requires state trading enterprises not to discriminate in their foreign trade.

Article XVIII recognises that developing countries may need tariff flexibility, and to be able to apply some quantitative restrictions to conserve foreign exchange and for development needs.

Article XIX prescribes when emergency action can be taken against import injuring domestic producers.

Article XX and **XXI** specify, respectively, general and security exceptions to the Agreement (e.g. to protect public health).

Article XXII deals with consultations, and **XXIII** with the settlement of disputes.

Part Three

Article XXIV regulates how customs unions and free trade areas may constitute exceptions to the most- favoured-nation rule.

Article XXV provides for action by the member governments. It is under this Article that waivers are granted.

Articles XXVI to **XXXV** are rules about the operation of GATT itself. They deal with its acceptance and entry into force (**XXVI**); withdrawal of tariff concessions from former members (**XXVII**); rules for tariff negotiations and changes in tariff schedules (**XXVIII**); the relationship between GATT and the stillborn Havana Charter (**XXIX**); amendment of the Agreement (**XXX**); withdrawal from GATT (**XXXI**); the definition of 'contracting parties' (members) (**XXXII**); accession to GATT (**XXXIII**); the annexes to the Agreement (**XXXIV**); and nonapplication of the GATT rules between particular members (**XXXV**).

Part Four

Articles XXXVI, XXXVII and **XXXVIII**, added in 1965, concern the special needs of the developing countries. **Article XXXVI** sets out GATT's principles and objectives in meeting these needs. **Article XXXVII** states commitments which members undertake to this end, and **Article XXXVIII** provides for joint action by them.

APPENDIX B

GATT: RULES OF THE ROAD FOR TRADE

[From GATT (1992) *GATT: What It Is, What It Does*, Geneva, GATT, pp. 6–11; reproduced with permission of the Information Division, GATT, Geneva].

The body of rules which together make up the multilateral trading system known as the GATT has three elements. First and foremost is the General Agreement itself and its 38 Articles. Added at later stages, particularly at the end of the Tokyo round, are associated agreements covering anti-dumping and subsidy rules and other non-tariff or sectoral issues. Although membership of these agreements is much more limited than for the General Agreement – ranging from less than twenty to about forty – the members nevertheless account for the majority of world trade in the relevant areas. Finally, the GATT system is completed by the Multi-Fibre Arrangement which is a negotiated exception to the normal disciplines of the General Agreement affecting the textiles and clothing sector.

Underlying the often complex Articles of the General Agreement are a number of simple principles.

Trade without discrimination

The first principle embodied in the famous 'most-favoured-nation' clause is that trade must be conducted on the basis of non-discrimination. All contracting parties are bound to grant to each other treatment as favourable as they give to any country in the application and administration of import and export duties and charges. Thus, no country is to give special trading advantages to another or to discriminate against it: all are on an equal basis and all share the benefits of any moves towards lower trade barriers. Most-favoured-nation treatment has been the vehicle which has ensured that developing countries and others with little economic leverage have been able to benefit freely and without question from the best trading condition negotiated by, and among, the strongest economic powers. Exceptions to this basic rule are allowed only in certain special circumstances. (See

'Regional trading arrangements', 'Special conditions for developing countries', pages 183–4).

A further article relating to non-discrimination requires that once goods have entered a market, they be treated no less favourably than equivalent domestically produced goods. This is referred to as 'national treatment'.

Protection through tariffs

GATT does not prohibit protection for domestic industries. However, a second basic principle is that where such protection is given, it should be extended essentially through the customs tariff, and not through other commercial measures. Among other things, the aim of this rule is to make the extent of protection clear and to minimize the trade distortion caused. (See page 184 'Quantitative restrictions on imports').

A stable basis for trade

A stable and predictable basis for trade is provided partly by the 'binding' of the tariff levels negotiated among the contracting parties. These bound items are listed, for each country, in tariff schedules which form an integral part of the General Agreement. Although provision is made for the renegotiation of bound tariffs, a return to higher tariffs is discouraged by the requirement that any increases be compensated for.

Promoting fair competition

Since it permits tariffs and other protection, in certain circumstances, the GATT is clearly not the 'free-trade organisation' it is sometimes described as. It is more concerned with open, fair and undistorted competition. Much of the GATT's work focuses on subsidies and dumping, for instance. The rules under which governments may respond to dumping in their domestic market by overseas competitors are contained in the GATT 'Anti-dumping Code'. Similarly, where export and domestic subsidies are alleged they can be challenged in the GATT. At the same time, GATT rules place disciplines on the use of 'countervailing' duties which can be imposed to negate the effects of a subsidy. Other distortions of international competition are being considered in the Uruguay round.

Quantitative restrictions on imports

A general prohibition of quantitative restrictions is a basic provision of GATT, which was established at a time when they were widespread and were perhaps the greatest single obstacle to international trade.

Quantitative restrictions are now less widespread in developed countries; nevertheless they affect trade in agricultural goods, textiles, steel and certain other products, many of which are of export interest to developing countries.

The main exception to the general GATT rules against quantitative restrictions allows their use in balance-of-payments difficulties (Article XII). Even then, restrictions must not be applied beyond the extent necessary to protect the balance of payments and must be progressively reduced and eliminated as soon as they are no longer required. This exception is broadened, for developing countries, by the recognition (Article XVIII) that they may impose quantitative restrictions to prevent an excessive drain on their foreign exchange reserves caused by the demand for imports generated by development, or because they are establishing or extending domestic production. Regular consultations in GATT are held with countries that introduce, maintain or intensify import restrictions for balance-of-payments reasons.

Where quantitative restrictions are permitted, they should be applied without discrimination (Article XIII).

The 'waiver' and possible emergency action

There are 'waiver' procedures (Article XXV) whereby a country may, when its economic or trade circumstances so warrant, seek a derogation from particular GATT obligations. Among others, the United States has a waiver relating to the implementation of certain agricultural policies which would otherwise be contrary to GATT.

It is also recognized that, on occasion, governments feel that they have no choice but to offer domestic industries temporary protection from imports. The 'safeguards' rule of GATT (Article XIX) permits such action in carefully defined circumstances. A contracting party may impose import restrictions or suspend tariff concessions on products which are being imported in increased quantities and which cause, or are likely to cause, serious injury to competing domestic producers.

In recent years, many GATT members have become concerned at the resort by some governments to discriminatory bilateral arrangements – often called 'voluntary' export restraints – which have avoided the disciplines of Article XIX. As a consequence, the question of safeguards forms an important negotiating issue in the Uruguay round.

Regional trading arrangements

Regional trading arrangements, in which a group of countries agree to abolish or reduce barriers against imports from one another, have been established in many parts of the world. The General Agreement recognises, in **Article XXIV**. The value of closer integration of national economies through freer trade. It therefore permits such **groupings**, as an exception to the general rule of most-favoured-nation treatment, provided that certain strict criteria are met. The rules are intended to ensure that the arrangements facilitate trade among the countries concerned, without raising barriers to trade with the outside world. In this way, regional integration should complement the multilateral trading system and not threaten it.

Regional trade groupings under Article XXIV may take the form of a customs union or a free-trade area. In both cases, duties and other barriers to substantially all trade between countries in the group are required to be removed. In a free-trade area, each member maintains its own external trade policy, including its tariff, towards non-members. A customs union adopts a unified customs tariff towards non-members. In either case, duties or other regulations affecting trade of members of the group with non-members are required to be no more restrictive than those which were applied before the group was set up.

Special conditions for developing countries

About two thirds of GATT's member countries are in the early stages of economic development and there is a constant stream of developing countries seeking accession. As a consequence, in 1965, a new chapter – Part IV – was added to the General Agreement. Three new Articles encouraged industrial countries to assist developing nations 'as a matter of conscious and purposeful effort'. Part IV recognised the need of developing countries to enjoy more favourable conditions of access to world markets for their products and for developed countries to refrain from introducing new barriers to exports of primary and other exports of special interest to less-developed nations. Industrial countries also accepted that they would not expect reciprocity for commitments they made in negotiations to reduce or remove tariff and other barriers to the trade of developing countries.

At the end of the Tokyo round in 1979 a decision was taken on differential and more favourable treatment, reciprocity and fuller participation of developing countries. The decision recognised developing countries as a permanent legal feature of the world trading system. This 'enabling clause' includes provision of a permanent legal basis for the extension of the generalised system of preferences (GSP) by developed countries to developing countries. It also permits special trade treatment for the least-developed countries.

Making an exception for textiles and clothing

Since 1974, much of world trade in textiles and clothing has been regulated by the Multi-Fibre Arrangement (MFA). Negotiated as an exception to normal GATT disciplines, the MFA has provided the basis on which industrial countries have established quotas on imports of textiles and clothing from more competitive developing countries. The Arrangement has been extended four times, most recently in July 1991 for a period of seventeen months. Some 41 countries or territories participated in the MFA (counting the EC as a single participant) prior to this extension.

In principle, the Arrangement is intended to reconcile the interests of importing and exporting countries by permitting the expansion and liberalisation of trade while avoiding disruption of markets. The safeguard provisions of the Arrangement may be invoked by participants if their domestic market is disrupted or threatened with disruption as a result of imports. Any restrictions introduced in this manner must permit exports from an affected supplying country to expand in an orderly and equitable manner. Most safeguard measures under the Arrangement have taken the form of bilateral agreements.

One major objective of the Uruguay round is to secure the eventual integration of the textiles and clothing sector into the post-Uruguay round GATT, thereby ending its status as an exceptional case.

APPENDIX C

THE FINAL ACT OF THE URUGUAY ROUND: A SUMMARY

[From: GATT (1993) GATT: The Final Act of the Uruguay Round: a Summary, *GATT Focus* 104: 5–15; reproduced with permission of the Information Division, GATT, Geneva].

The Final Act Embodying the Results of the Uruguay Round of Multilateral Trade Negotiations is 550 pages long and contains legal texts which spell out the results of the negotiations since the round was launched in Punta del Este, Uruguay, in September 1986. In addition to the texts of the agreements, the Final Act also contains texts of Ministerial Decisions and Declarations which further clarify certain provisions of some of the agreements.

The following summarizes all the components of the Final Act. These summaries are intended to provide an informal guide to the agreements and have no legal status.

The Final Act covers all the negotiating areas cited in the Punta del Este Declaration with two important exceptions. The first is the results of the 'market access negotiations' in which individual countries have made binding commitments to reduce or eliminate specific tariffs and non-tariff barriers to merchandise trade. These concessions are to be recorded in national schedules which will form an integral part of the Final Act. The second is the 'initial commitments' on liberalization of trade in services. These commitments on liberalization are also to be recorded in national schedules.

Agreement Establishing the World Trade Organization

The Agreement Establishing the World Trade Organization (WTO) envisages a single institutional framework encompassing the GATT, as modified by the Uruguay round, all agreements and arrangements concluded under its auspices and the complete results of the Uruguay round. Its structure will be headed by a Ministerial conference meeting at least once every two years. A General Council will be established to oversee the operation of the agreement and ministerial decisions on a regular basis. This General Council will itself act as a Dispute Settlement Body and a Trade Policy Review Mechanism, which will concern themselves with the full range of trade issues covered by the WTO, and will also establish subsidiary bodies such as a Goods Council, a Services Council and a TRIPs Council. The WTO framework will ensure a 'single undertaking approach' to the results of the Uruguay round – thus, membership in the WTO will entail accepting all the results of the round without exception.

General Agreement on Tariffs and Trade 1994

Texts on the interpretation of the following GATT Articles are included in the Final Act.

Understanding on the Interpretation of Article II: 1(b) (Schedules of Concessions). Agreement to record in national schedules 'other duties or charges' levied in addition to the recorded tariff and to bind them at the levels prevailing at the date established in the Uruguay Round Protocol.

Understanding on the Interpretation of Article XVII (State-trading Enterprises). Agreement increasing surveillance of their activities through stronger notification and review procedures.

Understanding on the Interpretation of Balance-of-Payments Provisions. Agreement that contracting parties imposing restrictions for balance-of-payments purposes should do so in the least trade-disruptive manner and should favour price-based measures, like import surcharges and import deposits, rather than quantitative restrictions. Agreement also on procedures for consultations by the GATT Balance-of-Payments Committee as well as for notification of BOP measures.

Understanding on the Interpretation of Article XXIV (Customs Unions and Free-Trade Areas). Agreement clarifying and reinforcing the criteria and procedures for the review of new or enlarged customs unions or free-trade areas and for the evaluation of their effects on third parties. The Agreement also clarifies the procedure to be followed for achieving any necessary compensatory adjustment in the event of contracting parties forming a customs union seeking to increase a bound tariff. The obligations of contracting parties in regard to measures taken by regional or local governments or authorities within their territories are also clarified.

Understanding on the Interpretation of Article XXV (Waivers). Agreement of new procedures for the granting of waivers from GATT disciplines, to specify termination dates for any waivers to be granted in the future, and to fix expiry dates for existing waivers. The main provisions concerning the granting of waivers are, however, contained in the Agreement on the WTO.

Understanding on the Interpretation of Article XXVIII (Modification of GATT Schedules). Agreement on new procedures for the negotiation of compensation when tariff bindings are modified or withdrawn, including the creation of a new negotiating right for the country for which the product in question accounts for the highest proportion of its exports. This is intended to increase the ability of smaller and developing countries to participate in negotiations.

Understanding on the Interpretation of Article XXXV (Non-application of the General Agreement). Agreement to allow a contracting party or a newly acceding country to invoke GATT's non-application provisions *vis-à-vis* the other party after having entered into tariff negotiations with each other. The WTO Agreement foresees that any invocation of the non-application provisions under that Agreement must extend to all the multilateral agreements.

Uruguay Round Protocol GATT 1994

The results of the market access negotiations in which participants have made commitments to eliminate or reduce tariff rates and non-tariff measures applicable to trade in goods will be recorded in national schedules of concessions which will be annexed to the Uruguay Round Protocol that forms an integral part of the Final Act.

The Protocol has five appendices: Appendix I, Section A: Agricultural Products – tariff concessions on a most-favoured nation basis; Section B: Agricultural Products – tariff quotas. Appendix II: Tariff Concessions on a Most-Favoured Nation Basis on Other Products. Appendix III: Preferential Tariff – Part II of Schedules (if applicable). Appendix IV: Concessions on Non-Tariff Measures – Part III of Schedules. Appendix V: Agriculture Products: Commitments Limiting Subsidization Part IV of Schedules (Section I: Domestic Support: Total AMS Commitments; Section II: Export Subsidies: Budgetary Outlay and Quantity Reduction Commitments; Section III: Commitments Limiting the Scope of Export Subsidies).

The schedule annexed to the Protocol relating to a member shall become a schedule to the GATT 1994 relating to that member on the day on which the Agreement Establishing the WTO enters into force for that member.

For non-agricultural products the tariff reduction agreed upon by each member shall be implemented in five equal rate reductions, except as may be otherwise specified in a member's schedule. The first such reduction shall be made effective on the date of entry into force of the

Agreement Establishing the WTO. Each successive reduction shall be made effective on 1 January of each of the following years, and the final rate shall become effective no later than the date four years after the date of entry into force of the Agreement Establishing the WTO. However, participants may implement reduction in fewer stages or at earlier dates than those indicated in the Protocol, if they so wish.

For agricultural products, as defined in Article 2 of the Agreement on Agriculture, the staging of reductions shall be implemented as specified in the relevant parts of the schedules. Details are given in the section of this Appendix concerning the Agricultural Agreement.

A related Decision on Measures in Favour of Least-Developed Countries establishes, among other things, that these countries will not be required to undertake any commitments and concessions which are inconsistent with their individual development, financial and trade needs. Alongside other more specific provisions for flexible and favourable treatment, it also allows for the completion of their schedules of concessions and commitments in Market Access and in Services by April 1995 rather than 15 December 1993.

Agreement on Agriculture

The negotiations have resulted in four main portions of the Agreement; the Agreement on Agriculture itself; the concessions and commitments members are to undertake on market access, domestic support and export subsidies; the Agreement on Sanitary and Phytosanitary Measures; and the Ministerial Decision concerning Least-Developed and Net Food-Importing Developing countries.

Overall, the results of the negotiations provide a framework for the long-term reform of agricultural trade and domestic policies over the years to come. It makes a decisive move towards the objective of increased market orientation in agricultural trade. The rules governing agricultural trade are strengthened which will lead to improved predictability and stability for importing and exporting countries alike.

The agricultural package also addresses many other issues of vital economic and political importance to many members. These include provisions that encourage the use of less trade-distorting domestic support policies to maintain the rural economy, that allow actions to be taken to ease any adjustment burden, and also the introduction of tightly prescribed provisions that allow some flexibility in the implementation of commitments. Specific concerns of developing countries have been addressed including the concerns of net food-importing countries and least-developed countries.

The agricultural package provides for commitments in the area of market access, domestic support and export competition. The text of the Agricultural Agreement is mirrored in the GATT Schedules of legal commitments relating to individual countries (as noted in the section of this Appendix that describes the Uruguay Round Protocol).

In the area of **market access**, non-tariff border measures are replaced by tariffs that provide substantially the same level of protection. Tariffs resulting from this 'tariffication' process, as well as other tariffs on agricultural products, are to be reduced by an average 36 per cent in the case of developed countries and 24 per cent in the case of developing countries, with minimum reductions for each tariff line being required. Reductions are to be undertaken over six years in the case of developed countries and over ten years in the case of developing countries. Least-developed countries are not required to reduce their tariffs.

The tariffication package also provides for the maintenance of current access opportunities and the establishment of minimum access tariff quotas (at reduced tariff rates) where current access is less than 3 per cent of domestic consumption. These minimum access tariff quotas are to be expanded to 5 per cent over the implementation period. In the case of 'tariffied' products 'special safeguard' provisions will allow additional duties to be applied in case shipments at prices denominated in domestic currencies below a certain reference level or in case of a surge of imports. The trigger in the safeguard for import surges depends on the 'import penetration' currently existing in the market, i.e. where imports currently make up a large proportion of consumption, the import surge required to trigger the special safeguard action is lower.

In order to facilitate the implementation of tariffication in particularly sensitive situations, a 'special treatment' clause was introduced into the Agreement on Agriculture. The special treatment allows a country, under certain carefully and strictly defined conditions, to maintain import restrictions up to the end of the implementation period. The conditions are: (i) that imports of the primary agricultural product, and its worked and/or prepared products, the so-called designated products, were less than 3 per cent of domestic consumption during the period 1986–88; (ii) no export subsidies have been provided for these products since 1986; (iii) effective production restricting measures are applied to the primary agricultural product; and (iv) minimum access opportunities are provided. The minimum access opportunities increase annually to reach 8 per cent in the sixth year. However, the final figure is lower if the designated products are tariffied before the end of the implementation period. For example, if the designated products are tariffied at the beginning of the third year of the implementation period the final minimum access opportunities are 6.4 per cent of domestic consumption of the designated products. Negotiations among trading partners on the possibility and terms of any continuation of special treatment beyond the implementation period must be completed by the end of the sixth year following the entry into force of the Agreement on Agriculture. In case of any continuation beyond the sixth year, additional commitments have to be taken.

A separate section in this context reflects the special and differential treatment applied to developing countries which is an integral element of all commitments taken in the Uruguay round, including in all areas of the Agreement on Agriculture. The provisions apply to a primary agricultural product that is the predominant staple in the traditional diet of the developing country which invokes this clause of the agreement.

Domestic support measures that have, at most, a minimal impact on trade ('green box' policies) are excluded from reduction commitments. Such policies include general government services, for example in the areas of research, disease control, infrastructure and food security. It also includes direct payments to producers, for example certain forms of 'decoupled' (from production) income support, structural adjustment assistance, direct payments under environmental programmes and under regional assistance programmes.

In addition to the green box policies, other policies need not be included in the Total Aggregate Measurement of Support (Total AMS) reduction commitments. These policies are direct payments under production-limiting programmes, certain government assistance measures to encourage agricultural and rural development in developing countries and other support which makes up only a low proportion (5 per cent in the case of developed countries and 10 per cent in the case of developing countries) of the value of production of individual products or, in the case of non-product-specific support, the value of total agricultural production.

The Total AMS covers all support provided on either a product-specific or non-product-specific basis that does not qualify for exemption and is to be reduced by 20 per cent (13.3 per cent for developing countries with no reduction for least-developed countries) during the implementation period.

Members are required to reduce the value of mainly direct **export subsidies** to a level 36 per cent below the 1986–90 base period level over the six-year implementation period, and the quantity of subsidised exports by 21 per cent over the same period. In the case of developing countries, the reductions are two-thirds those of developed countries over a ten-year period (with no reductions applying to the least-developed countries) and, subject to certain conditions, there are no commitments on subsidies to reduce the costs of marketing exports of agricultural products or internal transport and freight charges on export shipments. Where subsidised exports have increased since the 1986–90 base period, 1991–92 may be used, in certain circumstances, as the beginning point of reductions although the endpoint remains that based on the 1986–90 base period level. The Agreement on Agriculture provides for some limited flexibility between years in terms of export subsidy reduction commitments and contains provisions aimed at preventing the circumvention of the export subsidy commitments and sets out criteria for food aid donations and the use of export credits.

'Peace' provisions within the Agreement include: an understanding that certain actions available under the subsidies agree with commitments; an understanding that 'due restraint' will be used in the application of countervailing duty rights under the General Agreement; and setting out limits in terms of the applicability of nullification or impairment actions. These peace provisions will apply for a period of 9 years.

The Agreement sets up a committee that will monitor the implementation of commitments, and also monitor the follow up to the Decision on Measures Concerning the Possible Negative Effects of the Reform Programme on Least-Developed and Net Food-Importing Developing Countries.

The package is conceived as part of a continuing process with the long-term objective of securing substantial progressive reductions in support and protection. In this light, it calls for further negotiations in the fifth year of implementation which, along with an assessment of the first five years, would take into account non-trade concerns, special and differential treatment for developing countries, the objective to establish a fair and market-oriented agricultural trading system and other concerns and objectives noted in the preamble to the Agreement.

Agreement on Sanitary and Phytosanitary Measures

This Agreement concerns the application of sanitary and phytosanitary measures – in other words food safety and animal and plant health regulations. The Agreement recognises that governments have the right to take sanitary and phytosanitary measures but that they should be applied only to the extent necessary to protect human, animal or plant life or health and should not arbitrarily or unjustifiably discriminate between members where identical or similar conditions prevail.

In order to harmonise sanitary and phytosanitary measures on as wide a basis as possible, members are encouraged to base their measures on international standards, guidelines and recommendations where they exist. However, members may maintain or introduce measures which result in higher standards if there is scientific justification or as a consequence of consistent risk decisions based on an appropriate risk assessment. The Agreement spells out procedures and criteria for the assessment of risk and the determination of appropriate levels of sanitary or phytosanitary protection.

It is expected that members would accept the sanitary and phytosanitary measures of others as equivalent if the exporting country demonstrates to the importing country that its measures achieve the importing country's appropriate level of health protection. The Agreement includes provisions on control, inspection and approval procedures.

The Agreement also contains requirements on transparency, including the publication of regulations, the establishment of national enquiry points and notification procedures. It would establish a Committee on Sanitary and Phytosanitary Measures which, among other things, would provide a forum for consultations, discuss matters with potential trade impacts, maintain contact with other relevant organisations and monitor the process of international harmonisation.

The Decision on Measures Concerning the Possible Negative Effects of the Reform Programme on Least-Developed and Net Food-Importing Developing Countries

It is recognised that during the reform programme least-developed and net food-importing developing countries may experience negative effects with respect to supplies of food imports on reasonable terms and conditions. Therefore, a special decision sets out objectives with regard to the provision of food aid, the provision of basic foodstuffs in full grant form and aid for agricultural development. It also refers to the possibility of assistance from the International Monetary Fund and the World Bank with respect to the short-term financing of commercial food imports. The Committee of Agriculture, set up under the Agreement on Agriculture, will monitor the follow-up to the Decision.

Agreement on Textiles and Clothing

The object of this negotiation has been to secure the eventual integration of the textiles and clothing sector – where much of the trade is currently subject to bilateral quotas negotiated under the Multi-fibre Arrangement (MFA) – into the GATT on the basis of strengthened GATT rules and disciplines.

Integration of the sector into the GATT would take place as follows (on the assumption that the WTO enters into effect on I January 1995): first, on 1 January 1995; each party would integrate into the GATT products from the specific list in the Agreement which accounted for not less than 16 per cent of its total volume of imports in 1990. Integration means that trade in these products will be governed by the general rules of GATT.

At the beginning of Phase 2, on 1 January 1998, products which accounted for not less than 17 per cent of 1990 imports would be integrated. On 1 January 2002, products which accounted for not less than 18 per cent of 1990 imports would be integrated. All remaining products would be integrated at the end of the transition period on 1 January 2005. At each of the first three stages, products should be chosen from each of the following categories: tops and yarns, fabrics, made-up textile products, and clothing.

All MFA restrictions in place on 31 December 1994 would be carried over into the new Agreement and maintained until such time as the restrictions are removed or the products integrated into GATT. For products remaining under restraint, at whatever stage, the Agreement lays down a formula for increasing the existing growth rates. Thus, during Stage 1, and for each restriction previously under MFA bilateral agreements in force for 1994, annual growth should be not less than 16 per cent higher than the growth rate established for the previous MFA restriction. For Stage 2 (1998 to 2001 inclusive), annual growth rates should be 25 per cent higher than the Stage 1 rates. For Stage 3 (2002 to 2004 inclusive), annual growth rates should be 27 per cent higher than the Stage 2 rates.

While the Agreement focuses largely on the phasing-out of MFA restrictions, it also recognises that some members maintain non-MFA restrictions not justified under a GATT provision. These would also be brought into conformity with GATT within one year of the entry into force of the Agreement or phased out progressively during a period not exceeding the duration of the Agreement (that is by 2005).

It also contains a specific transitional safeguard mechanism which could be applied to products not yet integrated into the GATT at any stage. Action under the safeguard mechanism could be taken against individual exporting countries if it were demonstrated by the importing country that overall imports of a product were entering the country in such increased quantities as to cause serious damage – or to threaten it – to the relevant domestic industry, and that there was a sharp and substantial increase of imports from the individual country concerned. Action under the safeguard mechanism could be taken either by mutual agreement, following consultations, or unilaterally but subject to review by the Textiles Monitoring Body. If taken, the level of restraints should be fixed at a level not lower than the actual level of exports or imports from the country concerned during the twelve-month period ending two months before the month in which a request for consultation was made. Safeguard restraints could remain in place for up to three years without extension or until the product is removed from the scope of the Agreement (that is, integrated into the GATT), whichever comes first.

The Agreement includes provisions to cope with possible circumvention of commitments through transshipment, re-routing, false declaration concerning country or place of origin and falsification of official documents.

The Agreement also stipulates that, as part of the integration process, all members shall take such actions in the area of textiles and clothing as may be necessary to abide by GATT rules and disciplines so as to improve market access, ensure the application of policies relating to fair and equitable trading conditions, and avoid discrimination against imports when taking measures for general trade policy reasons.

In the context of a major review of the operation of the Agreement to be conducted by the Council for Trade in Goods before the end of each stage of the integration process, the Council for Trade in Goods shall by consensus take such decisions as it deems appropriate to ensure that the balance of rights and obligations in this Agreement is not upset. Moreover, the Dispute Settlement Body may authorise adjustments to the annual growth of quotas for the stage subsequent to the review with respect to members it has found not to be complying with their obligations under this Agreement.

A Textiles Monitoring Body (TMB) would be established to oversee the implementation of commitments and to prepare reports for the major reviews mentioned above. The Agreement also has provisions for special treatment to certain categories of countries – for example, those which have not been MFA members since 1986, new entrants, small suppliers, and least-developed countries.

Agreement on Technical Barriers to Trade

This Agreement will extend and clarify the Agreement on Technical Barriers to Trade reached in the Tokyo Round. It seeks to ensure that technical negotiations and standards, as well as testing and certification procedures, do not create unnecessary obstacles to trade. However, it recognises that countries have the right to establish protection, at levels they consider appropriate, for example for human, animal or plant life or health or the environment, and should not be prevented from taking measures necessary to ensure those levels of protection are met. The Agreement therefore encourages countries to use international standards where these are appropriate, but it does not require them to change their levels of protection as a result of standardisation.

Innovative features of the revised Agreement are that it covers processing and production methods related to the characteristics of the product itself. The coverage of conformity assessment procedures is enlarged and the disciplines made more precise. Notification provisions applying to local government and non-governmental bodies are elaborated in more detail than in the Tokyo Round Agreement. A Code of Good Practice for the Preparation, Adoption and Application of Standards by standardising bodies, which is open to acceptance by private sector bodies as well as the public sector, is included as an annex to the Agreement.

Agreement on Trade-Related Investment Measures

The agreement recognises that certain investment measures restrict and distort trade. It provides that no contracting party shall apply any TRIM inconsistent with Articles III (national treatment) and XI (prohibition of quantitative restrictions) of the GATT. To this end, an illustrative list of TRIMs agreed to be inconsistent with these articles is appended to the Agreement. The list includes measures which require particular levels of local procurement by an enterprise ('local content requirements') or which restrict the volume or value of imports such an enterprise can purchase or use to an amount related to the level of products it exports ('trade balancing requirements').

The Agreement requires mandatory notification of all non-conforming TRIMs and their elimination within two years for developed countries, within five years for developing countries and within seven years for least-developed countries. It establishes a Committee on TRIMs which will, among other things, monitor the implementation of these commitments. The Agreement also provides for consideration, at a later date, of whether it should be complemented with provisions on investment and competition policy more broadly.

Agreement on Implementation of Article VI (Anti-Dumping)

Article VI of the GATT provides for the right of contracting parties to apply anti-dumping measures, that is measures against imports of a product at an export price below its 'normal value' (usually the price of the product in the domestic market of the exporting country) if such dumped imports cause injury to a domestic industry in the territory of the importing contracting party. More detailed rules governing the application of such measures are currently provided in an Anti-Dumping Agreement concluded at the end of the Tokyo round. Negotiations in the Uruguay round have resulted in a revision of this Agreement which addresses many areas in which the current Agreement lacks precision and detail.

In particular, the revised Agreement provides for greater clarity and more detailed rules in relation to the method of determining that a product is dumped, the criteria to be taken into account in a determination that dumped imports cause injury to a domestic industry, the procedures to be followed in initiating and conducting anti-dumping investigations, and the implementation and duration of anti-dumping measures. In addition, the new Agreement clarifies the role of dispute settlement panels in disputes relating to anti-dumping actions taken by domestic authorities.

On the methodology for determining that a product is exported at a dumped price, the new Agreement adds relatively specific provisions on such issues as criteria for allocating costs when the export price is compared with a 'constructed' normal value and rules to ensure that a fair comparison is made between the export price and the normal value of a product so as not to create arbitrarily or inflate margins of dumping.

The Agreement strengthens the requirement for the importing country to establish a clear causal relationship between dumped imports and injury to the domestic industry. The examination of the dumped imports on the industry concerned must include an evaluation of all relevant economic factors bearing on the state of the industry concerned. The Agreement confirms the existing interpretation of the term 'domestic industry'. Subject to a few exceptions, 'domestic industry' refers to the domestic producers as a whole of the like products or to those of them whose collective output of the products constitutes a major proportion of the total domestic production of those products.

Clear-cut procedures have been established on how anti-dumping cases are to be initiated and how such investigations are to be conducted. Conditions for ensuring that all interested parties are given an opportunity to present evidence are set out. Provisions on the application of provisional measures, the use of price undertakings in anti-dumping cases, and on the duration of anti-dumping measures have been strengthened. Thus, a significant improvement over the existing Agreement consists of the addition of a new provision under which anti-dumping measures shall expire five years after the date of imposition, unless a determination is made that, in the event of termination of the measures, dumping and injury would be likely to continue or recur.

A new provision requires the immediate termination of an anti-dumping investigation in cases where the authorities determine that the margin of dumping is *de minimis* (which is defined as less than 2 per cent, expressed as a percentage of the export price of the product) or that the volume of dumped imports is negligible (generally when the volume of dumped imports from an individual country accounts for less than 3 per cent of the imports of the product in question into the importing country).

The Agreement calls for prompt and detailed notification of all preliminary or final anti-dumping actions to a Committee on Anti-

Dumping Practices. The Agreement will afford parties the opportunity of consulting on any matter relating to the operation of the Agreement or the furtherance of its objectives, and to request the establishment of panels to examine disputes.

Agreement on Implementation of Article VII (Customs Valuation)

The Decision on Customs Valuation would give customs administrations the right to request further information of importers where they have reason to doubt the accuracy of the declared value of imported goods. If the administration maintains a reasonable doubt, despite any additional information, it may be deemed that the customs value of the imported goods cannot be determined on the basis of the declared value, and customs would need to establish the value taking into account the provisions of the Agreement. In addition, two accompanying texts further clarify certain of the Agreement's provisions relevant to developing countries and relating to minimum values and importations by sole agents, sole distributors and sole concessionaires.

Agreement on Preshipment Inspection

Preshipment inspection (PSI) is the practice of employing specialised private companies to check shipment details – essentially price, quantity, quality – of goods ordered overseas. Used by governments of developing countries, the purpose is to safeguard national financial interests (prevention of capital flight and commercial fraud as well as customs duty evasion, for instance) and to compensate for inadequacies in administrative infrastructures.

The Agreement recognises that GATT principles and obligations apply to the activities of preshipment inspection agencies mandated by governments. The obligations placed on PSI-user governments include non-discrimination, transparency, protection of confidential business information, avoidance of unreasonable delay, the use of specific guidelines for conducting price verification and the avoidance of conflicts of interest by the PSI agencies.

The obligations of exporting members towards PSI users include non-discrimination in the application of domestic laws and regulations, prompt publication of such laws and regulations and the provision of technical assistance where requested.

The Agreement establishes an independent review procedure – administered jointly by an organisation representing PSI agencies and an organisation representing exporters – to resolve disputes between an exporter and a PSI agency.

Agreement on Rules of Origin

The Agreement aims at long-term harmonisation of rules of origin, other than rules of origin relating to the granting of tariff preferences, and to ensure that such rules do not themselves create unnecessary obstacles to trade.

The Agreement sets up a harmonisation programme, to be initiated as soon as possible after the completion of the Uruguay round and to be completed within three years of initiation. It would be based upon a set of principles, including making rules of origin objective, understandable and predictable. The work would be conducted by a Committee on Rules of Origin in the GATT and a technical committee under the auspices of the Customs Cooperation Council in Brussels.

Until the completion of the harmonisation programme, contracting parties would be expected to ensure that their rules of origin are transparent; that they do not have restricting, distorting or disruptive effects on international trade; that they are administered in a consistent, uniform, impartial and reasonable manner, and that they are based on a positive standard (in other words, they should state what *does* confer origin rather than what does not).

An annex to the Agreement sets out a 'common declaration' with respect to the operation of rules of origin on goods which qualify for preferential treatment.

Agreement on Import Licensing Procedures

The revised Agreement strengthens the disciplines on the users of import licensing systems – which, in any event, are much less widely used now than in the past – and increases transparency and predictability. For example, the Agreement requires parties to publish sufficient information for traders to know the basis on which licences are granted. It contains strengthened rules for the notification of the institution of import licensing procedures or changes therein. It also offers guidance on the assessment of applications.

With respect to automatic licensing procedures, the revised Agreement sets out criteria under which they are assumed not to have trade restrictive effects. With respect to non-automatic licensing procedures, their administrative burden for importers and exporters should be limited to what is absolutely necessary to administer the measures to which they apply. The revised Agreement also sets a maximum of 60 days for applications to be considered.

Agreement on Subsidies and Countervailing Measures

The Agreement on Subsidies and Countervailing Measures is intended to build on the Agreement on Interpretation and Application of Articles VI, XVI and XXIII which was negotiated in the Tokyo round.

Unlike its predecessor, the agreement contains a definition of subsidy and introduces the concept of a 'specific' subsidy – for the most part, a subsidy available only to an enterprise or industry or group of enterprises or industries within the jurisdiction of the authority granting the subsidy. Only specific subsidies would be subject to the disciplines set out in the Agreement.

The Agreement establishes three categories of subsidies. First, it deems the following subsidies to be 'prohibited': those contingent, in law or in fact, whether solely or as one of several other conditions, upon export performance; and those contingent, whether solely or as one of several other conditions, upon the use of domestic over imported goods. Prohibited subsidies are subject to new dispute settlement procedures. The main features include an expedited timetable for action by the Dispute Settlement body, and if it is found that the subsidy is indeed prohibited, it must be immediately withdrawn. If this is not done within the specified time period, the complaining member is authorised to take countermeasures.

The second category is 'actionable' subsidies. The Agreement stipulates that no member should cause, through the use of subsidies, adverse effects to the interests of other signatories, that is injury to domestic industry of another signatory, nullification or impairment of benefits accruing directly or indirectly to other signatories under the General Agreement (in particular the benefits of bound tariff concessions), and serious prejudice to the interests of another member. 'Serious prejudice' shall be presumed to exist for certain subsidies including when the total *ad valorem* subsidisation of a product exceeds 5 per cent. In such a situation, the burden of proof is on the subsidising member to show that the subsidies in question do not cause serious prejudice to the complaining member. Members affected by actionable subsidies may refer the matter to the Dispute Settlement body. In the event that it is determined that such adverse effects exist, the subsidising member must withdraw the subsidy or remove the adverse effects.

The third category involves non-actionable subsidies, which could either be non-specific subsidies, or specific subsidies involving assistance to industrial research and pre-competitive development activity, assistance to disadvantaged regions, or certain type of assistance for adapting existing facilities to new environmental requirements imposed by law and/or regulations. Where another member believes that an otherwise non-actionable subsidy is resulting in serious adverse effects to a domestic industry, it may seek a determination and recommendation on the matter.

One part of the Agreement concerns the use of countervailing measures on subsidised imported goods. It sets out disciplines on the initiation of countervailing cases, investigations by national authorities and rules of evidence to ensure that all interested parties can present information and argument. Certain disciplines on the calculation of the amount of a subsidy are outlined as is the basis for the determination of injury to the domestic industry. The Agreement would require that all relevant economic factors be taken into account in assessing the state of the industry and that a causal link be established between the subsidised imports and the alleged injury. Countervailing investigations shall be terminated immediately in cases where the amount of a subsidy is *de minimis* (the subsidy is less than 1 per cent *ad valorem)* or where the volume of subsidised imports, actual or potential, or the injury is negligible. Except under exceptional circumstances, investigations shall be concluded within one year after their initiation and in no case more than eighteen months. All countervailing duties have to be terminated within five years of their imposition unless the authorities determine on the basis of a review that the expiry of the duty would be likely to lead to continuation or recurrence of subsidisation and injury.

The Agreement recognises that subsidies may play an important role in economic development programmes of developing countries, and in the transformation of centrally-planned economies to market economies. Least-developed countries and developing countries that have less than $1,000 per capita GNP are thus exempted from disciplines on prohibited export subsidies, and have a time-bound exemption from other prohibited subsidies. For other developing countries, the export subsidy prohibition would take effect 8 years after the entry into force of the Agreement establishing the WTO, and they have a time-bound (though fewer years than for poorer developing countries) exemption from the other prohibited subsidies. Countervailing investigation of a product originating from a developing country member would be terminated if the overall level of subsidies does not exceed 2 per cent (and from certain developing countries 3 per cent) of the value of the product, or if the volume of the subsidised imports represents less than 4 per cent of the total imports for the like product in the importing signatory. For countries in the process of transformation from a centrally-planned into a market economy, prohibited subsidies shall be phased out within a period of seven years from the date of entry into force of the Agreement.

In anticipation of the negotiation of special rules in the **civil aircraft** sector under the Subsidies Agreement, civil aircraft sector, civil aircraft products are not subject to the presumption that *ad valorem* subsidisation in excess of 5 per cent causes serious prejudice to the interests of other members. In addition, the Agreement provides that where repayment of financing in the civil aircraft sector is dependent on the level of sales of a product and sales fall below expectations, this does not in itself give rise to such presumption of serious prejudice.

Agreement on Safeguards

Article XIX of the General Agreement allows a member to take a 'safeguard' action to protect a specific domestic industry from an unforeseen increase of imports of any product which is causing, or which is likely to cause, serious injury to the industry.

The Agreement breaks major ground in establishing a prohibition against so-called 'grey area' measures, and in setting a 'sunset clause' on all safeguard actions. The Agreement stipulates that a member shall not seek, take or maintain any voluntary export restraints, orderly marketing arrangements or any other similar measures on the export or the import side. Any such measure in effect at the time of entry into force of the Agreement would be brought into conformity with this Agreement, or would have to be phased out within four years after the entry into force of the Agreement establishing the WTO. An exception could be made for one specific measure for each importing member, subject to mutual agreement with the directly concerned member, where the phase-out date would be 31 December 1999.

All existing safeguard measures taken under Article XIX of the General Agreement 1947 shall be terminated not later than eight years after the date on which they were first applied or five years after the date of entry into force of the Agreement establishing the WTO, whichever comes later.

The Agreement sets out requirements for safeguard investigation which include public notice for hearings and other appropriate means for interested parties to present evidence, including on whether a measure would be in the public interest. In the event of critical circumstances, a provisional safeguard measure may be imposed based upon a preliminary determination of serious injury. The duration of such a provisional measure would not exceed 200 days.

The Agreement sets out the criteria for 'serious injury' and the factors which must be considered in determining the impact of imports. The safeguard measure should be applied only to the extent necessary to prevent or remedy serious injury and to facilitate adjustment. Where quantitative restrictions are imposed, they normally should not reduce the quantities of imports below the annual average for the last three representative years for which statistics are available, unless clear justification is given that a different level is necessary to prevent or remedy serious injury.

In principle, safeguard measures have to be applied irrespective of source. In cases in which a quota is allocated among supplying countries, the member applying restrictions may seek agreement with other members having a substantial interest in supplying the product concerned. Normally, allocation of shares would be on the basis of proportion of total quantity or value of the imported product over a previous representative period. However, it would be possible for the importing country to depart from this approach if it could demonstrate, in consultations under the auspices of the Safeguards Committee, that imports from certain contracting parties had increased disproportionately in relation to the total increase and that such a departure would be justified and equitable to all suppliers. The duration of the safeguard measure in this case cannot exceed four years.

The Agreement lays down time limits for all safeguard measures. Generally, the duration of a measure should not exceed four years although this could be extended up to a maximum of eight years, subject to confirmation of continued necessity by the competent national authorities and if there is evidence that the industry is adjusting. Any measure imposed for a period greater than one year should be progressively liberalised during its lifetime. No safeguard measure could be applied again to a product that had been subject to such action for a period equal to the duration of the previous measure, subject to a non-application period of at least two years. A safeguard measure with a duration of 180 days or less may be applied again to the import of a product if at least one year had elapsed since the date of introduction of the measure on that product, and if such a measure had not been applied on the same product more than twice in the five-year period immediately preceding the date of introduction of the measure.

The Agreement envisages consultations on compensation for safeguard measures. Where consultations are not successful, the affected members may withdraw equivalent concessions or other obligations under GATT 1994. However, such action is not allowed for the first three years of the safeguard measure if it conforms to the provisions of the Agreement, and is taken as a result of an absolute increase in imports.

Safeguard measures would not be applicable to a product from a developing country member, if the share of the developing country member in the imports of the product concerned does not exceed 3 per cent, and that developing country members with less than 3 per cent import share collectively account for no more than 9 per cent of total imports of the product concerned. A developing country member has the right to extend the period of application of a safeguard measure for a period of up to two years beyond the normal maximum. It can also apply a safeguard measure again to a product that had been subject to such an action after a period equal to half of the duration of the previous measure, subject to a non-application period of at least two years.

The Agreement would establish a Safeguards Committee which would oversee the operation of its provisions and, in particular, be responsible for surveillance of its commitments.

General Agreement on Trade in Services (GATS)

The Services Agreement which forms part of the Final Act rests on three pillars. The first is a framework agreement containing basic obligations which apply to all member countries. The second concerns national schedules of commitments containing specific further national commitments which will be the subject of a continuing process of liberalisation. The third is a number of annexes addressing the special situations of individual services sectors.

Part I of the basic agreement defines its scope – specifically, services supplied from the territory of one party to the territory of another; services supplied in the territory of one party to the consumers of any other (for example, tourism); services provided through the presence of service providing entities of one party in the territory of any other (for example, banking); and services provided by nationals of one party in the territory of any other (for example, construction projects or consultancies).

Part II sets out general obligations and disciplines. A basic most-favoured-nation (MFN) obligation states that each party 'shall accord immediately and unconditionally to services and service providers of any other Party, treatment no less favourable than that it accords to like services and service providers of any other country'. However, it is recognised that MFN treatment may not be possible for every service activity and, therefore, it is envisaged that parties may indicate specific MFN exemptions. Conditions for such exemptions are included as an annex and provide for reviews after five years and a normal limitation of ten years on their duration.

Transparency requirements include publication of all relevant laws and regulations. Provisions to facilitate the increased participation of developing countries in world services trade envisage negotiated commitments on access to technology, improvements in access to distribution channels and information networks and the liberalisation of market access in sectors and modes of supply of export interest. The provisions covering economic integration are analogous to those in Article XXIV of GATT, requiring arrangements to have 'substantial sectoral coverage' and to 'provide for the absence or elimination of substantially all discrimination' between the parties.

Since domestic regulations, not border measures, provide the most significant influence on services trade, provisions spell out that all such measures of general application should be administered in a reasonable, objective and impartial manner. There would be a requirement that parties establish the means for prompt reviews of administrative decisions relating to the supply of services.

The Agreement contains obligations with respect to recognition requirements (educational background, for instance) for the purpose of securing authorisations, licenses or certification in the services area. It encourages recognition requirements achieved through harmonisation and internationally agreed criteria. Further provisions state that parties are required to ensure that monopolies and exclusive service providers do not abuse their positions. Restrictive business practices should be subject to consultations between parties with a view to their elimination.

While parties are normally obliged not to restrict international transfers and payments for current transactions relating to commitments under the Agreement, there are provisions allowing limited restrictions in the event of balance-of-payments difficulties. However, where such restrictions are imposed they would be subject to conditions, including that they are non-discriminatory, that they avoid unnecessary commercial damage to other parties and that they are of a temporary nature.

The Agreement contains both general exceptions and security exceptions provisions which are similar to Articles XX and XXI of the GATT. It also envisages negotiations to the develop disciplines on trade-distorting subsidies in the services area.

Part III contains provisions on market access and national treatment which would not be general obligations but would be commitments made in national schedules. Thus, in the case of market access, each party 'shall accord services and service providers of other Parties treatment no less favourable than that provided for under the terms, limitations and conditions agreed and specified in its schedule'. The intention of the market access provision is progressively to eliminate the following types of measures: limitations on numbers of service providers, on the total value of service transactions or on the total number of service operations or people employed. Equally, restrictions on the kind of legal entity or joint venture through which a service is provided or any foreign capital limitations relating to maximum levels of foreign participation are to be progressively eliminated.

The national treatment provision contains the obligation to treat foreign service suppliers and domestic service suppliers in the same manner. However, it does provide the possibility of different treatment being accorded the service providers of other parties to that accorded to domestic service providers. However, in such cases the conditions of competition should not, as a result, be modified in favour of the domestic service providers.

Part IV of the Agreement establishes the basis for progressive liberalisation in the services area through successive rounds of negotiations and the development of national schedules. It also permits, after a period of three years, parties to withdraw or modify commitments made in their schedules. Where commitments are modified or withdrawn, negotiations should be undertaken with interested parties to agree on compensatory adjustments. Where agreement cannot be reached, compensation would be decided by arbitration.

Part V of the Agreement contains institutional provisions, including consultation and dispute settlement and the establishment of a Council on Services. The responsibilities of the Council are set out in a Ministerial decision.

The first of the annexes to the Agreement concerns the movement of labour. It permits parties to negotiate specific commitments applying to the movement of people providing services under the Agreement. It requires that people covered by a specific commitment shall be allowed to provide the service in accordance with the terms of the commitment. Nevertheless, the Agreement would not apply to measures affecting employment, citizenship, residence or employment on a permanent basis.

The annex on financial services (largely banking and insurance) lays down the right of parties, notwithstanding other provisions, to take prudential measures, including for the protection of investors, deposit holders and policy holders, and to ensure the integrity and stability of the financial system. However, a further understanding on financial services would allow those participants who choose to do so to undertake commitments on financial services through a different method. With respect to market access, the understanding contains more detailed obligations on, among other things, monopoly rights, cross-border trade (certain insurance and reinsurance policy writing as well as financial data processing and transfer), the right to establish or expand a commercial presence, and the temporary entry of personnel. The provisions on national treatment refer explicitly to access to payments and clearing systems operated by public entities and to official funding and refinancing facilities. They also relate to membership of, or participation in, self-regulatory bodies, securities or futures exchanges and clearing agencies.

The annex on telecommunications relates to measures which affect access to and use of public telecommunications services and networks. In particular, it requires that such access be accorded to another party, on reasonable and non-discriminatory terms, to permit the supply of a service included in its schedule. Conditions attached to the use of public networks should be no more than is necessary to safeguard the public service responsibilities of their operators, to protect the technical integrity of the network and to ensure that foreign service suppliers do not supply services unless permitted to do so through a specific commitment. The annex also encourages technical cooperation to assist developing countries in the strengthening of their own domestic telecommunications sectors.

The annex on air-transport services excludes from the Agreement's coverage traffic rights and directly related activities which might affect the negotiation of traffic rights. Nevertheless, the annex, in its current form, also states that the Agreement should apply to aircraft repair and maintenance services, the marketing of air-transport services and computer reservation services. The operation of the annex would be reviewed at least every five years.

In the final days of the services negotiations, three Decisions were taken – on Financial Services, Professional Services and the Movement of Natural Persons. The Decision on Financial Services confirmed that commitments in this sector would be implemented on an MFN basis, and permits members to revise and finalise their schedules of commitments and their MFN exemptions six months after the entry into force of the Agreement. Contrary to some media reports, the audio-visual and maritime sectors have not been removed from the scope of the GATS.

Agreement on Trade-Related Aspects of Intellectual Property Rights, Including Trade in Counterfeit Goods

The Agreement recognises that widely varying standards in the protection and enforcement of intellectual property rights and the lack of a multilateral framework of principles, rules and disciplines dealing with international trade in counterfeit goods have been a growing source of tension in international economic relations. Rules and disciplines were needed to cope with these tensions. To that end, the Agreement addresses the applicability of basic GATT principles and those of relevant international intellectual property agreements; the provision of adequate intellectual property rights; the provision of effective enforcement measures for those rights; multilateral dispute settlement; and transitional arrangements.

Part I of the Agreement sets out general provisions and basic principles, notably a national treatment commitment under which the nationals of other parties must be given treatment no less favourable than that accorded to a party's own nationals with regard to the protection of intellectual property. It also contains a most-favoured-nation clause, a novelty in an international intellectual property agreement, under which any advantage a party gives to the nationals of another country must be extended immediately and unconditionally to the nationals of all other parties, even if such treatment is more favourable than that which it gives to its own nationals.

Part II addresses each intellectual property right in succession. With respect to copyright, parties are required to comply with the substantive provisions of the Berne Convention for the protection of literary and artistic works, in its latest version (Paris 1971), though they will not be obliged to protect moral rights as stipulated in Article 6bis of that Convention. It ensures that computer programs will be protected as literary works under the Berne Convention and lays down on what basis databases should be protected by copyright. Important additions to existing international rules in the area of copyright and related rights are the provisions on rental rights. The draft requires authors of computer programmes and producers of sound recordings to be given the right to authorise or prohibit the commercial rental of their works to the public. A similar exclusive right applies to films where commercial rental has led to widespread copying which is materially impairing the right of reproduction. The draft also requires performers to be given protection from unauthorised recording and broadcast of live performances (bootlegging). The protection for performers and producers of sound recordings would be for no less than 50 years. Broadcasting organisations would have control over the use that can be made of broadcast signals without their authorisation. This right would last for at least 20 years.

With respect to trademarks and service marks, the Agreement defines what types of signs must be eligible for protection as a trademark or service mark and what the minimum rights conferred on their owners must be. Marks that have become well known in a particular country shall enjoy additional protection. In addition, the Agreement lays down a number of obligations with regard to the use of trademarks and service marks, their term of protection, and their licensing or assignment. For example, requirements that foreign marks be used in conjunction with local marks would, as a general rule, be prohibited.

In respect of geographical indications, the Agreement lays down that all parties must provide means to prevent the use of any indication which misleads the consumer as to the origin of goods, and any use which would constitute an act of unfair competition. A higher level of protection is provided for geographical indications for wines and spirits, which are protected even where there is no danger of the public's being misled as to the true origin. Exceptions are allowed for names that have already become generic terms, but any country using such an exception must be willing to negotiate with a view to protecting the geographical indications in question. Furthermore, provision is made for further negotiations to establish a multilateral system of notification and registration of geographical indications of wines.

Industrial designs are also protected under the agreement for a period of 10 years. Owners of protected designs would be able to prevent the manufacture, sale or importation of articles bearing or embodying a design which is a copy of the protected design.

As regards patents, there is a general obligation to comply with the substantive provisions of the Paris Convention (1967). In addition, the Agreement requires that 20-year patent protection be available for all inventions, whether of products or processes, in almost all fields of technology. Inventions may be excluded from patentability if their commercial exploitation is prohibited for reasons of public order or morality; otherwise, the permitted exclusions are for diagnostic, therapeutic and surgical methods, and for plants and (other than microorganisms) animals and essentially biological processes for the production of plants or animals (other than microbiological processes). Plant varieties, however, must be protectable either by patents or by a *sui generis* system (such as the breeder's rights provided in a UPOV Convention). Detailed conditions are laid down for compulsory licensing or governmental use of patents without the authorisation of the patent owner. Rights conferred in respect of patents for processes must extend to the products directly obtained by the process; under certain conditions alleged infringers may be ordered by a court to prove that they have not used the patented process.

With respect to the protection of layout designs of integrated circuits, the agreement requires parties to provide protection on the basis of the Washington Treaty on Intellectual Property in Respect of Integrated Circuits which was opened for signature in May 1989, but with a number of additions: protection must be available for a minimum period of 10 years; the rights must extend to articles incorporating infringing layout designs; innocent infringers must be allowed to use or sell stock in hand or ordered before learning of the infringement against a suitable royalty: and compulsory licensing and government use is only allowed under a number of strict conditions.

Trade secrets and know-how which have commercial value must be protected against breach of confidence and other acts contrary to honest commercial practices. Test data submitted to governments in order to obtain marketing approval for pharmaceutical or agricultural chemicals must also be protected against unfair commercial use.

The final section in this part of the Agreement concerns anticompetitive practices in contractual licences. It provides for consultations between governments where there is reason to believe that licensing practices or conditions pertaining to intellectual property rights constitute an abuse of these rights and have an adverse effect on competition. Remedies against such abuses must be consistent with the other provisions of the Agreement.

Part III of the Agreement sets out the obligations of member governments to provide procedures and remedies under their domestic law to ensure that intellectual property rights can be effectively enforced, by foreign right holders as well as by their own nationals.

Procedures should permit effective action against infringement of intellectual property rights but should be fair and equitable, not unnecessarily complicated or costly, and should not entail unreasonable time limits or unwarranted delays. They should allow for judicial review of final administrative decisions. There is no obligation to put in place a judicial system distinct from that for the enforcement of laws in general, nor to give priority to the enforcement of intellectual property rights in the allocation of resources or staff.

The civil and administrative procedures and remedies spelled out in the text include provisions on evidence of proof, injunctions, damages and other remedies which would include the right of judicial authorities to order the disposal or destruction of infringing goods. Judicial authorities must also have the authority to order prompt and effective provisional measures, in particular where any delay is likely to cause irreparable harm to the right holder, or where evidence is likely to be destroyed. Further provisions relate to measures to be taken at the border for the suspension by customs authorities of release, into domestic circulation, of counterfeit and pirated goods. Finally, parties should provide for criminal procedures and penalties at least in cases of wilful trademark counterfeiting or copyright piracy on a commercial scale. Remedies should include imprisonment and fines sufficient to act as a deterrent.

The Agreement would establish a Council for Trade-Related Aspects of Intellectual Property Rights to monitor the operation of the Agreement and governments' compliance with it. Dispute settlement would take place under the integrated GATT dispute settlement procedures as revised in the Uruguay round.

With respect to the implementation of the Agreement, it envisages a one-year transition period for developed countries to bring their legislation and practices into conformity. Developing countries and countries in the process of transformation from a centrally-planned into a market economy would have a five-year transition period, and least-developed countries eleven years. Developing countries which do not at present provide product patent protection in an area of technology would have up to ten years to introduce such protection. However, in the case of pharmaceutical and agricultural chemical products, they must accept the filing of patent applications from the beginning of the transitional period. Though the patent need not be granted until the end of this period, the novelty of the invention is preserved as of the date of filing the application. If authorisation for the marketing of the relevant pharmaceutical or agricultural chemical is obtained during the transitional period, the developing country concerned must offer an exclusive marketing right for the product for five years, or until a product patent is granted, whichever is shorter.

Subject to certain exceptions, the general rule is that the obligations in the Agreement would apply to existing intellectual property rights as well as to new ones.

Understanding on Rules and Procedures Governing the Settlement of Disputes

The dispute settlement system of the GATT is generally considered to be one of the cornerstones of the multilateral trade order. The system has already been strengthened and streamlined as a result of reforms agreed following the Mid-Term Review Ministerial Meeting held in Montreal in December 1988. Disputes currently being dealt with by the Council are subject to these new rules, which include greater automaticity in decisions on the establishment, terms of reference and composition of panels, such that these decisions are no longer dependent upon the consent of the parties to a dispute. The Uruguay Round Understanding on Rules and Procedures Governing the Settlement of Disputes (DSU) will further strengthen the existing system significantly, extending the greater automaticity agreed in the Mid-Term Review to the adoption of the panels' and a new Appellate Body's findings. Moreover, the DSU will establish an integrated system permitting WTO members to base their claims on any of the multilateral trade agreements included in the Annexes to the Agreement Establishing the WTO. For this purpose, a Dispute Settlement Body (DSB) will exercise the authority of the General Council and the Councils and committees of the covered agreements.

The DSU emphasises the importance of consultations in securing dispute resolution, requiring a member to enter into consultations within 30 days of a request for consultations from another member. If after 60 days from the request for consultations there is no settlement, the complaining party may request the establishment of a panel. Where consultations are denied, the complaining party may move directly to request a panel. The parties may voluntarily agree to follow alternative means of dispute settlement, including good offices, conciliation, mediation and arbitration.

Where a dispute is not settled through consultations, the DSU requires the establishment of a panel, at the latest, at the meeting of the DSB following that at which a request is made, unless the DSB decides by consensus against establishment. The DSU also sets out specific rules and deadlines for deciding the terms of reference and composition of panels. Standard terms of reference will apply unless the parties agree to special terms within 20 days of the panel's establishment. Where the parties do not agree on the composition of the panel within the same 20 days, this can be decided by the Director-General. Panels normally consist of three persons of appropriate background and experience from countries not party to the dispute. The Secretariat will maintain a list of experts satisfying the criteria.

Panel procedures are set out in detail in the DSU. It is envisaged that a panel will normally complete its work within six months or, in cases of urgency, within three months. Panel reports may be considered by the DSB for adoption 20 days after they are issued to members. Within 60 days of their issuance, they will be adopted, unless the DSB decides by consensus not to adopt the report or one of the parties notifies the DSB of its intention to appeal.

The concept of appellate review is an important new feature of the DSU. An Appellate Body will be established, composed of seven members, three of whom will serve on any one case. An appeal will be limited to issues of law covered in the panel report and legal interpretations developed by the panel. Appellate proceedings shall not exceed 60 days from the date a party formally notifies its decision to appeal. The resulting report shall be adopted by the DSB and unconditionally accepted by the parties within 30 days following its issuance to members, unless the DSB decides by consensus against its adoption.

Once the panel report or the Appellate Body report is adopted, the party concerned will have to notify its intentions with respect to implementation of adopted recommendations. If it is impracticable to comply immediately, the party concerned shall be given a reasonable period of time, the latter to be decided either by agreement of the parties and approval by the DSB within 45 days of adoption of the report or through arbitration within 90 days of adoption. In any event, the DSB will keep the implementation under regular surveillance until the issue is resolved.

Further provisions set out rules for compensation or the suspension of concessions in the event of non-implementation. Within a specified time-frame, parties can enter into negotiations to agree on mutually acceptable compensation. Where this has not been agreed, a party to the dispute may request authorisation of the DSB to suspend concessions or other obligations to the other party concerned. The DSB will grant such authorisation within 30 days of the expiry of the agreed time-frame for implementation. Disagreements over the proposed level of suspension may be referred to arbitration. In principle, concessions should be suspended in the same sector as that in issue in the panel case. If this is not practicable or effective, the suspension can be made in a different sector of the same agreement. In turn, if this is not effective or practicable and if the circumstances are serious enough, the suspension of concessions may be made under another agreement.

One of the central provisions of the DSU reaffirms that members shall not themselves make determinations of violations or suspend concessions, but shall make use of the dispute settlement rules and procedures of the DSU.

The DSU contains a number of provisions taking into account the specific interests of the developing and the least-developed countries. It also provides some special rules for the resolution of disputes which do not involve a violation of obligations under a covered agreement but where a member believes nevertheless that benefits are being nullified or impaired. Special decisions to be adopted by Ministers in 1994 foresee that the Montreal Dispute Settlement Rules which would otherwise have expired at the time of the April 1994 meeting are extended until the entry into force of the WTO. Another decision foresees that the new rules and procedures will be reviewed within four years after the entry into force of the WTO.

Decision on Achieving Greater Coherence in Global Economic Policy-making

This Decision will set out concepts and proposals with respect to achieving greater coherence in global economic policy-making. Among other things, the text notes that greater exchange rate stability based on more orderly underlying economic and financial conditions should contribute to 'the expansion of trade, sustainable growth and development, and the timely correction of external imbalances'. It recognises that while difficulties whose origins lie outside the trade field cannot be redressed through measures taken in the trade field alone, there are nevertheless interlinkages between the different aspects of economic policy. Therefore, WTO is called upon to develop its cooperation with the international organisations responsible for monetary and financial matters. In particular, the Director-General of WTO is called upon to review, with his opposite numbers in the World Bank and the International Monetary Fund, the implications of WTO's future responsibilities for its cooperation with the Bretton Woods institutions.

Trade Policy Review Mechanism

An agreement confirms the Trade Policy Review Mechanism, introduced at the time of the Mid-term Review, and encourages greater transparency in national trade policy-making. A further Ministerial decision reforms the notification requirements and procedures generally.

New Agreement on Government Procurement

In parallel with the conclusion of the Uruguay round, negotiators agreed on 15 December 1993 a new Agreement on Government Procurement which will open up to international competition government purchases worth several hundred billion dollars each year.

The new Agreement will supersede the current Code which has been in force since 1981. It will, for the first time, cover services, including construction services; procurement at the sub-central level (e.g. states, provinces, departments and prefectures); and procurement by public utilities. The new Agreement expands by some ten-fold the current coverage.

The new Agreement will also reinforce rules guaranteeing fair and non-discriminatory conditions of international competition. For example, governments will be required to put in place domestic procedures by which aggrieved private bidders can challenge procurement decisions and obtain redress in the event such decisions are inconsistent with the Agreement.

National treatment

The cornerstone of the new rules is national treatment: foreign suppliers and foreign goods and services must be given no less favourable treatment in government procurement than national suppliers and goods and services. Thus, the Agreement deals in some detail with tendering procedures; the use of technical specifications in invitations to bid; the conditions of the qualifications of suppliers eligible to bid; the publication of invitations to tender; time limits for tendering and delivery; the contents of tender documentation provided to potential suppliers; the submission, receipt and opening of tenders; and awarding of contractions and *ex post* information regarding the award of contracts.

In addition to the 35 or so pages containing these rules to secure open and non-discriminatory procurement, the Agreement contains in 200 pages of Annexes lists of the procuring entities of participating governments which will be subject to the rules of the Agreement. Annex 1 lists central government entities. Annex 2 lists covered entities at the sub-central government level and Annex 3 other entities subject to the rules of the Agreement, such as public utilities. Annexes 4 and 5 define the services and construction services whose procurement by the covered entities is subject to the Agreement's rules.

The Agreement applies to contracts which are above certain thresholds in value. In the case of central government purchases of goods and services, the threshold is SDR 130,000 (some $176,000). For purchases of goods and services by sub-central government entities, the threshold varies but is generally in the region of SDR 200,000. For utilities, the threshold is generally in the area of SDR 400,000. For construction contracts, in general the threshold is SDR 5 million.

Although the Agreement is considered a balanced package as it stands, participants intend to expand further the coverage of commitments prior to its signature in April 1994 and subsequently prior to its entry into force at the beginning of 1996. This applies in particular to a negotiated settlement commitment to each other in these areas. Improvements will be applied on a non-discriminatory basis to all participants.

The new Agreement will constitute part of the WTO, being a plurilateral agreement that not all WTO members will be asked to accept. The participants in the negotiations were: Austria, Canada, the EC, Finland, Hong Kong, Israel, Japan, the Republic of Korea, Norway, Sweden, Switzerland and the United States. Other governments will of course be able to negotiate their accession to the New Agreement.

BIBLIOGRAPHY

Anderson, K. and Tyers, R. (1987) 'Japan's Agricultural Policy in International Perspective', *Journal of the Japanese & International Economies*, I (2): 131–46.

Baldwin, R.E. (1989) 'On the Growth Effect of 1992', *Economic Policy*, 9: 3–54.

—— (1992a) 'Measurable Dynamic Gains from Trade', *Journal of Political Economy*, 100: 162–74.

—— (1992b) *An Eastern Enlargement of EFTA: Why the East Europeans should Join and the EFTANs Should Want Them*, CEPR Occasional Paper, 10, London, CEPR.

—— (1993) *The Potential for Trade Between the Countries of EFTA and Central and Eastern Europe*, EFTA Occasional Paper, 44, Geneva, EFTA

—— (1994) *Towards an Integrated Europe*, London, CEPR.

Bayard, T.O. and Elliott, K.A. (1992) '"Aggressive Unilateralism" and Section 301: Market Opening or Market Closing', *The World Economy*, 15(6): 685–706.

Belderbos, R. (1991) 'On the Advance of Japanese Electronics Multinationals in the EC', paper presented at INSEAD Conference, Fontainebleau, October.

Bergstrand, J.H. (1985) 'The Gravity Model – Some Microeconomic Foundations and Empirical Evidence', *Review of Economics and Statistics*, 67: 474–81.

BEUC (1992a) *Parallel Markets for Cars in the EC*, BEUC 222/92.

—— (1992b) *Price Surveys*, BEUC 377/92.

Bhagwati, J. (1988) *Protectionism*, Cambridge MA and London, Massachusetts Institute of Technology Press.

—— (1989) 'Is Free Trade Passé After All?', *Weltwirtschaftliches Archiv*, 125(1): 17–44.

—— (1990a) 'Aggressive Unilateralism', in J. Bhagwhati and H.T. Patric (eds), *Aggressive Unilateralism: America's 301 Trade Policy and the World Trading System*, Ann Arbor, University of Michigan Press.

—— (1990b) 'Multilateralism at Risk: The GATT Is Dead. Long Live the GATT', *World Economy*, 13: 149–169.

—— (1991) *The World Trading System at Risk*, London, Harvester Wheatsheaf.

Butler, A. (1992) 'Environmental Protection and Free Trade; Are they Mutually Exclusive?', *Federal Reserve Bank of St. Louis Review*. May–June: 2–16.

CEC (1985) *Completing the Internal Market* (the white paper) COM (85) 310, Brussels, 14 June.

—— (1986) *Single European Act*, Bulletin of the European Communities, Supplement 2/86, Luxembourg, OOPEC.

—— (1988a) 'The Economics of 1992', *European Economy*, 35, March, Luxembourg, OOPEC.

—— (1988b) *Research on the Cost of Non-Europe: Basic Findings*, Brussels.

—— (1988c) *Note to the Members of other 113 Committee: Definition of the NICs*, Brussels.

—— (1989a) 'International Trade of the European Community', *European Economy*, 39, Luxembourg, OOPEC.
—— (1989b) *First Survey on State Aids in the European Community*, Luxembourg, OOPEC.
—— (1991a) *Opening up the Internal Market*, Luxembourg, OOPEC.
—— (1991b) 'EC Trade with Eastern and Central Europe: Trade rather than Aid?', Mimeo, Brussels, CEC.
—— (1991c) *The European Electronics and Information Technology Industry: States of Play, Issues at Stake and Proposals for Action*, Luxembourg, OOPEC.
—— (1992a) *Seventh Report of the Commission to the Council and the European Parliament Concerning the Implementation of the White Paper on the Completion of the Internal Market*, COM (92) 383 final, Brussels, 2 September.
—— (1992b) *Third Survey on State Aids in the EC*, Luxembourg, OOPEC.
—— (1992c) *European Motor Vehicle Industry: Situation, Issues at Stake and Proposals for Action*, COM (92) 166 final, Brussels.
—— (1992d) *Twenty-first Report on Competition Policy*, SEC (92) 756 final, Brussels.
—— (1993) 'The European Community as a World Trade Partner', *European Economy*, 52, Luxembourg, OOPEC.
—— (1994) '1994 Broad Economic Policy Guidelines', *European Economy*, 58, Luxembourg, OOPEC.
Cecchini, P. (1988) *The European Challenge: 1992 – The Benefits of a Single Market*, Aldershot, Wildwood House.
CEPR (1992) *Is Bigger Better? The Economics of EC Enlargement*, Monitoring European Integration 3, London, CEPR.
Coffey, P. (1993) *The EC and the United States*, London, Pinter.
Collins S. and Rodrik, D. (1991) *Eastern Europe and the Soviet Union in the World Economy*, Washington, DC, Institute for International Economics.
Costello, D. and Pelkmans, J. (1991) 'The Removal of National Quotas and "1992"', in P. Ludlow *et al.* (eds), *The Annual Review of European Community Affairs*, Centre for European Policy Studies, London.
Davenport, M. and Page, S. (1991) 'The External Policy of the Community and its Effects upon the Manufactured Goods of Developing Countries', *Journal of Common Market Studies*, 29: 181–200.
Deardorff, A.V. (1984) 'Testing Trade Theories and Predicting Trade Flows', in R.W. Jones and P.B. Kenen (eds), *Handbook of International Economics*, Amsterdam, North-Holland Publishing Company.
Deardorff, A.V. and Stern, R.N. (1984) *Methods of Measurement of Non-Tariff Barriers*, University of Michigan, Institute of Public Policy Studies, Discussion Paper, 203.
DTI (Department of Trade and Industry) Department for Enterprise (1993) *The Single Market: Progress on Commission White Paper*, London, DTI.
ECE (1993) *Economic Bulletin for Europe*, 45, Geneva, UN.
Economist (1989a) 'The Joy of High Costs', 4 March: 81.
—— (1989b) 'The EEC and EFTA: Unequal Partners', 11 March: 50–52.
—— (1991) 'Management Focus: What Makes Yoshio Invent?', 12 January: 75.
—— (1992a) 'Economics Focus: Japan's Troublesome Imports', 11 January: 69.
—— (1992b) 'Trade Watch: A Good Tanning', 22 February: 78.
—— (1993) 'Economics Focus: Japan's Trade Surplus Returns to Haunt It', 30 January: 68.
Economists' Advisory Group (1988) 'The Cost of non-Europe: The Pharmaceutical

Industry', in CEC, *Research on the Cost of Non-Europe: Basic Findings*, 1, 7, Brussels.

EFTA (1994) *Bulletin*, January, Geneva, EFTA.

Eurostat (1991) *EC–NICs Trade: A Statistical Analysis*, Luxembourg, OOPEC.

—— (1993) *External Trade and Balance of Payments, Statistical Yearbook*, Recapitulation 1958–1992, Luxembourg, OOPEC.

Evans, P. and Walsh, J. (1994) *The EIU Guide to the New GATT*, Research Report, London, Economist Intelligence Unit.

Faini, R. *et al.* (1992) *A Primer on the MFA Maze*, CEPR Discussion Paper, 716, September.

Financial Times (1993) 'The GATT Deal', 16 December: 4–5.

Finger, M. and Murray, T. (1990) 'Policing Unfair Imports: The United States Example', *Journal of World Trade*, August.

Freeman, C. *et al.* (eds) (1991) *Technology and the Future of Europe: Global Competition and the Environment*, London, Pinter.

Gardener E.P.M. and Teppett, J.L. (1992) *The Impact of 1992 on the Financial Services Sectors of EFTA Countries*, Occasional Papers, 33, Geneva, EFTA.

GATT (1991) *Trade Policy Review: The European Communities*, (1st Review) Geneva, GATT.

—— (1992a) *Trade Policy Review: United States* (2nd Review) Geneva, GATT.

—— (1992b) *GATT: What It Is – What It Does*, Geneva, GATT.

—— (1992c) 'Trade and the Environment', in *International Trade 1990–91*, I: 19–47.

—— (1993a) *International Trade Statistics*, Geneva, GATT.

—— (1993b) *Trade Policy Review: The European Communities* (2nd Review) Geneva, GATT.

—— (1993c) *Trade Policy Review, Japan* (2nd Review) Geneva, GATT.

—— (1993d) *Final Act Embodying the Results of the Uruguay Round of Multilateral Trade Negotiations*, UR-93-0246, Geneva, GATT.

—— (1993e) 'The Final Act of the Uruguay Round: A Summary', *GATT Focus*, 104: 5–15.

—— (1994a) 'The Final Act of the Uruguay Round: Press Summary', *News of the Uruguay Round*, NUR, 084, April, Geneva, GATT.

—— (1994b) 'Increases in Market Access Resulting from the Uruguay Round', *News of the Uruguay Round*, April.

Greenaway, D. (1993) 'Trade and Foreign Direct Investment', *European Economy*, 52: 103–27.

Grubel, H.G. and Lloyd, J.P. (1975) *Intra-Industry Trade: The Theory and Measurement of International Trade in Differentiated Products*, New York, John Wiley & Sons.

Guieu, P. and Bonnet, C. (1987) 'Completion of the Internal Market and Indirect Taxation', *Journal of Common Market Studies*, 25, 3: 209–22.

Haaland, J.I. and Norman, V.D. (1992) 'Global Production Effects of European Integration', in L.A. Winters (ed.), *Trade Flows and Trade Policy after '1992'*, Cambridge, Cambridge University Press.

Hamilton, C.B. (1991) *The Nordic EFTA Countries' Options: Seeking Community Membership or a Permanent EEA–Accord*, CEPR Discussion Paper, 524, London, CEPR.

Henrikson, S. (1992) *European Economic Integration – Effects of '1992' on the Manufacturing Industries of the EFTA Countries* EFTA Occasional Paper, 38, Geneva; EFTA.

Hindley, R. (1992) 'Trade Policy of the European Community', in P. Minsford (ed.), *The Cost of Europe*, Manchester and New York, Manchester University Press.

Hindley, B. (1993) *Helping Transition Through Trade? EC and US Policy towards exports from Eastern and Central Europe*, EBRD Working Paper, 4, London, EBRD.

Hufbauer, G.C. (1990) *Europe 1992: An American Perspective*, Washington DC, Brookings Institution.

IFS (1982) *Differentials between Car Prices in the UK and Belgium*, IFS Report Series, 2.

IMF (1993) *Direction of Trade Statistics Yearbook*, Washington DC, IMF.

ITC (1989) *The Effects of Greater Economic Integration Within the European Community on the United States*, Washington DC, July.

—— (1990) *The Economic Effects of Significant US Import Restraints, Phase II: Agricultural Products and Natural Resources*, USITC Publication, 2314, Washington DC, September.

Ito, T. (1992) *The Japanese Economy*, Cambridge, Massachusetts Institute of Technology Press.

Jacquemin, A. and Sapir, A. (1990) *Competition and Imports in the European Market*, CEPR Discussion Paper, 474.

—— (1991) 'Western Europe, Eastern Europe and the World Economy', *American Economic Review, Papers & Proceedings*, 81(2): 166–70.

Japanese Ministry of Foreign Affairs (1992) *The Role of Keiretsu in Business: Separating Facts from Friction*, Tokyo.

Kay, J.A. (1989) 'Myths and Realities', in E. Davis *et al. Myths and Realities*, London, London Business School.

Kay, J.A. and Posner, M.V. (1989) 'Routes to Economic Integration', *National Institute Economic Review*, August: 55–68.

Klepper, G. (1992) *Pharmaceuticals – Who's afraid of '1992'?*, CEPR Discussion paper, 675.

Krugman, P. (1987) 'Pricing to Market when the Exchange Rate Changes', in S.W. Arndt and J.D. Richardson (eds), *Real – Financial Linkages among Open Economics*, Cambridge, Massachusetts Institute of Technology Press.

—— (1988) *EFTA and 1992*, EFTA Occasional Paper, 23, June, Geneva, EFTA.

—— (1989) 'Re-Thinking International Trade', *Business Economist*, Spring: 4–15.

Langhammer, R. and Sapir, A. (1987) *Economic Impact of Generalised Tariff Preferences*, London, Trade Policy Research Centre.

Lawrence, R.Z. (1987) *Imports in Japan: Closed Markets or Minds?* Brookings Papers on Economic Activity, Washington DC, Brookings Institute.

—— (1991a) *Efficient or Exclusionist? The Import Behaviour of Japanese Corporate Grounds*, Brookings Papers on Economic Activity, Washington DC, Brookings Institute.

—— (1991b) 'How Open is Japan?', In P. Krugman (ed.), *Trade with Japan: Has the Door Opened Wider*? Chicago and London, University of Chicago Press.

Lincoln, E.J. (1990) *Japan's Unequal Trade*, Washington DC, Brookings Institution.

Lindström, S.G. (1994) 'The Idea of Pan-European Cumulation, *Bulletin*, 2/94: 1–3, Geneva, EFTA.

Linnemann, H. (1966) *An Economic Study of International Trade Flows*, Amsterdam, North-Holland Publishing Company.
Lintner, V. (1989) *1992: The EC Customs Union in Theory and Reality*, London, Polytechnic of North London Press.
Loertscher, R. and Wolter, F. (1980) 'Determinants of Intra-Industry Trade Among Countries and Across Industries', *Weltwirtschaftliches Archiv*, 116(2): 280–93.
Messerlin, P.A. (1989) 'The EC Anti-Dumping Regulations: A First Economic Appraisal 1980–85', *Weltwirtschaftliches Archiv*, 125: 563–87.
Mishan, E.J. (1976) *Elements of Cost Benefit Analysis* (2nd edn) London, Allen & Unwin.
MMC (1992) *New Motor Cars: A Report on the Supply of Motor Cars within the UK*, London, HMSO, Cmd 1808.
Mobius, V. and Schumacher, D. (1990) *Eastern Europe and the EC: Trade Relations and Trade Policy with Regard to Industrial Products*, Mimeo, Berlin, German Institute for Economic Research (DIW).
NCC (1990) 'Consumer Electronics and the ECs' Anti-dumping Policy', Working Paper 1, *International Trade and the Consumer*, London, NCC.
Nello, S.S. (1991) *The New Europe: Changing Economic Relations between East and West*, New York and London, Harvester, Wheatsheaf.
Nerb, G. (1988) 'The Completion of the Internal Market: A Survey of European Industry's Perception of the Likely Effects', in CEC, *Research on the Cost of Non-Europe: Basic Findings*, 3, 16, Brussels.
Neven, D.J. (1990) 'EC Integration towards 1992: Some Distributional Aspects', *Economic Policy*, 10: 13–62.
Neven, D.J. and Roeller, L.H. (1990) *European Integration and Trade Flows*, CEPR Discussion Paper, 367.
N'Guyen, G.D. and Owen, R.F. (1992) 'High-Tech Competition and Industrial Restructuring in Light of the Single Market', *American Economic Review, Papers & Proceedings*, 82(2): 97–101.
Nguyen, T. *et al.* (1993) 'An Evaluation of the Draft Final Act', *Economic Journal*, 103: 1540–9.
Norman, V.D. (1989) 'EFTA and the Internal European Market', *Economic Policy*, 9: 423–66.
—— (1991) '1992 and EFTA', in A.L. Winters and A.J. Venables (eds), *European Integration: Trade and Industry*, Cambridge, Cambridge University Press.
OECD (1976) *Economics of Transfrontier Pollution*, Paris, OECD.
—— (1979) *The Impact of Newly-Industrialising Countries*, Paris, OECD.
—— (1993) *Assessing the Effects of the Uruguay Round*, Trade Policy Issues No. 2, Paris, OECD.
Ohlin, B. (1933) *Inter-Regional and International Trade*, Cambridge MA, Harvard University Press.
Ostrey, S. (1990) *Governments and Corporations in a Shrinking World: Trade and Innovation Policies in the United States, Europe and Japan*, New York, Council on Foreign Relations.
Owens, R. and Dynes, M. (1989) *1992 – Britain in a Europe without Frontiers*, Aldershot, Wildwood House.
Pelkmans, J. (1988) 'The North American Internal Market', in CEC, *Research on the Cost of Non-Europe: Basic Findings*, 2, 24, Brussels.
Pelkmans, J. and Winters, L.A. (1988) *Europe's Domestic Market*, London, Routledge.

Porter M. (1990) *The Competitive Advantage of Nations*, London, Macmillan.
Posner, M.V. and Sargent, J.R. (1987) 'A Case of Eurosclerosis', *Midland Bank Review*, Winter: 9–17.
Rosati, D.K. (1992) 'Problems of Post-CMEA Trade and Payments', in J. Fleming and J.M.C. Rollo (eds), *Trade, Payments and Adjustments in Central and Eastern Europe*, London, Royal Instititute of International Affairs and EBRD.
Saxonhouse, G.R. (1991) 'Comment on Lawrence, R.Z., How Open is Japan?', in P. Krugman (ed.), *Trade with Japan: Has the Door Opened Wider?* Chicago and London, University of Chicago Press.
Schoneveld, F. (1992) 'The European Community Reaction to the "Illicit Commercial Trade Protection of Other Countries"', *Journal of World Trade*, 26(2): 17–34.
Servant-Schreiber, J. (1967) *Le Défi Américain*, Paris, Deonël.
Smith, A. (1989) 'The Market for Cars in an Enlarged European Community', *European Economic Review*, 32: 1501–25.
Smith, A. and Venables, A.J. (1988) 'The Cost of Non-Europe: An Assessment Based on a Formal Model of Imperfect Competition and Economies of Scale', in CEC, *Research on the Cost of Non-Europe: Basic Findings*, 2, 21, Brussels.
Swann, D. (1992) (ed.) *The Single European Market and Beyond – A Study of the Wider Implications of the Single European Act*, London, Routledge.
Thomsen, S. and Nicolaides, P. (1990) *Foreign Direct Investment: 1992 and Global Markets*, London, Royal Institute of Internal Affairs.
Tyers, R. and Anderson, K. (1986) *Distortions in World Food Markets: A Quantitative Assessment*, World Bank Development Report Background Paper, Washington DC, World Bank.
Tyson, L.D. (1992) *Who's Bashing Whom: Trade Conflict in High-Technology Industries*, Washington, DC, Institute for International Economics.
Van Bergeijk, P. and Oldersma, H. (1990) 'Détente, Market-oriented Reform and German Unification: Potential Consequences for the World Trade System', *Kyklos*, 43 (4): 566–609.
Vincent, D. (1989) 'Effects of Agricultural Protection in Japan: An Economy Wide Analysis', in A.B. Stoeckel *et al.* (eds), *Macroeconomic Consequences of Farm Support Policies*, Canberra, Centre for International Economics.
Wieser, T. (1989) *Price Differentials in the European Economic Space*, EFTA Occasional Paper, 29, Geneva, EFTA.
Winch, D.M. (1971) *Analytical Welfare Economics*, Harmondsworth, Penguin.
Winters, L.A. (1987) *Patterns of World Trade in Manufactures: Does Trade Policy Matter*, CEPR Discussion Paper, 160.
—— (1992a) (ed.) *Trade Flows and Policy after '1992'*, Cambridge, Cambridge University Press.
—— (1992b) 'The Europe Agreements: With a Little Help from Our Friends', in CEPR, *The Association Process: Making it Work – Central Europe and the European Community*, CEPR Occasional Paper, 11, London, CEPR.
Winters, L.A. and Brenton, P.A. (1988) *VERs: UK Restrictions on Imports of Leather Footwear from Eastern Europe*, CEPR Discussion Paper, 283.
Winters, L.A. and Hamilton, C. (1992) 'The Trading Potential of Eastern Europe', *Economic Policy*, 14 May: 77–116.
Winters, L.A. and Wang, Z.K. (1994) *Eastern Europe's International Trade*, Manchester and New York, Manchester University Press.

Woolcock, S. (1991) *Market Access Issues in EC–US Relations: Training Partners or Trading Blows*, London, Pinter.
World Bank/OECD (1993) *Trade Liberalisation: The Global Economic Implications*, Washington and Paris, World Bank and OECD.

TERMS

Acquis Communautaire – Term for primary EU law (the Treaty of Rome and other such treaties) and secondary EU law adopted under the Rome Treaty (regulations, directives and decisions).

Ad Valorem Tariff – A tariff calculated as a p.c. of the value of a traded good.

Anti-dumping Duties – Duties imposed where dumping of low-priced goods by a foreign supplier causes 'material injury' to domestic producers. Usually the difference between the price charged in the exporting firm's home market and the price set on the export market.

Balance of Payments – Account representing all transactions between residents of one country and residents of the rest of the world over a specific period of time, generally a year.

Barter (or Counter) Trade – Trade involving some element of reciprocity between countries: in exchange for being able to export to country A, country B agrees to import from country A.

Bilateralism – Attempt by any two countries to balance their trade flows instead of seeking to balance their trade with the world as a whole (multilateralism).

Cassis de Dijon – Basic principle governing the free movement of goods within the EU. A product approved in one EU member state should also be allowed in other EU countries unless importing the product endangers the environment, the health and life of humans, animals or plants, consumers' interests in general.

Cecchini Report (1988) – Findings of a study by a group of experts (conducted at the request of the European Commission and chaired by Paolo Cecchini) into the 'cost of non-Europe' and the potential benefits of the internal market ('1992').

Comparative Advantage – Principle (developed by David Ricardo in the 19th century) demonstrating that differences in the relative costs of production of any two goods between any two countries lead to a situation in which both countries benefit from trade if each country exports that product which it cán produce at comparatively lower costs than the other country.

Customs Union – Group of countries maintaining free trade among themselves and establishing a common external tariff in trading with the rest of the world.

Dumping – A situation when a country charges a lower price on the export market than on the home market (selling at 'less than fair value').

Economic Union – Agreement among a group of countries to establish some degree of harmonisation in their budgetary and monetary systems (in addition to forming a customs union and allowing mobility of capital and labour among the members).

Economic and Monetary Union – Extension of the internal market by means of a common currency, a common monetary policy and co-ordination of fiscal policy.

ECU – Abbreviation for the European currency unit, made up of a 'basket' comprising differing proportions of the currencies of each member state of the EU. At present only a unit of account, but envisaged to become the common currency within the EU.

Export Restraint Agreement – An agreement between two countries limiting the exports of one to the other.

Export Subsidy – Payment to domestic producer linked to his/her export performance.

Free Trade Area – Group of countries arranging free movement of goods and services among themselves.

Foreign Direct Investment – Foreign investment by a multinational enterprise which either establishes a wholly-owned foreign subsidiary or acquires the controlling interest in a foreign company.

Generalised System of Preferences – Scheme to grant favourable trading conditions to developing countries enabling them to export specified goods at low or zero tariffs to the developed world.

Heckscher-Ohlin Theorem – Principle (developed by the Swedish Economists Heckscher and Ohlin in the 1920s) according to which international trade flows are determined by the fact that countries differ in their factor endowments and that different goods require different relative factor inputs: countries will export those goods that require large inputs of its relatively abundant factor of production.

Import Penetration – Measured by the ratio of imports to home market sales (of domestic and foreign suppliers).

Infant Industry Protection – Protection of domestic industry from foreign competition to foster its development tends to be justified on the grounds that an industry's initial costs will be high but that the 'infant industry' will be able to compete against imports once costs have declined following the protectionist phase.

Inter-Industry Trade – Trade between countries involving the exchange of products that belong to different industries (example: food products being exported in exchange for consumer durables).

Internal Market – Area without internal frontiers in which the free movement of goods, persons, services and capital is ensured in accordance with the provisions of a treaty (such as, for example, The Single European Act).

Intra-Firm Trade – Trade between a multinational enterprise and its affiliate(s) in other countries.

Intra-Industry Trade – Situation in which a country both exports and imports products that belong to the same industry (example: a country both exports and imports motor vehicles).

Invisibles – Intangibles that appear in the current account of a country's balance of payments: trade in services (banking and insurance, tourism, transport, etc.); cross-border flows of investment income (property income from abroad); and non-commercial transfers. To be distinguished from trade in tangible goods (visible trade).

J-Curve Effect – Argument that after a devaluation or depreciation a country's trade balance will initially deteriorate rather than improve because the value effect of the devaluation/depreciation will precede its volume effect.

Law of One Price – Assertion that trade will tend to eliminate price differentials for the same good in different countries provided markets are competitive.

Managed (or Controlled) Trade – Any trade that is subject to some degree of control via non-tariff measures (by the exporting country, the importer or both trading partners).

Marshall-Lerner Conditions – Argument that certain elasticity of demand and supply conditions have to be fulfilled for a devaluation or depreciation of a country's currency to lead to an improvement of that country's trade balance.

Most-favoured Nation Principle – Central pillar of the GATT agreement according to which a country undertakes to offer equal treatment to all trading partners to which it has extended this principle: the country thus agrees to refrain from discriminating against any third country to which it has bestowed MFN status.

Multi-fibre Agreement – System of (bilateral) quotas for trade in textiles and clothing regulating exports from countries of the 'South' and transition economies to the industrialised world.

Multilateralism – Situation whereby countries seek to regulate their commercial policies at a global level and balance their overall transactions with the world as a whole rather than focusing on trade with a particular country (or group of countries) and seeking to balance their bilateral payments with individual trading partners (bilateralism).

New Commercial Policy Instrument – Procedural framewok allowing the EU to respond to any illicit commercial practices and to remove the 'injury' caused by such practices or to exercise the Union's rights with regard to third countries' commercial measures that violate international trade agreements or inhibit EU trade.

Newly Industrialising Countries – Term used to refer to those Third World countries that have, as a result of expanding exports of manufactured goods to developed countries, achieved fast growth and rapid industrialisation (examples: Taiwan, Hong Kong, Singapore and South Korea – the Asian NICs).

New Protectionism – Term referring to the type of protectionism which unlike the old protectionism relies on non-tariff barriers rather than tariffs to interfere with trade.

Non-Tariff Barriers – Any commercial policy other than a tariff designed to impede imports and protect domestic suppliers (examples: quotas, discriminatory public procurement practices, domestic content regulations, technical and health standards, voluntary export restraints etc.).

Orderly Marketing Agreement – Name given to a bilateral measure whereby an exporting country agrees to limit the volume of export of a particular good to an importing country. Similar in scope to an export restraint agreement.

Quota – Commercial policy limiting the volume of imports of a specific product over a particular period of time.

Rules of Origin – Formal criteria laid down for determining the 'nationality' of a product. Usually a minimum percentage of a good's value must have been added in the exporting country.

Reciprocity – GATT principle applying to trade policy according to which countries must, in international tariff negotiations, reciprocate, i.e. offer tariff concessions in return for receiving tariff concessions.

Screwdriver Operation – Production process whereby a manufacturer, instead of exporting a finished product, exports the components to a subsidiary or joint venture company in another country where they are being assembled in a plant and then put on the market.

Section 301 – Provision of US Trade Law which allows the United States trade representative to take (unilateral) action against the imports into the USA from countries which make use of unfair trade practices.

Specific Tariff – A tariff calculated as a fixed amount of money per physical unit imported.

Strategic Trade Policy – Type of commercial policy (including protectionist measures) used in order to foster the growth of those domestic industries for which growing world markets exist and in which rapid technical advances exist.

Tariff – A tax imposed on imports (or exports).

Tariffication – Converting non-tariff barriers into tariff barriers.

Terms of Trade – Ratio of a country's export prices to its import prices. Terms of trade improve for a country if its export prices rise faster than its import prices. Favourable terms of trade for a country mean that it derives large gains from trade, and vice versa.

Trade Balance – A country's total export receipts minus its total import expenditure over a specific period of time, generally a year.

Trade Creation – Welfare gain accruing to a country replacing supply from less efficient domestic producers by more efficient producers from trading partners.

Trade Deflection – Imports to a free trade from third countries via the member state with the lowest external tariff rate.

Trade Diversion – Welfare loss experienced by a country as a result of its consumers buying goods (or services) from less efficient domestic producers instead of more efficient trade partners.

Trade Policy Review Mechanism – Gatt procedure set up during the Uruguay Round to monitor contracting parties' trade policies and practices.

Trade Related Aspects of Intellectual Property Rights – Extension of established rules on copyright to other aspects of intellectual property rights (patents, trade marks, etc.).

Trade-Related Investment Measures – Domestic regulations permitting foreign direct investment only if the investing firm accepts certain constraints such as local content requirements, equity participation rules.

Transfer Pricing – Pricing policy used by multinational companies in selling goods (or services) from one unit of the multinational to another. Transfer prices may differ from market prices in order to reduce bills for (ad valorem) tariffs, or in order to shift profits within a multinational from a high rate tax country to a low rate tax country.

Visible Trade – Trade in tangible goods distinct from invisibles which are trade in intangible items.

Voluntary Export Restraint – Bilateral measure whereby an exporting country 'voluntarily' agrees to restrict its exports of a particular good to a trading partner, frequently in order to avoid less acceptable protectionist policies by the importing country.

Voluntary Import Expansion – Bilateral measure amounting to 'export protectionism'. Trade agreement whereby the importing country 'voluntarily' agrees to expand the market share for imports of a particular good from the exporting country to a specified percentage, frequently in order to avoid retaliatory commercial policies by the exporting country.

INDEX